Animal World

THE PENGUIN

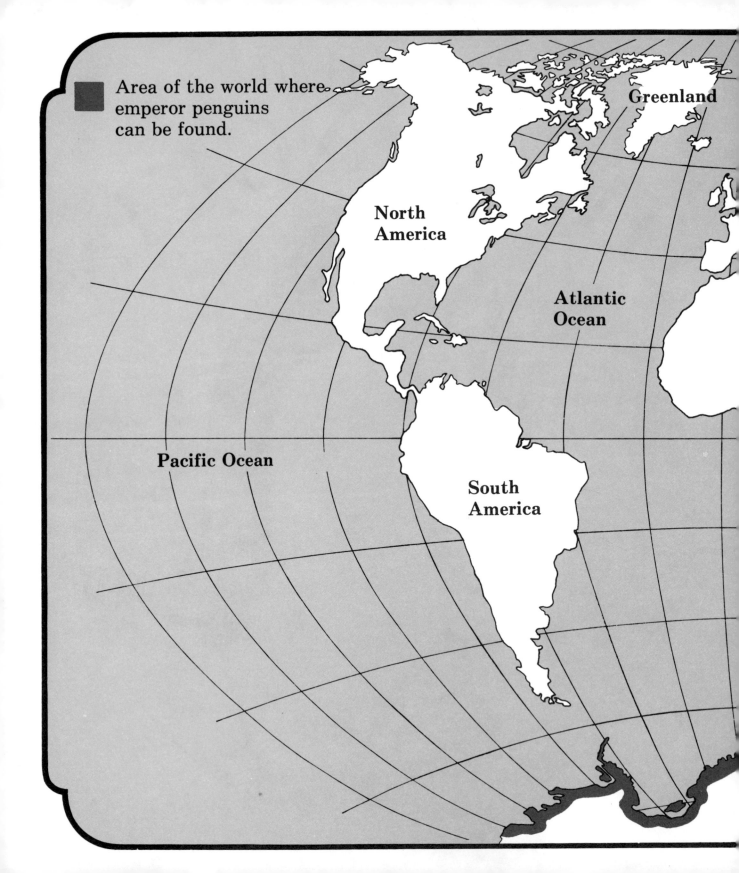

Area of the world where emperor penguins can be found.

Greenland

North America

Atlantic Ocean

Pacific Ocean

South America

Published by Watermill Press
Copyright © 1983 by The Rourke Enterprises, Inc. All copyrights reserved. No part of this book may be reproduced in any form without written permission from the publisher. Printed in the United States of America.

Library of Congress Cataloging in Publication Data

Dalmais, Anne-Marie, 1954-
  The penguin.

  (Animal world)
  Translation of: Le manchot.
  Reprint. Originally published: London : Macdonald
Educational, 1979.
  Summary: Text and illustrations introduce the natural environment, physical characteristics, and habits of the emperor penguin.
  1. Emperor penguin—Juvenile literature.   [1. Emperor]
penguin.   2. Penguins]   I. Weaver, Norman, ill.
II. Title.   III. Series.
QL696.S473D3413   1984   598.4'41   83-9784
ISBN 0-86592-854-1

Animal World

THE PENGUIN

illustrated by
Norman Weaver

Watermill Press

On the ice of Antarctica

A big mass of ice sparkles in the summer sun. It is floating near the coast of the Antarctic continent. This continent is in the Southern Hemisphere. It is as large as Europe but no one lives on it. The climate is too harsh. In winter the temperature falls to minus 160°F. Even in summer it does not rise higher than 32°F.

The landscape is partly mountains of rock. Some of them are 19,000 feet high. There are also vast plains and steep cliffs. Everything is covered with a thick layer of ice that never melts. It is difficult to reach this frozen continent because there are gigantic icebergs in the way, as well as sheets of ice that are carried along by the currents.

The sheets of ice are where the emperor penguins live for part of the year. These large birds cannot fly. They have small wings but they use them for swimming. Look at the group in the picture. You can tell they are penguins from a long way off because they stand up so straight.

A pair of penguins

Here is a pair of emperor penguins, one male and the other female. You can see that they are very alike. They have the same long, pointed beaks, black on top and orange underneath. They both have strong, rounded bodies and their narrow stiff wings are the same. So is their thick black and white plumage. Their legs are short and black and have webbed feet. The male is a little bigger than the female.

Penguins look clumsy when they walk. When they see the ground sloping down in front of them, they throw themselves flat on their bellies and slide along as if they were tobogganing.

In the water

Penguins are happiest when they are in the water. They are splendid swimmers. They can compete with such champions as seals and porpoises, leaping gracefully out of the water and diving deep. They push themselves forward with their wings and steer with their feet. They can reach a speed of 25 miles per hour.

Here you see the male coming to the surface, while the female leaps into the air and lands on the ice.

Penguins find all their food in the sea. They eat fish and squid, but they like shrimps best of all.

Enemies of the penguin

Penguins have few natural enemies. The only animals in the sea that can swim fast enough to attack them are killer whales and leopard seals.

On the left of the picture you can see a leopard seal lifting its head above the drifting ice. This creature belongs to the seal family. It is fierce, greedy and a very fast, agile swimmer. When it sees a penguin, it swims in a circle around it. The penguin cannot escape from the circle because it cannot fly. When it is exhausted, the leopard seal pounces on it.

The killer whale on the right is the largest and fiercest member of the dolphin family. It goes after penguins and slashes them with its sharp teeth.

On land

At the beginning of autumn the penguins leave the floating ice and swim ashore. Thousands of them gather there.

Every year the penguins come back to the same places to lay their eggs. But once they leave the sea, they have to do without food because there is none on land for them. For weeks they eat nothing. They live on the fat that is stored in their bodies.

The eggs are laid

Now it is time for the penguins to mate. Males and females do a dance which is called a mating display. Two months later, the females lay their eggs. Each female lays a single white egg weighing about 15 ounces. Then she goes back to the sea to feed. She leaves the male to hatch the egg.

The male balances the egg on his feet and keeps it warm under a fold of the skin on his belly. It is very cold now and the males need protection from the blizzards. They all huddle together taking turns to stand in the sheltered places in the middle of the group.

The penguin chicks

The eggs hatch two months later. At the same time the females return from the sea and take over for the males. Now it is the fathers' turn to go in search of food, which they so badly need. They have lost nearly 33 pounds in weight.

While the fathers are away, the mothers look after the chicks. Each baby penguin stays hidden in its mother's plumage for another 2 to 3 weeks. The chicks are funny to look at with their light gray downy feathers. Their mothers feed them on juices and fats produced by their own digestive tubes.

Watching over the young

When the fathers have eaten enough to regain their
full weight, they come back to help look after the chicks.
The young penguins grow up in large groups. Hundreds
of them are gathered together and are watched over by
the adult penguins. They are now old enough to eat fish.
The parents catch the fish in the sea and bring them
back in their crops, which are pouches below their gullets
for storing food. Then they put the fish into the infants'
beaks. This goes on for three months. Soon the ice
begins to crack and the parents do not have so far to go
in search of fish for their young.

Back to the sea

At last, summer comes to Antarctica. The penguins lose their old feathers and grow new ones. This is called molting. With their new plumage, all the birds return to the sea. The young live on their own now, swimming and diving happily in the ice cold waters of the Antarctic Ocean.

SOME INTERESTING FACTS ABOUT PENGUINS

Species:

Penguins belong to the scientific family of Spheniscidae. They have been around for 50 million years. The first penguins lived in the Antarctic, New Zealand and South America. The biggest fossil penguin ever discovered stood 5 feet 8 inches tall. No modern penguin is that tall.

Penguins are birds. However, they differ from other birds in two respects: one, their wings are really flippers and two, they do not fly.

There are 17 species of penguins. Two of them live in the Antarctic. The rest are scattered throughout the Southern Hemisphere. There are no penguins in the Northern Hemisphere.

Description:

The word *penguin* is Welsh. It means "whitehead." Penguins have a white front and a black back. They look like they are wearing tuxedos.

Penguins are flightless birds that "fly" through the water. They are great swimmers. They live in water and come on land only to breed and raise their young.

Their bodies are well designed for swimming. Their feathers are so small and tightly packed that they look like scales. Because of this, they can move through the water sleekly. Feathers also provide insulation. Penguins swim in very cold water. Their feet are used for steering. Powerful flippers provide propulsion. Those flippers enable them to swim with great strength. Sometimes a penguin will surface so forcefully that it will soar through the air. On land, the flippers are used for fighting. Penguins look comical when they walk. They have a waddle. Sometimes they flop on their bellies and slide.

In 1975 an American scientist named Kooyman studied the diving habits of penguins. He found that they can dive much deeper than people imagined. They go to depths of 800 feet and can stay down for 18 minutes.

The largest penguin is the emperor penguin. An adult stands 4 feet tall and weighs about 60 pounds. It lives in the Antarctic. Some people think that it is the most beautiful of all penguins. It has a purple bill and its "bib" is golden and shiny.

The macaroni penguin is not well known. It lives in the sub-Antarctic and the islands in the cold regions of all three oceans. It is very different in appearance from the emperor. At 2 feet tall and weighing only about 10 pounds, it is one of the smaller penguins. It has long, bright, yellow plumes growing from the top of its head. It looks like it is wearing a crown.

The Galapagos penguin is very rare. There are only about 4,000 of these in the world. It lives on the Galapagos Islands. It is the only penguin to live so near the equator. It likes to live close to the warm sea waters, in caves or cliffs.

The rockhopper penguin is named for its habit of jumping or hopping from rock to rock while holding its feet together. It was savagely massacred in the millions by men who wanted its oil.

Family Life:

Males and females live apart, except during the breeding season. Most penguins have similar mating habits. The breeding season begins on October and extends into the six-month-long polar night.

Both males and females will spend the months prior to October swimming and fishing. They want to eat as much as possible at this time. They will not be able to eat later.

In October, the males will climb on shore and head for the breeding grounds. These are called "rookeries." All penguins have established rookeries that they go to year after year. The male will go to the nest and wait for the female to arrive. When she gets there, they greet each other. This is done with neck stretches and flipper waves. This is called the "mutual display." It is part of their ritual.

In November, the female lays one egg. Some penguins, like the Adelie, lay two. She then goes back to the sea to feed. Unlike some fathers, the male penguin plays a vital role in the birth of his young. If the egg were left alone at this point, it would surely freeze. The father incubates the egg by carrying it on his large feet. His body temperature keeps it warm. To keep from freezing himself, he gathers in a huddle with all the other fathers. It is a long vigil. The temperatures can reach 70 degrees below zero, and it is always dark. In some species the female returns to incubate the egg. This is called the "changing of the guard." They greet each other with excited "mutual displays." The male quickly goes off to sea. He has not eaten in about 6 weeks.

The incubation period is about 40 days. One exception, the king penguin, takes as long as 54 days. The baby weighs about 11 ounces and is covered with gray down. Since there is nothing for it to eat in this frozen place, the parents must feed their babies in a strange manner. They take turns going to sea and collecting fish in their bills. They do not swallow the fish. They return to the nest and allow the baby to pick the fish out of their bills. This is the only food the baby has.

It is now January. It is still dark and very cold. All the babies huddle together as their fathers did. This huddle is called a "creche." Soon the ice will begin to break up and parents and young will head for the open sea.

Penguins are noisy, social creatures. They will gladly take care of each other's young. Most penguins are mature at 4 years of age. They live between 25 and 30 years.

Conservation:

Penguins love to be in the water. They spend most of their time there. If a hunter is after them, he will go to their breeding grounds. Because penguins always return to the same rookery every year, he knows where to find them. Penguins do not move quickly on land, so they are nearly helpless. Some penguins, like the rockhopper, have valuable stores of oil. For this reason they were preyed on and killed in the millions.

Penguin chicks are in danger from the leopard seal. Leopard seals will wait just under the ice. They pounce on young penguins just as they are about to take their first swim.

Men cannot do much about the threat of leopard seals, but they can control human hunters. The people of 11 nations of the Southern Hemisphere have banded together to protect the penguin. Their rookeries are now protected by international law. Many of them are bird sanctuaries.

Tyler M. Paetkau

Entrepreneur
MAGAZINE'S

LEGAL
GUIDE

Hiring
and Firing

Ep
Entrepreneur.
Press

Editorial director: Jere L. Calmes
Cover design: Desktop Miracles, Inc.
Composition and production: MillerWorks

This publication is designed to provide accurate and authoritative information in regard to
the subject matter covered. It is sold with the understanding that the publisher is not engaged
in rendering legal, accounting, or other professional services. If legal advice or other expert
assistance is required, the services of a competent professional person should be sought.

Scales ©Rzymu

Library of Congress Cataloging-in-Publication Data
Paetkau, Tyler M.
   Hiring and firing / by Tyler M. Paetkau.
     p. cm.
   ISBN-13: 978-1-59918-070-0 (alk. paper)
   ISBN-10: 1-59918-070-7 (alk. paper)
     1. Employee selection. 2. Employees—Dismissal of. I. Title.
HF5549.5.S38P32 2007
658.3'11—dc22   2007004074

Printed in Canada

12 11 10 09 08 07   10 9 8 7 6 5 4 3 2 1

Contents

Appendix: Sample Policies and Forms

Introduction

O n an airplane, the take-off and the landing are the
most dangerous parts of the flight. Similarly, in
business, the most treacherous part of an employment
relationship is the beginning and the end. Why?
Because they can claim you discriminated against
them and sue you, get injured and sue you, and steal
from you and (after you fire them) sue you. But you
can and should avoid legal problems with your
employees.

This book is a road map to help you navigate the
journey that is the employment relationship process.
The goal is to help you avoid unexpected explosions and
your most valuable asset—your human capital. The

employment relationship need not be an adversarial one, but employers need to understand that it can quickly become adversarial and plan accordingly. This book is not a substitute for sound legal advice from an experienced labor and employment lawyer, but it will help small and "start-up" employers recognize the legal issues raised by their labor and employment law practices and policies.

With increased scrutiny on employers—of all sizes and in all types of industries—in the wake of recent corporate scandals (for example, Tyco, Arthur Andersen, Enron, Quest, Wal-Mart, JP Morgan, and many others), and with the accompanying potential exposure both from a liability and an employee morale standpoint, employers cannot afford simply to "roll the dice." It is critical for small and start-up employers to get it right at the outset of the employment relationship, and to continue to monitor the employment relationship from beginning to end. Fortunately, many of the concepts discussed in this book fall under the category of common sense. Some of them will seem intuitive, even to small and start-up businesses. For example, most entrepreneurs and small business owners were themselves subordinate employees at one point in their careers. In planning and managing the employment relationship, think about what worked and did not work when *you* were an employee:

- How did you like to be treated when you were an employee?
- What things could your prior employers, managers, and supervisors have done better to make you a more productive, efficient, and happy employee?
- What things did your prior employers, managers, and supervisors do that really motivated you and made you want to perform to your maximum capability?
- What prior employer conduct made you want to quit on the spot?
- How could your prior employers have done a better job communicating with their employees?
- What things did your prior employers do that you felt were unfair, dishonest, or less than straightforward?

In short, the time-honored "Golden Rule"—treat others as you would like to be treated—has an important role in managing the employment relationship.

Studies have shown that most employees simply want to be treated fairly, honestly, and in a straightforward manner. Employees sue when they feel mistreated, lied to, manipulated, and used by their employers. Motivated and happy employees will make your business grow and succeed. Employee morale can be much more important than your wonderful products, your loyal customers, your cutting-edge technology, and your industry experience. The lesson for employers? Invest in your most important asset—your employees—as much if not more than you invest in these other important components of your business plan. Indeed, happy and motivated employees can help you immeasurably in improving all other aspects of your business. First and foremost, you need and want a happy, loyal, motivated, and stable workforce!

> Your family is important. Protecting the life of your business is crucial to preserving your family's income.

Of course, some employment laws and requirements are not so intuitive. Sometimes the legal requirement for employers are obscure, inconsistent, ambiguous, and elusive. Accordingly, this book also will help you avoid potential traps, where the legal requirements are not so obvious.

Hiring the Best and Brightest

Football coach Paul "Bear" Bryant is famous for saying, "I don't hire anybody not brighter than I am. If they're not smarter than me, I don't need them." Neither does your business. The best investment you can make in a new employee is taking the time to make a smart, well-informed hiring decision. You will avoid dealing later with the problem employee, that employee's problems, and, when you finally get fed up, the employee's wrongful termination or other lawsuit.

The First Question: Do You Want an Employee or an Independent Contractor?

The initial decision for many employers is whether to hire an employee or an independent contractor. Due to the penalties associated with misclassifying employees as independent contractors (discussed below), and the increased government scrutiny in this area, employers should be cautious in treating a worker as an independent contractor. A court or administrative agency could later find that the worker was actually an employee and impose substantial penalties (including back wages, employment benefits and taxes, and statutory penalties) on the employer.

The following is a brief overview of the independent contractor versus employee determination. The key issue is the degree of control exercised by the would-be employer. Thus, for example, the fact that the contractor works for others, brings his or her own tools, sets his or her own work hours, carries his or her own tools and equipment, etc., is helpful. Unfortunately, no one factor is controlling.

Legal Definition

The law generally provides that a worker may be considered an independent contractor if:

1. The worker has the right to control the performance of services;
2. The result of the work is the primary factor bargained for, and not the means by which it is accomplished;
3. The worker has an independently established business;
4. The worker's independent contractor status is not a subterfuge to avoid employee status.

The law further states that independent contractor status is evidenced if the worker:

1. Has a substantial investment in the business other than personal services;
2. Purports to be in business for himself or herself;
3. Receives compensation by project rather than by time;
4. Has control over the time and place the work is performed;

5. Supplies the tools used in the work;
6. Hires his or her own employees;
7. Performs work that is not ordinarily in the course of the employer's work;
8. Performs work that requires a particular skill;
9. Holds a business license;
10. Intends to establish an independent contractor relationship;
11. Agrees that the relationship is not terminable at will.

Again, there is no easy-to-apply formula or test for determining when a worker is (or becomes) an employee rather than an independent contractor.

> ### The Six-Month Rule of Thumb
>
> Although no length of time worked will tip the balance from independent contractor to employee, a general rule of thumb for employers is that if the worker works for you for six continuous months, you should seriously consider whether he or she is in fact an employee subject to your control. The longer that a worker performs the same services for you, the more likely a court or an administrative agency will find that he or she was in fact an employee rather than an independent contractor. Generally the more "control" that you exercise over the worker, the more likely he or she will be considered an employee.

Independent Contractor Agreements

The first step an employer should take to define the relationship is to have the parties execute a well-written independent contractor agreement. This agreement should state that the employer is only interested in the results to be achieved, and that the manner and method of accomplishing the results are left to the control of the independent contractor. However, the mere existence of an independent contractor agreement alone will not compel a court or agency to conclude that an independent contractor relationship exists. Instead, all of the relevant factors must be reviewed before any decisions are made. (See sample Independent Contractor Agreement in the Appendix.)

To determine whether a worker can be properly classified as an independent contractor, the employer should carefully review the checklist in Figure 1.1. It is important to remember that no single factor is determinative. Instead, the employer must consider all of these factors when making this crucial decision.

FIGURE 1–1. **Independent Contractor Checklist**

The greater the number of yes responses to the questions set forth below, the greater the likelihood that the worker may be considered an independent contractor.

❑ *Intent of the Parties.* Did you and the worker clearly intend to create an independent contractor relationship? Is there a written independent contract agreement signed by both you and the worker? Do you and the worker not have the right to terminate the relationship at will, i.e., a 30-day notice or "cause" required for termination of the contract?

❑ *Right to Control.* Do you have little or no control over the worker? Does the worker have the right to control the manner and means of accomplishing the results desired? Does the worker use his or her own initiative and judgment when performing the services?

❑ *Separate Business.* Does the worker hold himself or herself out as an independent contractor instead of an employee? Is the worker engaged in a separately established business distinct from that of your business? Does the worker perform services for other people and companies besides you/your business?

❑ *Other Employees.* Does the worker performing the services have the right to hire and terminate employees working for him or her? Do you not have the ability to hire or fire the employees of the worker? Does the worker have no authority to supervise employees of your company?

❑ *Specialized Services.* Does the worker provide specialized services that no other employee of yours can perform? Is the worker providing services that require a great deal of skill? Is the work being performed by the worker not part of your regular business? Does the worker have a work-related license, degree, or certificate?

❑ *Services Performed.* Does the work have a set time period in which it must be completed? Is the length of time for which the worker is to perform the services short? Does the worker provide the tools, instrumentalities, and supplies to perform the work? Does the worker provide services at a location other than at your premises? Does the worker enter your premises on an infrequent basis, or not at all?

❑ *Payment for Services.* Is the method of payment by the job instead of by the hour? Is the worker being paid a high rate for his or her services? Do you issue invoices for the worker's services? Are the payments to the worker charged to accounts other than your own labor and salary accounts? Is the worker not listed on your payroll? Do you not withhold taxes from payments to the worker? Do you issue a 1099 Form for the services provided by the worker?

Employers should recognize that merely placing an independent contractor label on a worker is not sufficient under the law. A court or administrative agency will look behind such labels to the practical realities of the working relationship. Furthermore, a court or administrative agency is unlikely to be sympathetic to the small or start-up employer's defense that it planned to reclassify the independent contractor as an employee once it obtained funding, or once it obtained more employees, or became more established, or hired additional workers, or obtained a sufficient number of customers. There is no start-up employee exemption for basic employee obligations, such as minimum wage and employment taxes.

The independent contractor versus employee determination is a fine example of how misapplied labels can get you in trouble. Don't assume that a label will cover up the realities of the situation. Put another way, if it walks like a duck, quacks like a duck, and acts like a duck, it is a duck even if you call it something else. Similarly, if you exercise a sufficient degree of control over your workers, if they work alongside your regular employees, report to and take direction from the same supervisors as your regular employees, and work regular hours over a long period of time (for example, longer than the six-month rule of thumb

The Danger in Labels

Don't make the common but often costly mistake of using labels to cover up the realities of the employment relationship. Whether it is an "independent contractor" or "partner" label to avoid payment of wages and employment taxes, or a "manager" label to avoid the payment of overtime to employees who are actually not managers and thus not exempt from the payment of overtime—or any other easy label—when challenged a court or administrative agency will likely ignore or give short shrift the employer-chosen "label" and instead evaluate the practical realities of the employment relationship. Along the same lines, employers should be careful not to assume that merely having nice, well-articulated policies in place (for example, internal complaint procedures for whistleblowers and victims of discrimination and unlawful harassment) means that you are protected from legal claims and liability. The best employment policies in the world won't protect you if you don't take them seriously and fail to implement and/or enforce them! Once again, a court or an administrative agency will not be impressed by a well-drafted policy on a piece of paper if, in practice, you don't enforce the policy. In short, what you do is much more important than what you *say* you do!

> ### Microsoft's Problem with Independent Contractors
>
> A few years ago, one of the world's most respected employers, Microsoft Corporation, got into trouble for misclassifying a large group of temporary employees as independent contractors (*Vizcaino v. Microsoft Corp.*, 173 F.3d 713 [9th Cir. 1999]). The problem for Microsoft was that these temps worked alongside the company's regular full-time employees, were subject to the same level of supervision as its full-time employees, and worked regular hours over long periods of time. Although Microsoft had independent contractor agreements with these temps, the practical reality was that they were doing the same work and receiving the same treatment as Microsoft's regular employees. Ultimately, a court found that Microsoft had misclassified these temps as independent contractors instead of employees, and ordered the company to pay those workers back wages and employment benefits (including the retroactive right to participate in the company's lucrative stock option benefits!), as well as employment taxes and substantial statutory penalties. Although Microsoft saved some money in the short term by classifying these temps as independent contractors, it paid dearly in the long term (approximately $20 million), and had to reclassify the workers as employees. The Microsoft example demonstrates that even large, sophisticated employers can and do make costly mistakes by incorrectly labeling employees as independent contractors. Don't make the same mistake.

mentioned previously), then a court or an administrative agency is likely to find that they were in fact your employees, despite the label that you placed on them and the independent contractor agreement that you had them sign.

Penalties for Misclassifying Workers

The penalties for misclassifying an employee as an independent contractor can be quite severe. They may include an intrusive government audit, which frequently leads to the employer having to pay back taxes and fines to the government. Also, workers who were misclassified as independent contractors may bring civil lawsuits to recover lost wages and benefits from the employer, and may even recover their attorneys' fees and costs of suit. Finally, there has been a recent trend toward class action lawsuits against employers in this area, which can be quite expensive to defend.

Joint Employer Problems

Problems arise when temporary staffing firms make mistakes with temporary employees, or where they are insolvent. The courts and governmental administrative agencies (such as the Equal Employment Opportunity Commission [EEOC], the IRS, Workers' Compensation, and the Occupational Safety and Health Act [OSHA]), generally will treat the temp as an employee of *both* the staffing firm and its customer (the employer). Accordingly, it is sound practice to audit the staffing firm's labor and employment policies and forms, and to ensure its financial solvency.

The Audition: Employment Interviews

It's a try-out, so let the interviewee audition. There is no overwhelming need to sell an applicant on your company. The applicant *wants* the job. *They* spent the time filling out an application form, submitting a résumé, and coming in for the interview. That awkward pause in the interview conversation is your friend. Just curb the urge to jump in. The interviewee will do it for you and you will gain valuable information in the process. If you talk to someone long enough, odds are you will get a warning signal if something is not right. You can only uncover those hidden secrets if you dig a little, since their goal is to try to keep them hidden. A little diligence and self-control will serve you in the end.

An excellent technique to help you find someone who is serious about working for you and plans to stay awhile is to try to talk them *out* of the job. If they still want the job after you tell them how hard the work is, how the hours can be long, how some parts are just downright tedious, that's a good sign!

> ### Stop Talking
>
> Use the 75/25 Rule: Listen more, talk less. Many interviewers have an unnecessary and seemingly uncontrollable urge to talk during an interview. This is a bad idea. While talking, the interviewer is not gathering information, not keenly observing the applicant, not picking up important clues that just might avert a frustrating, expensive, and time-consuming bad hire. After all, the reason you are there is because you want to find out if the person sitting in front of you is the one for the job.

Don't Make Promises You Can't Keep

Just because a promise is not in writing, doesn't mean it's not enforceable. Oral promises made to job applicants or employees can be enforced against an employer if the person to whom the promise was made reasonably relied on the promise to their detriment. What your recruiter or hiring manager says to the applicant can create liability for the company. An employee can claim fraud against an employer if, during the hiring process, the employee reasonably relied on misrepresentations made during the hiring process. The false statements have to be specific and not just statements of opinion like the company is "anticipating solid growth and a stable, profitable future" (*Everts vs. Matteson*, 21 Cal. 2d 437, 451 [1942]).

No Moving Van Unless You Are Darn Sure about It

Inducing someone to change their residence by making misrepresentations during the hiring process can create serious issues. In fact, in some states, such as California (see California Labor Code § 970], there are specific statutes that provide punitive damages and even make it a crime for an employer to fraudulently misrepresent the terms and conditions of employment.

Avoid this scenario by emphasizing the at-will nature of the employment relationship as much as possible. Make it very clear in the offer letter that although you would like them to join your company, there are absolutely no guarantees of any length of continued employment in the job they are accepting, and, in fact, the job itself may cease to exist at any time in the future, even if they are doing a fantastic job. This "no promises" mindset should be emphasized even more when someone is physically moving his or her residence to take the job.

Cut through the Fluff: Be Efficient

Interview to extract the most information in the least amount of time. Focusing questions on pertinent traits and skills keeps you on the appropriate legal track and avoids throwing you into dangerous waters. Innocently talking about things like the interviewee's family, ethnic background, and other areas

Relocation Nightmare

Joe Boxliter is a star in the field of pharmaceutical sales. He works for DrugCo, but PharmCo wants him in a bad way, so the latter offers Joe a lucrative incentive compensation package along with a guaranteed salary and generous benefits. The only complication is that Joe is currently based in Arizona, but PharmCo needs him for a new territory in California. No problem. The icing on the compensation package is that all moving expenses will be paid for by PharmCo. When sales dip and there is a need to cut jobs, it is determined that Joe has got to go. Big problem. Joe just sold his house in Tucson, pulled his kids out of their schools, and purchased a home in Los Angeles based on the promise that he would get a substantial raise in one year. He has no intention of going anywhere. In fact, his plan was to retire from PharmCo—and no one ever gave him any reason to plan differently. In fact, Joe distinctly remembers his boss telling him that "here at PharmCo, we are one big family." (You can't fire your family, right?) Joe feels secure. PharmCo has a problem.

Under California law (Labor Code sections 970-972), an employer (or person) is liable for double damages and is guilty of a misdemeanor if it/he/she "influence(s), persuade(s), or engage(s) any employee to move from another state to California, from California to another state, or even within California "through or by means of knowingly false representations ... concerning either: a) the kind, character, or existence of such work; b) the length of time such work will last, or the compensation ..."

Many states have similar "Grapes of Wrath" era laws, and many states' laws recognize a separate "tort" claim for "fraudulent inducement" to accept employment through misrepresentation. Victims can recover emotional distress damages, lost wages, reliance on false promises damages, and punitive damages.

that the government has determined may be discriminatory, can inadvertently lead you into a forbidden area. The law assumes that if you ask a question, then you care about the answer. This is not a time to make small talk.

What Are You Looking For?

If you don't know what you're looking for, how do you expect to find it? Do your homework. Sit down and figure out exactly what skills, background, edu-

FIGURE 1–2. **Employment Inquiries**

ACCEPTABLE	SUBJECT	UNACCEPTABLE
Name	Name	Maiden name
Place of residence	Residence	Questions regarding owning or renting.
Statements that hire is subject to verification that applicants meet legal age requirements.	Age	Age, birth date, date of attendance/completion of school, or questions that tend to identify applicants over 40.
Statements/inquiries regarding verification of legal right to work in the United States.	Birthplace, Citizenship	Birthplace of applicant or applicant's parents, spouse or other relatives; requirements that applicant produce naturalization or alien card prior to employment.
Languages applicant reads, speaks or writes if use of language other than English is relevant to the job for which applicant is applying.	National Origin	Questions as to nationality, lineage, ancestry, national origin, descent or parentage of applicant, applicant's parent or relative.
Statement by employer of regular days, hours, or shifts to be worked.	Religion	Questions regarding applicant's religion or religious days observed.
Name and address of parent or guardian if applicant is a minor. Statement of company policy regarding work assignment of employees who are related.	Sex, Marital Status, Family	Questions to indicate applicant's sex, marital status, number/ages of children or dependents, or regarding pregnancy, childbirth, or birth control. Name/address of relative, spouse, or children of adult applicant.
	Race, Color, Sexual Orientation	Questions to applicant's race, color, or sexual orientation, or regarding applicant's complexion, color of eyes or hair, or sexual orientation.
Statement that a photograph may be required after employment.	Physical Description Photographs, Fingerprints	Questions as to applicant's height/weight. Requiring applicant to affix a photograph to application or submit one at his/her option, or require a photograph after interview but before employment.
Employer may inquire if applicant can perform job-related functions or make statement that employment offer may be made contingent upon passing a job-related mental/physical examination.	Mental/Physical Disability,Mental Condition (Applicants)	Any inquiry into the applicant's general health, medical condition, or mental/physical disability, or requiring a psychological/medical examination of any applicant.
A medical/psychological examination/inquiry may be made as long as it is job-related and consistent with business necessity and all applicants for the same job classification are subject to the same.	Mental/Physical Disability, Medical Condition (Post-Offer/Pre-Employment)	Any inquiry into the applicant's general health, medical condition, or physical/mental disability, if not job-related and consistent with business necessity.
A medical/psychological examination/inquiry may be made as long as the examination is job-related and consistent with business necessity.	Mental/Physical Disability, Medical Condition (Employees)	Any inquiry into the employee's general health, medical condition, or mental/physical disability, if not job-related and consistent with business necessity.
Job-related questions about convictions, except those that have been sealed, expunged, or statutorily eradicated.	Arrest, Criminal Record	General questions regarding arrest record.
Questions regarding relevant skills acquired during U.S. military service.	Military Service	General questions regarding military service such as dates/type of discharge, or questions regarding service in a foreign military.
Requesting lists of job-related organizations, clubs, or professional societies omitting indications of protected bases.	Organizations, Activities	General questions regarding organizations, clubs, societies, and lodges.
Name of persons willing to provide professional and/or character references for applicant.	References	Questions of applicant's former employers or acquaintances that elicit information specifying applicant's race, etc.
Name and address of person to be notified in case of accident or emergency.	Notice In Case of Emergency	Name, address, and relationship of relative to be notified in case of accident or emergency.

cation, and experience you need in the position. Then write a job description—or at least jot down the essential functions of the job, the tasks, duties, and functions that you need the employee to perform, including all the physical and mental requirements that go along with it. This will help you get the right person for the job.

The reality, however, is that time is rarely on your side when in comes to filling a position. More often than not, there is not much time to sit and ponder. The new employee was needed yesterday. The very reason you are hiring is because the company is experiencing a dramatic increase in work or because a key employee has up and left. So much for leisurely searching, but that doesn't mean that you hire the first person who walks through the door. That is a recipe for disaster.

Why Is a Job Description so Important?

Under the Americans with Disabilities Act, an individual with a disability who is able to perform the essential functions of the job, with or without reasonable accommodation, cannot be discriminated against (42 U.S. Code § 12111 [8]). If we don't know the essential functions of the job, how can we determine who is or is not qualified? If someone brings a discrimination claim, it is very likely that the job description will be reviewed to determine if discrimination occurred. A complete and thorough job description that includes all the essential functions will help protect the company from unfounded disability discrimination claims. Note, however, that poor job descriptions (i.e. inadequate, incomplete, inaccurate, etc.) can be powerful evidence *against* employers.

Behavior-based and Personality-based Interviewing

Behavior-based interviewing relies on the theory that past behavior is a good predictor of future behavior. Set up a few situations or dilemmas that typically occur in the work environment of the job applicant. Example: An important customer complains about poor service and threatens to send her business elsewhere. The complaint is about employer's specialized services, industry, products, processes, technology, etc. How would the applicant handle the situation?

Personality-based interviewing attempts to uncover the applicant's true character, traits, and qualities. Examples of good questions: What are your strongest skills? What do you do in your spare time? Why are you interested in market research on XYZ? Although many applicants can easily rehearse

When you need someone *really bad*, that is precisely when you are going to get someone *really bad*. If you dread going through a series of interviews, ask yourself this question: If you don't have the time to do it right this time, when are you going to have the time to do it again?

answers, it is worth a shot. See which works for you and for the position in which you are interviewing.

Interviewing Is Time Well Spent

Despite the fact that interviewing can feel like a non-productive, time-consuming exercise that eats up numerous hours and even days, often leading to a dead end, it is critically important in the long term. A good, solid hire will serve to either produce huge benefits or cost the company in terms of lost productivity, disruption, negative employee morale, and even the possibility of legal liability. Think of it like going to the dentist—no one likes to spend the time doing it, but it undoubtedly can save you from future pain.

Still not convinced that it is worth all the time and effort involved? How about the bottom line—money! The cost of making a bad hire by not making the requisite effort can add up to a large loss to your company when that new hire who wasn't thoroughly checked out either quits or is fired shortly after being hired. The company must foot the bill for another round of advertising, interviewing, and training. In addition to the lost time involved in redoing those tasks, there is also the potential loss of business when customers become dissatisfied with uneven service or quality due to staff changes.

To see how much you spend when you have to re-hire, check out the free "Turnover Cost Calculator" at www.chally.com/turnover_cost_calculator.htm.

Conclusion

The most important investment you can make in the business is recruiting, hiring, training, developing, and retaining employee talent. It starts with practical and legally sound interviewing practices.

CHAPTER 2

The Value of Applications

E mployers should use the application process to avoid hiring bad employees. Of course, employers need to ask job-related questions that are designed to determine whether the applicant has the skills, education, and experience required for the open position. Employers also should focus on finding the right fit. In weeding out applicants who are potential trouble, employers should focus on identifying periods of unemployment and the applicant's reasons for leaving his or her former employers. Also make sure to include a verification and acknowledgment that the applicant has provided truthful information in the application and that *any* significant misrepresentation is ground for immediate termination of employment or revocation of any offer of employment.

Avoiding Illegal Questions and Inquiries

The law provides that employers may not discriminate against any applicant based on that applicant's protected status, including race, national origin, ancestry, citizenship, gender, age, religion, disability, and other protected characteristics. As a practical matter, these prohibitions make it illegal to ask questions during the application or interview process that will elicit information that identifies the applicant's protected characteristic or membership in a protected group. A few examples illustrate how even well-intentioned employers can violate the law. It is customary, for example, to ask an applicant about his or her educational background and history in the application itself and/or during the interview process. In doing so, however, employers should be mindful that they cannot ask an applicant the date of graduation from high school, as such information would tend to reveal the applicant's age-protected status. Also avoid asking about:

- Whether the applicant intends to become a United States citizen, as this tends to reveal citizenship. Instead, you can ask, "If hired, can you provide evidence of your legal right to work in the U.S.?"
- How the applicant acquired the ability to read, write, or understand a foreign language, as this tends to reveal national origin and ancestry.
- Clubs, societies, lodges, or organizations to which the applicant belongs, as this tends to reveal race, national origin, and other protected characteristics. Instead, ask only for job-related activities and organizations.
- The number and kinds of arrests an applicant has had, which is prohibited by statute; employers can ask about convictions, but must add that any conviction does not necessarily disqualify the applicant from employment.
- The contact information for the "nearest relative" in case of emergency, which tends to reveal family status. Instead, simply request the name of

a person to contact in case of an emergency.

See Figure 1.2 for a list of prohibited questions during the application and interview process. The Appendix of this book also contains guidelines for acceptable interview and application questions.

The Critical Importance of At-Will Employment Disclaimers

Another critical item that employers should consider including in their employment application is an "at-will statement," confirming that this is the status of the employment relationship. But what does at-will employment really mean? At-will employment allows either the employee or the employer to end the employment relationship at any time without advance notice or good reason. It provides maximum flexibility to both parties, although many people believe it favors employers who use it to terminate employment without any good reason. In many of other countries, such as those in Western Europe, at-will employment is not the rule. Generally, these other countries require "good cause" or reason for discharge, borrowing from the union context, where the collective bargaining agreements typically require "good" or "just cause," or simply "cause," for termination.

The majority of states recognize employment is at-will, unless the employee and the employer make a different or contrary agreement concerning the duration or other conditions of employment. Missouri and Montana do not recognize at-will employment.

Employers might rightfully question why at-will employment is so important, given that "we always have a good reason anyway" to terminate an employee's employment. The reason is that employers need to retain maximum

> **Legally Protected Characteristics: Title VII and State Law Counterparts**
>
> Employers should review the laws in very state where they do business, as some states' laws include additional protected characteristics. For example, California law (Fair Employment and Housing Act) prohibits sexual orientation discrimination, whereas federal law (Title VII) does not contain a similar prohibition. In general, employers must comply with the law that provides greater protection to employees. See the Appendix, page 183: Employment Discrimination Laws by State.

Avoiding Implied Promises of Long-Term Employment

Many statements by employers can give rise to "implied" promises of long-term employment. For example, avoid statements or promises such as the following:

- "This is a career position."
- "We are a family here," or "This is a family atmosphere."
- "As long as you do a good job, you can stay here as long as you like."
- "You will be a permanent employee."
- "Your annual salary will be $50,000" implies at least a one-year term of employment.
- "You have lifetime employment."
- "We won't fire you unless you steal from us."
- "You will be eligible for an annual bonus."

flexibility to respond to changing business conditions and requirements. Even if you, the employer, always have a good reason to terminate an employee when you decide to do so, you want to avoid any claims or litigation by the employee over the adequacy or validity of your reasons. In addition, you need to maintain maximum flexibility in case there is a major downturn in you business or other conditions beyond your control that make it necessary to terminate a group of employees with a minimal amount of notice. By including at-will disclaimers in their employment applications and other policies, you can avoid major headaches and even litigation over the meaning of "good cause" and whether you had sufficient reason to terminate a particular employee.

Courts and arbitrators have ruled that the presumption of at-will employment status may be overturned by evidence of contrary intent on the part of the employer and the employee. For example, an employer's promises about the duration of employment may override the statutory presumption, particularly when the employer makes such promises in writing. As an employer, you should not use statements such as "You are part of the family," "This is a career position," "Do your job and you'll be here for life." Avoid mention of annual salary (use weekly or bi-weekly salary) and terms such as "permanent" employee (use "full-time" if necessary). Avoid making predictions of future growth and job longevity, and train managers to not make promises about the anticipated duration of employment.

In evaluating whether an employee has overcome the presumption of at-will employment, courts often look to various factors including the personnel

---

The Federal WARN Act and Title VII

Employers should note that in the case of a mass layoff or plant closing, 60 days advance notice of termination is required by the federal WARN Act (Worker Adjustment Retraining Notification). Some states also have similar laws requiring advance notice of mass layoffs. Further, employers who desire to obtain a release of all employment-related claims in connection with a mass layoff must provide the affected employees who are 40 years old or older with information about the selection criteria and the federal Older Workers Benefits Protection Act (OWBPA), which is part of the Age Discrimination in Employment Act (ADEA), in order to obtain a valid release of age discrimination claims.

---

policies or practices of the employer, the employee's longevity of service, actions or communications (written or verbal) by the employer reflecting assurances of continued employment, and the practices of the industry.

To minimize these risks of an employee claiming (and a judge or a jury later agreeing) that the employer did not have good or just cause to terminate a particular employee's employment, employers should consider including an at-will policy in the employment application and any offer letter or employment contract, including in any stock option agreement, and also in the employee handbook. Here is an example of how the policy may be expressed in an offer of employment contract:

As noted in the application form and in the *Employee Handbook*, employment with the Company is at the mutual consent of each employee and the Company. Accordingly, while the Company has every hope that employment relationships will be mutually beneficial and rewarding, employees and the Company retain the right to terminate the employment relationship at will, at any time, with or without cause. Please note that no individual has the authority to make any contrary agreement or representation. This constitutes a final and fully binding integrated agreement with respect to the at-will nature of the employment relationship.

It is also important to train supervisors and managers to not make any promises to employees regarding continued employment or the anticipated length of the employment relationship.

Other Information to Seek in Applications

In addition to the above information, employers should consider including in the employment application the following:

- A consent to a background check (see Chapter 5);

- A consent to drug or fitness-for-duty testing;

- An agreement to arbitrate all employment-related disputes;

- A provision affirming the employer's respect for any prior employer's trade secrets or other confidential and/or proprietary information, and confirming protection for the employer's own trade secrets and confidential and proprietary information (see Chapter 7);

- A commitment to a discrimination-free work environment (also known as an equal employment opportunity or EEO commitment);

- Prior employment history;

- Educational background;

- Special skills, training, or knowledge that would assist the applicant in performing the job for which he or she is applying;

- Personal information about the applicant, including name and contact information;

- Whether the applicant is willing to work overtime, if the job requires it;

- Whether the applicant, if hired, can provide proof of his or her legal right to work in the U.S.;

- Reference information, particularly from prior employers; and

- How the applicant found out about the job opening, whether by referral by another employee, advertisement, etc.

With regard to compliance with immigration laws, employers should note that they cannot knowingly hire or continue to employ people who do not have the legal right to work in the U.S. It is therefore very important for you, as an employer, to verify every employee's legal right to work in the U.S.

through the use of the "I-9" verification process, and periodically to audit immigration law compliance by, for example, checking to make sure all I-9 forms are completed and kept in each employee's personnel file. In particular, you should promptly complete the I-9 verification forms for each new employee, and retain all paperwork supporting such verifications. In addition, you also should pay attention to expiring work permits and work visas for foreign employees.

> **Verification of Information Statement**
>
> I certify that the information I have provided in this Application is true, correct, and complete, and that I have not omitted any material information. I agree that a material misstatement or omission on this Application is grounds for immediate termination of employment.

Finally, it is very important to include in the application statements to the effect that the applicant is certifying that the information that he or she provides is true, correct, and complete; that the applicant authorizes the employer to verify the information provided; that the applicant fully releases the employer from any legal liability for seeking to verify or relying on such information; and that the provision of materially false information in the application is grounds for immediate termination of employment or revocation of any employment offer if discovered before hiring.

Employers should consider including the following statements in their applications:

The statements set forth above are true and complete. I authorize Employer to obtain information about me from previous employers, including relevant facts and opinions about my work and work habits, and I release from liability or responsibility all persons or entities requesting or supplying such information. I release Employer from liability for considering, relying on, or taking into account the information it receives from such persons or entities.

I expressly authorize any educational institutions that I have attended to provide transcripts and degree status. I release from liability or responsibility all persons or entities requesting or supplying such information. I release

Employer from liability for considering, relying on, or taking into account the information it receives from such persons or entities.

I understand that any false information or significant omissions on this application may disqualify me from further consideration for employment, and that if employed, false information or significant omissions on this application shall be grounds for immediate termination of employment.

A sample application for employment can be found in the Appendix. Employers should consult with an experienced labor and employment law attorney to verify the legal requirements in the states in which they intend to use such applications.

Conclusion

A well-designed application will assist you in achieving your ultimate goal of hiring and retaining the best and brightest employees. Employers should note that some bad applicants may be discouraged from even applying by the employer's thorough (and legal) background check. A good application will confirm at-will employment, authorize legal background checks, protect employers from unfair competition and trade secret theft claims by former employers, and screen out poor candidates for employment.

CHAPTER 3

Avoid
Liability

in the Recruitment and Interview Process

Applicants, and not just employees, enjoy various legal protections even during the recruitment and pre-hire process. Employers therefore must pay attention to the various legal protections, most notably the protection against discrimination in the recruiting, interviewing, and hiring process. There are many traps for the unwary employer discussed in this chapter.

Interviewing a prospective employee is not akin to speed dating, so take your time and be careful. There is a lot to be gained in an interview by posing methodical and well-thought-out questions.

Prepare for the Interview

Here are some important steps to ensure an efficient and effective interview process:

- Does the person applying for the position have all the requisite skills and minimal educational background for the position? If not, don't waste your time interviewing.
- Review the applicant's application, résumé, and any other information that the applicant provided. Make sure all portions of the application are filled out. Look for inconsistencies between the application and the résumé, as well as gaps in employment. If you find inconsistencies or gaps, be sure to ask the applicant about it. He or she could have a logical explanation, or give you reason to be cautious in hiring this person.
- If you will be conducting a reference check and/or background check, have you, pursuant to the Fair Credit Reporting Act, informed the applicant of the process and informed him or her that an acceptable background report is a prerequisite to employment?
- If you will require a medical exam and/or drug screen, has the applicant been informed that successful completion of these also are conditions of employment?

There is a lot that could be lost in terms of both time and money if the screening process is less than adequate. Some of the danger areas to watch out for include claims of discrimination, violation of privacy, and negligent hiring.

Avoiding Discrimination Claims Means Never Having to Say "But I Didn't Mean Anything by It!"

We all just talk sometimes. We say things that are simply forgotten almost the moment they are out of our mouths. A job interview is definitely not the place for this type of conversation. You can be sure that if you ask an applicant a question, that person believes you really care about the answer. And the law tends to back up an applicant on that conclusion.

Illegal Interview Questions Can Get a Company into Trouble

If you make a discriminatory statement or ask a discriminatory question during an interview, it is not something the applicant is likely to forget when that person is not offered the job. That discriminatory statement will be used as evidence of discrimination if the applicant decides to claim that is the reason the job was not offered to them.

What Did You Mean by That?

You will have to have a credible explanation of why you made the statement and why nothing was meant by it. That explanation will have to be believed by a judge, a jury, or an administrative agency. You should be able to clearly and logically explain the reason you chose to hire the person that got the job, and why you didn't hire the person who is now claiming that a legally impermissible reason was why they didn't get the job. Always be able to state the legitimate, non-discriminatory, business reason for your hiring decision.

What a lot of work! Why not just make sure that discriminatory statements or questions never make it into the job interview? It is such a better approach. If you don't need to know the answer, or if it is better not to know the answer, then don't ask the question.

The key is to keep all interview and application questions related to the job in question. If the question doesn't help you evaluate whether this applicant is the right person for this job, then don't ask it. Straying from this fundamental goal might get you into legal trouble.

Examples of Job-Related Interview Questions

1. What part of your education best prepared you for this job?
2. What recent work experience have you had that best prepared you for this job?
3. What special skills do you have for this job that aren't reflected in your résumé?
4. Can you tell us about your recent work experiences that will help you perform this job better?
5. What unique qualities will you bring to this job?

So What Exactly Can You Be Accused of?

Over 40 years ago, Congress enacted a law called Title VII of the Civil Rights Act of 1964. A few years later came the Age Discrimination in Employment Act (ADEA) and then, in 1990, the Americans with Disabilities Act. These laws prohibit discrimination based on sex, race, color, religion, national origin, age, and disability.

Title VII and the ADA cover all private employers, state and local governments, and educational institutions that employ 15 or more individuals. These laws also cover private and public employment agencies, labor organizations, and joint labor management committees controlling apprenticeship and training.

The ADEA covers all private employers with 20 or more employees, state and local governments (including school districts), employment agencies, and labor organizations.

Numerous State Laws Add Areas to Avoid

In addition to the federal anti-discrimination provision discussed briefly above, individual states pass their own laws prohibiting discrimination, some of which provide broader protection to employees than the federal laws. For example, categories like genetic traits, gender identity, sexual orientation, and marital status are protected in some states in addition to those covered by the federal laws. See the Appendix for a table of employment discrimination laws for each state (page 183).

So what does all this mean to you when you are hiring? Don't ask questions or encourage discussion of those topics. Why would you want to do so? None of those areas have anything to do with what you are hiring someone to do. Stick to the areas that you really care about. How much experience do they have in the position you are offering? What is their educational background? What kind of past success have they had? Are they available to work when you need them?

The general rule is that employers must avoid questions during the recruitment, application, and interview process that require applicants to

FIGURE 3–1. **Ten Questions to Absolutely Avoid During an Interview**

1. **How old are you?** It doesn't really matter unless you are casting a teenage sitcom. Don't try to be sly about it, either, with questions like: "When did you graduate from high school?" "When were you born?" "You are about the same age as me, right?" They all can be used to establish an age discrimination claim if the person is not hired and turns out to be 40 years old or older.

2. **Have you ever been arrested?** In the United States, we are presumed innocent until proven guilty. Any questions regarding arrests that did not result in a conviction should be avoided, as should any questions regarding criminal records that have been sealed, eradicated, or expunged. In fact, even actual convictions should not necessarily disqualify someone from employment. Convictions can be taken into consideration while making the employment decision, but factors like age at the time of the offense, seriousness and nature of the offense, and whether the person was rehabilitated should all go into the decision-making process.

3. **Where were you born?** How did you learn how to speak English so well? Any question that illicits a person's country of origin, lineage, ancestry, or nationality, are illegal. The one appropriate question to ask is based on immigration requirements: "Are you prevented from being employed in the United States because of your visa or immigration requirements?" Likewise, don't comment on their charming accent or the unique spelling of their name. Also, don't ask any of these questions about the applicant's spouse or relatives.

4. **Have you ever filed a workers' compensation claim?** Questions involving filing workers' compensation claims are not a valid basis to make an employment decision. The law provides this remedy for injured workers. Penalizing someone for exercising such a right is illegal.

5. **Are you disabled?** Employers should not make any inquiries about medical conditions, disabilities, the amount of sick time an applicant took from a prior job, or require an applicant to take a medical exam before making a conditional offer of employment.

6. **How many children do you have?** This question has no relevance to anything in a job interview. You'll see the family photos on the desk in due time. Be patient.

7. **Are you married? Single? Divorced? Engaged?** Likewise, these questions have no place in an interview, especially if you are—or can seem to be—asking for personal reasons. Don't go there. Under some states' laws, employers are strictly liable for managers' and supervisors' sexual harassment. That means if you do it and it is proven, you, as an agent of the company, have brought a liability against the company.

8. **Are you pregnant? Do you plan to become pregnant?** Pregnancy discrimination is a form of sex discrimination. It is illegal for an employer to refuse to hire an applicant because she is pregnant if she is able to work and is qualified for the position. Once you have the knowledge that someone is pregnant and you don't hire them, it is very difficult to convince a jury that you did not take that fact into account at all when making the hiring decision. Better not to know and not to have to defend yourself.

9. **What is your religion?** There is really no reason to talk about this either. If you are concerned about covering all work shifts, then simply explain when your company is open, and ask if the applicant can work all shifts.

10. **What is your sexual preference?** Certainly no one should ever ask this in an interview—but they have. Please don't become one of the statistics.

reveal information about their protected characteristics. Here are a few more examples:

- *Do you need any accommodations to perform your job?* Note, however, that it is acceptable to ask an applicant, "If hired, could you perform the essential functions of the job, with or without a reasonable accommodation?"
- *Where were your parents/relatives/family born?* This opens employers to claims of national origin, ancestry, and citizenship discrimination.
- *What language do you speak at home?* Employers can ask about language skills only if relevant to the job (for example, international relations position, interpreter).
- *What is your mother tongue?* (ethnicity, national origin)
- *What is your maiden name?* (marital status)
- *How did you get that name?* (ethnicity, national origin)
- *Who will take care of your family?* (marital status)
- *Which holidays will you need to take off?* (religion) Note, however, that employers generally can ask whether the applicant is available to work on weekends or evenings under certain circumstances.
- *What is your height and weight?*
- *What is your birth date?* (Age; note, however, that employers can ask whether the applicant can submit proof of age or whether the applicant is over 18 years old.)
- *What year did you graduate from high school?* (age)

Employers must avoid discrimination in the recruitment and application process. Therefore, in seeking out applicants, in communications with recruiters and headhunters, in job postings, want ads, advertising, and job descriptions, employers should avoid statements such as the following:

- "Employer looking for a thoughtful but aggressive woman as an assistant."
- "Employer looking for someone who takes an interest in her work."
- "Employer desires a salesman [use "salesperson" or "sales representative"], waitress [server], stewardess [flight attendant], fireman [firefighter]..."

- "Employer desires a recent [college or high school] graduate." This can be seen as age discrimination.
- "Employer desires a customer service girl with no accent" implicates the employer on gender and ethnicity/national origin discrimination.
- "Employer desires a 'family man' or a single/married employee" can instigate marital status discrimination claims.

Collecting Required Applicant Flow Data

Employers with federal (and in some cases, state) government contracts need to track and retain background information about applicants. The federal Office of Federal Contract Compliance Programs (OFCCP) issued new regulations on February 6, 2006, amending federal contractors' recordkeeping requirements for internet-based job applications. Such data is used with affirmative action programs and responsibilities, and for determining whether a particular job requirement, test, or practice has a "disparate impact" on a protected group of applicants. Employers may not, however, use such information as a basis for making the hiring decision. Also, employers must keep such information separate from the employee's personnel file and others responsible for personnel decisions. Employers who are required to retain such applicant flow data must retain it for two years.

Negligent Hiring

Negligent hiring can create liability for a company if it hires an employee who is incompetent, dangerous, or unfit for the job, and this creates an unreasonable risk of harm to others. Negligent hiring, according to agency law, is based on the following theory:

> A person conducting an activity through servants or other agents is subject to liability for harm resulting from his conduct if he is negligent or reckless … in the employment of improper persons or instrumentalities in work involving risk of harm to others. (American Law Institute Restatement of Agency [Second] section 213 [1958] at 458).

For example, in one case, the employer, a school district, hired an administrator who had been forced to resign from four prior school districts based on allegations of child sexual abuse and inappropriate relationships with young students (*Randi W. v. Muroc Unified Sch. Dist.*, 14 Cal. 4th 1066 [1997]). The parents of a student at the school sued the employer and the four prior school districts on a negligent hiring claim. All four of the prior school districts had provided unqualified positive recommendations for the administrator. Ultimately, the California Supreme Court held that an employer has no legal duty to provide any recommendation for a former employee, but if an employer undertakes to provide some recommendation it must include negative information if there is a foreseeable risk of personal injury. The case is a good example of "bad facts making bad law," as now many employers are reluctant to say anything about former employees for fear of being sued, which makes it even more difficult for employers to obtain information from prior employers concerning applicants. This means that a company hiring someone is required to reasonably investigate the background of applicants. At a minimum, this means checking references and completing criminal background checks.

Conclusion

As discussed in this chapter, you need to be thinking about employment law compliance even before hiring anyone. Careful recruitment and interview planning will go a long way toward avoiding claims of unfair treatment or discrimination. They also will get you off to a good start with promising new employees.

Offer
Letters
and Required Documents

Offer letters may create a binding contract between the employer and the employee, depending on the wording. An offer letter also may be evidence of limitations on the employer's discretion to discipline or discharge the employee. Courts may scrutinize an employer's offer letters for evidence of uniformity and consistency in the employer's treatment of its employees. Generally, employers use offer letters to make the terms of employment clear at the outset of the employment relationship in order to avoid disputes later. Therefore, it is a good idea to have an experienced employment lawyer review your offer letter to make sure that it is clear and does not

Be Careful What You Say: It May Create a Binding Employment Contract

Employers should recognize that anything and everything they say in applications, advertisements, offer letters, employees handbooks, and other communications with applicants and employees, has the potential to create a binding legal (contractual) obligation. Accordingly, employers should exercise extreme care to say things that they will be proud of later. Don't say it and don't write about it if it's not true, or if it's misleading or unclear to applicants or employees.

unwittingly bind the employer to a term or condition of employment to which the employer was unaware.

Make It Clear

The offer letter is extremely important because it establishes the initial terms and conditions of employment. For example, many employers prefer to establish an at-will employment relationship, which means that either the employer or the employee may terminate the employment at any time, with or without cause or advance notice. Courts have ruled that the presumption of at-will employment may be overcome by evidence of contrary intent, such as promises about the duration of employment, particularly when the employer makes such promises in a written offer letter. For this reason, employers desiring to maintain a policy of at-will employment should consider avoiding the mention of an annual salary and use "weekly" or "bi-weekly" salary instead. Similarly, employers should avoid terms such as "permanent" employee (use "full-time" if necessary), and avoid predictions of future growth and the anticipated duration or longevity of the employment relationship (for example, "This is a *career* position"). Employers desiring to maintain an at-will employment policy also should train managers not to make promises about the duration of employment. What managers and supervisors say to employees can bind the employer.

Among the factors that courts sometimes consider in determining whether the employee has overcome the statutory presumption of at-will employment are the following:

• The personnel policies or practices of the employer.

- The employee's longevity of service.
- Actions or communications (written or verbal) by the employer reflecting assurances of continued employment.
- The practices of the industry.

Include an at-will policy in any offer letter, even if the application, the stock option agreement, and the employee handbook also include one. Here is a sample provision:

> As noted in the application form and in the Employee Handbook, employment with the Company is at the mutual consent of each employee and the Company. Accordingly, while the Company has every hope that employment relationships will be mutually beneficial and rewarding, employees and the Company retain the right to terminate the employment relationship at will, at any time, with or without cause. Please note that no individual has the authority to make any contrary agreement or representation. This constitutes a final and fully binding integrated agreement with respect to the at-will nature of the employment relationship.

How Much Detail to Include in Offer Letters

In general, offer letters should confirm only the employment benefits and avoid any reference to a specified term of employment unless, of course, you want to establish a set length of time for the employment.

In discussing salary and benefits in particular, be aware that some courts have suggested that a definite employment term may be inferred from the period designated for the measure of compensation. For example, in one case, *Swaffield v. Universal Ecsco Corp.*, (271 Cal. App. 2d 147, 168 {1969}) the court ruled that a company's board of directors' minutes providing for an "annual salary" of the employee might be evidence of a one-year employment contract. Similarly, employers should be careful when making references to stock vesting schedules or other waiting periods for accrual of rights to deferred compensation not to create an implied agreement of employment for any specified term.

With regard to employment benefits, it also is generally a good idea to refer in the offer letter to the terms and conditions of the employer's benefit plans and insurance policies, and a disclaimer to the effect that the terms and conditions of the actual benefits plans control over any contrary or inconsistent statement in the offer letter, or elsewhere.

Employers should consider having the employee acknowledge and accept the offer in writing. Employers also should consider making the employment offer contingent on satisfactory results of any background or reference check, or drug test or medical examination in appropriate cases—and never allow an employee to start working until all of the background checks and test results are obtained.

Regarding the content of offer letters, employers should focus on what to avoid, as much as on what to include. Here are some no-nos:

- "You will be entitled to an annual bonus." This statement implies long-term employment.

- "Your annual salary will be $75,000." A better strategy would be to use the bi-monthly salary figures and include an at-will disclaimer.

- "You will be responsible for restoring ABC Company's profitability." This suggests that employee will be given sufficient time to complete the long-term task of restoring company's profitability.

- "This is a career position."

- "We look forward to a long and successful/mutually rewarding relationship."

Employers should avoid "puffery," or promises of certain terms and conditions of employment, even in a tight labor market. Many state laws impose potential criminal and civil liability for knowingly making false representations to induce employees to move from one location to another, either within the state or between states. There also is potential liability in tort for "fraudulent inducement" of employment.

FIGURE 4–1. **An Example of a *Bad* Offer Letter**

> Dear Joe:
>
> We were very impressed with you during our recent interview and strongly believe you are the man to lead our lagging sales division into the next millennium. Accordingly, I am pleased to confirm your offer of employment at an annual salary of $230,000. As discussed, you will also be entitled to an annual discretionary bonus. Annual guaranteed bonuses for the past five years have ranged between $20,000 and $100,000 depending on sales, profitability, and performance.
>
> In addition, you will be entitled to exercise your stock options at annual intervals. We promise to make every effort to make sure you have the resources at your disposal to turn sales around over the next five years. Welcome aboard!
>
> Very truly yours,
> Jane Smith
> Human Resources Director

Arbitration and Other Legal and Practical Considerations for Offer Letters

There are a number of other legal and practical issues that employers should consider at the pre-employment stage. For example, some employers may want to include provisions requiring employees to arbitrate all employment-related disputes. Arbitration raises a number of practical and legal issues, including the effect on employee morale from requiring employees to waive their rights to a jury trial and enforcement/validity of the arbitration program. Furthermore, the laws in each state vary as to the enforceability of arbitration agreements.

Arbitration is generally perceived as cheaper and less likely to receive large damages awards. The process is private, protecting trade secrets, adverse publicity, and embarrassing facts. It is more flexible and faster than litigation. There are, however, disadvantages to arbitration to consider before bringing it into the employment relationship, including:

- Escalation of a conflict;
- Can result in an inability to obtain necessary information through discovery (depends on arbitrators' discretion to allow such discovery).
- Takes decision-making power away from participants (compared to, for example, mediation).
- Informal and potentially unjust (as compared to more formal court procedures such as pleading challenges, summary judgment motions, and appeals; arbitration is final except under very limited statutory exceptions, including fraud and corruption).

Employers desiring to implement mandatory arbitration as a tool to control litigation costs should be careful not to overreach. In particular, employers should avoid provisions that unduly favor the employer's rights over the employee's rights, such as exceptions for employers to go to court to obtain a restraining order or a preliminary injunction. A court may find this provision unfair to employees as the employer, but not the employee, can go to court to seek injunctive relief to prevent misappropriation of trade secrets. For example, see *Ingle v. Circuit City Stores, Inc.* (328 F.3d 1165, 1169 n.2 [9th Cir. 2003]). Courts will continue to scrutinize whether the employer has attempted to tilt the playing field in deciding whether to enforce arbitration agreements. Poorly drafted arbitration agreements invite litigation, precisely what they seek to avoid.

Although the Federal Arbitration Act and most federal courts favor enforcement of arbitration agreements in the employment context, some state courts have refused to enforce employment arbitration agreements where there is evidence of "overreaching" by the employer, such as an attempt to force the employee to pay more administrative fees in arbitration than he or she would have to pay if the claim had been filed in court. Courts will examine an employer's actions to determine if, in arbitration, they have gained an unfair advantage over the employee, such as by limiting remedies available to the employee, imposing large administrative fees on employees, and shortening the applicable statutes of limitations (such as the deadlines for employees to file employment-related claims against their employers).

For those employers who desire to require arbitration as a condition of employment, it is critical to review the latest court decisions regarding conditions of enforceability in the specific states where enforcement is sought, because the laws vary from state to state. In general, it is best to have a separate, stand-alone arbitration agreement to increase the chances that a court will enforce the parties' arbitration agreement. Employers desiring to implement an arbitration program should consult with an experienced labor and employment law attorney to determine the best practices to increase the chances of judicial enforcement. Other considerations for employers drafting offer letters include the following:

- Whether to include a post-offer, pre-employment "fitness for duty" or medical examination requirement (see Chapter 5 regarding background checks and pre-employment medical examinations)
- Whether the position is exempt or non-exempt from the payment of overtime
- Work schedule, full-time or part-time position, reporting structure
- Any conditions of the offer, such as favorable background checks and post-offer medical examination or drug test
- Benefits reference and benefits disclaimer; in other words, where the offer letter and the benefits plan(s) conflict, the benefits plan(s) will take precedence and apply
- Starting pay rate and eligibility for bonuses, profit-sharing, stock options, and other inventive compensation
- Deadline for accepting the offer
- Reporting-to-work date
- Job title and description, or list of job duties

Due to the importance of the offer letter, employers should consider having an experienced labor and employment law attorney review it. Employers should retain the originals and copies of all signed offer letters; for current employees, employers should retain them during employment and for at least six years after termination of employment.

Conclusion

Offer letters may seem like a formality, but they are a critical start to the employment relationship. The words and promises in offer letters can create legal binding obligations, so choose your words wisely. Think about the effect of your promises on the average reader. It is important to be as clear and concise as possible in your offer letters, as they will set the stage for the remainder of the employment relationship, including termination.

Background Checks

As discussed below and in Chapter 6, there is an increasingly complex patchwork of federal, state, and local privacy laws affecting all employers. Several well-known employers have experienced breaches of their computer networks, requiring large-scale notices to affected employees. Employers should, therefore, proceed with caution in the area of background checks, in compliance with all legal requirements.

Another critical component of the hiring process, which will assist an employer in its ultimate goal to hire qualified and reliable employees, is a thorough background check of all applicants for employment. Background checks can take many forms, and delve

Increased Focus on Privacy Rights and Identity Theft

Due to increased concern over identity theft and individual privacy rights, it is very important for employers to safeguard the personally identifying information garnered in interviews, such as names, social security numbers, dates of birth, home addresses and telephone numbers, health insurance information, etc. In general, this means limiting access to those who have a true need to know, keeping some personal information (for example, medical leave of absence), separate from the employee's personnel file and encrypting and/or firewall protecting certain personally identifying information.

into as much detail as an employer desires. Limitations on the scope and detail of background checks include the legal requirements and prohibitions (discussed below), and the financial resources of the employer. In general, investing in a thorough background check pays dividends in the form of a better, more reliable workforce. In this area, like in many other aspects of the employment hiring process, it is advisable not to be "penny wise and pound foolish."

The Legal Framework and Requirements

Due to increased focus on the protection of personal privacy, it is critical that employers carefully obey the federal and state laws governing background checks. In general, this means obtaining from each applicant written consent to the planned background check, full disclosure of the nature of the background check to which the applicant is consenting, full disclosure of the applicants' legal rights under the applicable federal and state laws, and careful use of any information discovered during the background checks.

The federal law governing background checks, the Fair Credit Reporting Act (FCRA), has been in effect for almost 35 years. Since its enactment, the FCRA has governed the collection and use of certain information for employment purposes.

FCRA Requirements

Under the FCRA, an employer is now required to notify an applicant or employee that it may obtain a "consumer report" or an investigative consumer report for employment purposes. The FCRA defines consumer reports as those reports that include information bearing on an individual's "character, general reputation, personal characteristics, or mode of living" and that are used or expected to be used for establishing employment eligibility. (See U.S. Code 15, § 1681[a].) Investigative consumer reports include interviews with an applicant's or employee's friends, neighbors, associates, and references. Notification must be in writing, must be clear and conspicuous, must be in a separate document that contains no other content, and must be given to the applicant or employee *before* the employer orders the report (U.S. Code 15. § 1681[b]). In addition, the employer must obtain the applicant or employee's written authorization before obtaining a consumer report or an investigative consumer report. Employers must also comply with special certification of use and legal compliance requirements if they wish to obtain an investigative consumer report.

Employers intending to take action against an applicant or employee based in whole or in part on information they receive from a consumer report must first provide the applicant or employee with a copy of the report. Employers must notify applicants and employees of their legal rights under the FCRA in writing, using a form approved by the Federal Trade Commission (FTC). If an employer obtains an investigative consumer report, the employer must notify the applicant or employee of his or her rights no later than three days after ordering the report. Such notice must include a statement of the applicant or employee's right to a complete and accurate disclosure of the nature and scope of the investigation the employer has requested, and a summary of individual consumer's rights. The employer need not disclose the names and sources of the information, but cannot erase or otherwise obliterate privileged matter (even contents protected by the attorney-client privilege and/or the attorney-work product privilege).

In 1996, Congress adopted sweeping amendments to the FCRA, which imposed substantial new procedural requirements on users of consumer reports for employment purposes. Congress removed the exemption for workplace investigations and added many other disclosure and notification requirements.

Based on these and other legal requirements and concerns, employers should obtain the affected employees' consent at the start of employment. In

FIGURE 5–1. **Federal Fair Credit Reporting Act Requirements**

Form	Requirements under FCRA if Investigation is Related to Individual's Credit Worthiness, Credit Standing, or Credit Capacity	Requirements under FCRA for All Other Third-party Investigations
Written Disclosure	If no Credit Reporting Agency (CRA) used, no disclosure requirement. If CRA used: Notify employee of possibility of obtaining a "consumer" or "investigative consumer report." (Must be separate document and can be obtained in advance from all prospective and current employees.) • If investigative consumer report, also notify employee within three days of request for report. Include a statement of the employee's right to request by writing a complete and accurate disclosure of nature and scope of investigation and a summary of employee's rights. • If consumer report, employer must also certify that employer has made the above disclosures to the consumer; if an adverse action is taken, the employer will comply with relevant disclosures; and the information will not be used in violation of any applicable federal or state equal employment opportunity law or regulation. • If investigative consumer report, certify that employer has made the above disclosures to the consumer and will comply with the further disclosure requirement if the consumer so requests.	No disclosure requirement
Written Consent	IF no CRA used, no consent requirement. If CRA used, obtain written consent from the employee (can be obtained in advance from all prospective and current employees and can be on disclosure form).	No consent requirement
Copy of Public Record/ Report to Employee	No copy requirement unless use CRA and take adverse action, see below.	No copy requirement
If Adverse Action Taken As Result of Report	If no CRA used, no requirements if employer takes adverse action. If CRA used, before adverse action taken, notify the employee: • of the adverse action; • of the name, address, and phone number of the CRA making the report; • that the CRA did not make the adverse action and cannot explain it. Provide employee a copy of report with no redactions except sources of information, and a summary of his/her consumer rights.	If no CRA used, no requirements if take adverse action. If CRA used, provide employee a summary of the communications upon which any adverse action is based, including the nature and substance of communications. The summary need not include sources such as identity of individuals interviewed.

particular, employers should ask all current employees to sign a FCRA consent form. (See page 175 in Appendix for FCRA background checks information and forms.)

The FCRA does not apply to investigations that employers conduct themselves through their own personnel, or to third-party investigators who do not regularly engage in preparing such reports.

State Statutes and Privacy Laws

Many states have separate statutes that govern the collection of information about applicants, employees, and consumers. Employers generally must comply with both federal and state law in this increasingly complex area, as well as with an emerging patchwork of privacy-related laws and regulations.

Practical Tips for Background Checks

The increased concern about individual privacy interests and the rapidly evolving legal requirements in this area are compelling reasons for employers to proceed with caution when conducting background checks. There are now many reputable companies that are familiar with the legal requirements of privacy protection and will conduct background checks for a fee.

The FACTs about Consumer Reports

The term "consumer report" means any written, oral, or other communication of any information by a consumer reporting agency bearing on a consumer's credit worthiness, credit standing, credit capacity, character, general reputation, personal characteristics, or mode of living. The term "investigative consumer report" means a consumer report or portion thereof in which information on a consumer's character, general reputation, personal characteristics, or mode of living is obtained through personal interviews with neighbors, friends, or associates of the consumer. See U.S. Code 15 § 1681a(d)(1) and U.S. Code 15 § 1681a(e).

The FACT Act, effective December 4, 2003, excludes from the definition of "consumer reports" or "investigative consumer reports" communications made to employers in connection with an investigation of 1) suspected misconduct relating to employment; and 2) compliance with federal, state, or local laws and regulations, the rules of a self-regulatory organization, or any preexisting written policies of the employer. Employers are thus free to hire outside consultants, investigators, or law firms to investigate and report on most workplace issues without having to comply with the FCRA's notice and consent requirements.

In addition to providing a safeguard against legal hassles, it is often also more cost-effective to use an outside company that specializes in such background checks. Many states also have distinct laws that regulate background checks, giving employers additional reason to consider retaining a reputable background check firm. It is not sufficient, however, for employers merely to outsource the background check function to any third party. Employers should check the firm's references carefully, and independently investigate the firm's professional reputation. Has the firm been involved in any litigation concerning background checks?

Employers should consider carefully the type of information to obtain in conducting background checks and try to focus on issues that correlate to future job performance. For example, when considering a recent high school or college graduate, grades and fields of study can be indicators of future job performance. Checking for criminal history, and contacting former employers—whether provided by the applicant or not—to ask about performance issues is also important. Employers may encounter difficulty in obtaining information from former employers, however, given the increased concern over privacy, defamation, and related legal exposure arising from statements about former employees (see "Responding to Employment References" on the next page).

Above all, employers should focus on obtaining only job-related information about applicants and employees. Whether

The Employment Reference Paradox

You might rightfully ask, "Wait a minute. You're telling us to get as much information as possible about our potential new hires, but not to reveal anything about our former employees. How can we do both?" You are correct. Generally, the law does not require you to say anything at all about your former employers, and if you do you might be sued for defamation, blacklisting, interference with prospective economic advantage, invasion of privacy, and a host of other claims. On the other hand, the risk of negligent hiring claims, and the risk of hiring bad employees, compels most employers to conduct some form of background check. Accordingly, employers must adopt and enforce a conservative reference policy (for example, only revealing name, dates of employment, and last position held, and only then if affected former employee consents and releases all claims against employer in writing), and at the same time pursue legal background checks on applicants and employees, as needed.

talking with former employers or deciding what to include in a background check, avoid invading the applicant's privacy, the risk of which increases exponentially when employers seek clearly irrelevant information.

Responding to Employment References

Employers also need to be careful in responding to reference requests from prospective employers of former employees. Former employees sometimes sue for defamation, "blacklisting," and interference with contractual relations—among other claims—based on employers' statements about them to prospective employers. Due to the privacy and legal concerns discussed above, and also because there is generally no legal duty to respond to such employment reference inquiries, employers should adopt and enforce a "no comment" policy about former employees.

If employers are inclined to provide any information, they should consider obtaining a "release of all claims" agreement signed by former employees to provide any background information, and carefully limit what is said and by whom at the company. (See Appendix for sample agreement.) Employers desiring to provide references also should centralize the employment reference inquiry and response process, expressly prohibit all off-the-record references—nothing is ever off the record—and consider adopting "no comment" or similar limited provision of reference information regarding former employees to avoid defamation and intentional interference with contractual relations claims.

Pre-employment Physicals, Medical Histories, and Drug Tests

In general, state and federal laws prohibit pre-employment physicals or medical inquiries intended to determine the existence of a disability or its nature or severity. The purpose of these laws is to prevent the screening out of individuals with disabilities because of the employer's prejudice or outmoded stereotypes. Employers must exercise caution to evaluate each candidate for employment individually, and to that end may ask only questions designed to predict future job performance. As noted above, at the pre-hire stage, employers may generally inquire as to an applicant's ability to perform the essential functions of the job with or without a reasonable accommodation. Employers also may generally ask applicants about their physical condition or medical history if it is *directly related* to the position or necessary to determine if the applicant would endanger others, or his or her own health or safety in the workplace.

In general, employers may condition offers of employment on a medical examination under five conditions:

1. The examination must be completed before the employee starts work.
2. The examination is to determine the employee's fitness for the job.
3. All employees in similar positions are subjected to the same examination.
4. If the examination results would disqualify the applicant, the employer must provide the applicant an opportunity to submit results of an independent medical examination.
5. The results of the examination must be kept confidential.

Employers may withdraw offers of employment where the post-offer, pre-employment medical examination reveals that even with reasonable accommodations, the applicant is not qualified for the position.

In general, employers can inform supervisors of an employee's work restrictions and need for accommodations, but employers must be careful in this sensitive area to limit the information provided on a need-to-know basis.

With respect to the sensitive issue of drug tests, there are several different types, and the law governing their use is complex and evolving. "Suspicionless" or random drug testing is the most risky in light of privacy concerns. Other types of drug testing, such as "post-accident" or "post-mishap" testing, anniversary date testing, "suspicion" testing, are more likely to withstand court scrutiny. Given the complexities of the law and the substantial privacy issues at stake, employers should consult with an experienced labor and employment law attorney before implementing any drug testing program.

When Suspicious Drug Testing is Not Okay

Loder v. City of Glendale, 14 Cal. 4th 846 (1997) was the first case in which the supreme court of California considered (under Article I, Section 1 of the

California Constitution guaranteeing California citizens the right to privacy) the constitutionality of suspicionless (random) drug testing in the employment context. *Loder* was a taxpayer challenge, brought by a woman who never worked or sought to work for the city of Glendale but who was offended by the city's drug testing program and sought to stop the use of taxpayer dollars to fund it. At the time the plaintiff filed suit, the city required all applicants for employment, and all employees being considered for promotion, to submit to mandatory urinalysis drug testing as part of a preplacement medical examination. The drug tests were conducted without regard to the nature of the position being sought, and without regard to whether the city had any reason to suspect the applicant or employee was using or abusing drugs. City officials testified that the city implemented this policy after personnel officers reported seeing a dramatic increase in the number of disciplinary cases in which substance abuse appeared to be an issue and a corresponding increase in the number of city employees who voluntarily sought treatment for substance abuse.

The plaintiff in *Loder* challenged the city's drug testing program on both federal and state constitutional grounds, claiming it violated U.S. citizens' Fourth Amendment rights to be free from unreasonable searches and seizures and California citizens' Article 1, Section 1 privacy rights. The trial court concluded that the city's drug testing program was overbroad and unconstitutional to the extent that it authorized suspicionless drug testing of applicants and employees seeking to be placed in positions that were not "involved with public safety, related to drug interdiction, involved [with] access to highly sensitive or classified information, or [possessing] other factors that could affect the reasonable expectation of privacy of persons seeking employment in a particular position." The city appealed the trial court's decision and lost again, with the appellate court concluding that, as a matter of both federal and state constitutional law, suspicionless drug testing was valid "only as to positions in which the regular duties involve some special and obvious physical or ethical demand, and the compromise of the employee's ability to meet such demands could have an immediate and disastrous consequence upon public safety or security." The city appealed to the California Supreme Court.

Noting that it had never addressed the issue of whether employment-related drug testing was valid as a matter of state constitutional law, the California Supreme Court elected to defer consideration of that issue until after it determined whether the city's drug testing program could be upheld as valid under the federal constitution. After a lengthy analysis of the federal cases that addressed the constitutionality of employment-related drug testing under the Fourth Amendment, the California Supreme Court determined that while the city's suspicionless pre-employment testing of all applicants was valid as a matter of federal constitutional law, its suspicionless testing of all candidates for promotion was not. Accordingly, the Court determined that the issue of whether the city's prepromotional drug testing program was valid under the state constitution was moot, and addressed *and rejected* the plaintiff's state constitutional challenge only as it related to pre-employment testing. The Court stated: "Balancing the employer's substantial interest in conducting suspicionless drug testing of a job applicant against the relatively minor intrusion upon such an applicant's reasonable expectations of privacy when the drug testing is conducted as part of a general pre-employment medical examination, we conclude that, as applied to such job applicants, the city's drug testing program does not violate the privacy provision of the state Constitution." However, in a portion of its opinion that was not necessary to its holding, the California Supreme Court made several statements that, collectively, shed some light on how it might rule if forced to address the viability of suspicionless employee drug testing under the California Constitution in the future. First, expressing its general disdain for suspicionless drug testing of current employees, the Supreme Court stated:

> Although [the employer's] interest [in increasing productivity and decreasing absenteeism, health insurance costs, and employee turnover] logically could support drug testing of current employees as well as job applicants, an employer generally need not resort to suspicionless drug testing to determine whether a current employee is likely to be absent from work or less produc-

tive or effective as a result of current drug or alcohol abuse: an employer can observe the employee at work, evaluate his or her work product and safety record, and check employment records to determine whether the employee has been excessively absent or late. *If a current employee's performance and work record provides some basis for suspecting that the employee presently is abusing drugs or alcohol, the employer will have an individualized basis for requesting that the particular employee undergo drug testing, and current employees whose performance provides no reason to suspect that they currently are using drugs or abusing alcohol will not be compelled to sustain the intrusion on their privacy inherent in mandatory urinalysis testing* [emphasis added].

The Supreme Court nonetheless acknowledged the potential need for suspicionless drug testing in certain instances, and chastised the appellate court for setting too restrictive a standard for determining which types of positions were sufficiently safety or security sensitive to warrant such testing:

> Although we do not determine the validity of suspicionless, prepromotional testing as applied to any particular job category, we believe it is appropriate to observe that, in our view, the Court of Appeal in [*Loder*] set forth too restrictive a standard in holding that such testing is permissible only for positions in which an employee's inability to perform his or her duties could have an "immediate disastrous consequence upon public safety or security."

Finally, in separate opinions, both Justice Mosk and Justice Kennard vehemently objected to the majority's categorization of urinalysis drug testing as only minimally more invasive of privacy than the standard, widely accepted pre-employment/preplacement medical examination and suggested that they would require employers conducting suspicionless drug testing to demonstrate that a *substantial public safety interest* is served by such testing. Justices Mosk and Kennard cited with approval federal cases that permit suspicionless drug testing only in positions where "even a momentary lapse of attention can have disastrous effects" and noted that "[n]onspecific governmental, symbolic interests such as the 'integrity of the workforce,' or interest in a 'drug free workplace,' although laudable, do not justify the invasion of privacy inherent in a drug test." They concluded: "I do not doubt that employees performing certain types of work [for example, tree trimmers using chain saws] endanger their own safety and that of others when they work while under the influence of alcohol or drugs; urinalysis testing [in such instances] is certainly permissible to determine substance abuse."

These statements, read collectively, suggest that if and when the California Supreme Court is forced to define the parameters under which California companies can lawfully conduct suspicionless drug testing of current employees, it would follow the federal standard applied to Fourth Amendment drug testing challenges, and restrict such testing to employees who work in positions that directly and substantially impact public safety or security.

Under state and federal law, it is difficult to justify random drug testing because of privacy concerns. In addition to the common law, some states, such as California, have specific state statutes and/or constitutional provisions recognizing the right of privacy (for example, see California Constitution, Article 1, §1). As a result, the courts have held that random testing is permissible only in safety-sensitive positions. The bases that have been upheld upon a showing of appropriate concern for privacy are pre-employment screening, "reasonable suspicion," and post-accident testing.

Any type of random testing is severely scrutinized in courts for privacy concerns. In *Smith v. Fresno Irrigation District*, 72 Cal. App. 4th 147, 161 [1999] for example, random drug testing of construction and maintenance employees working in ditches and operating heavy equipment was upheld. In determining if the position was safety sensitive, the court focused on the degree, severity, and immediacy of the harm posed and the fact that a single misperformed duty could have irremediable consequences, that is, consequences resulting from an employee being unable to rectify his or her mistake, and the employee's coworkers having no opportunity to intervene before harm occurs. Finally, the court noted that both the hazardous nature of the working environment and hazards inherent in the work itself should be considered when designating a position as safety sensitive. Some examples of random drug tests that courts have upheld are: an operating room scrub technician responsible for laying out the proper instruments for surgery; a medical resident; a teacher; and a school custodian who regularly uses hazardous substances and operates potentially dangerous equipment.

Pre-employment screening, which usually takes the form of an offer of employment conditioned on passing a drug screen, has been approved. In *Wilkinson v. Times Mirror Corp.*, 215 Cal. App. 3d 1034, 1051 (1989), the court upheld an employer's requirement that applicants provide a urinalysis sample for drug testing in the course of a regular pre-employment physical examination. The court applied a general "reasonableness" balancing test and found that the requirement did not violate the privacy provision of the California Constitution. The court considered relevant the fact that the test was designed to minimize the intrusiveness of the procedure and that access to test results was restricted. In *Loder v. City of Glendale*, the supreme court of California upheld a distinction between the testing of applicants and the testing of current employees and found that job applicants could be required by an employer to undergo a drug test when that test is part of an already mandated pre-employment medical examination that is required of every applicant. Although *Loder* was a case involving government employers, the California Constitution's privacy provision (which was considered in *Loder*) applies to private employers. Accordingly, it would appear that such testing is allowed for private employers as well.

Where an employer maintains a policy of testing on "reasonable suspicion," the courts balance the employee's reasonable expectation of privacy and the level of the intrusion upon that expectation against the employer's legitimate interest in maintaining a safe and drug-free work environment (*Hill v. National Collegiate Athletic Association*, 7 Cal. 4th 1 [1994]). However, "reasonable suspicion" drug testing is not without limitation. In *Kraslawsky v. Upper Deck Co.* (56 Cal. App. 4th 179, 182 [1997]), the employer fired an employee after the latter refused urinalysis under the defendant's reasonable cause drug testing program. The court found that the existence of reasonable cause was relevant to determining the constitutionality of the employer's drug test demand and that the plaintiff had successfully created a factual issue as to

Balancing Employer Rights Against Employees' Reasonable Expectations of Privacy

In the drug-testing context, as in other areas that implicate personal privacy rights (such as background checks, monitoring of employee internet and e-mail usage, and desk inspection policies), the courts balance the employer's asserted need to engage in the challenged practice or to enforce the challenged policy against the affected employees' *reasonable* expectation of privacy. It is therefore important for employers to *diminish* employees' reasonable expectation of privacy by adopting and enforcing appropriate policies. For example, and as we discuss in chapter 6, employers who desire to monitor employee use of e-mail and the internet should have a written policy acknowledged by all employees that the computers and laptops (and any other electronic media provided by the employer) remain the property of the employer and that the employer reserves the right to monitor that equipment for legitimate business purposes, including to prevent unlawful harassment and discrimination from occurring in the workplace. Similarly, in the drug-testing context, employers should consider whether applicants or employees have a reasonable expectation of privacy in certain areas.

whether the defendant had reasonable cause to conduct the test. The court observed that it is not enough that an employer maintain a constitutionally valid suspicion-based testing policy if the employer cannot demonstrate that suspicion actually existed in the individual case. Indeed, even nonvisual monitoring (such as by a nurse listening for urination sounds outside toilet area) may be sufficiently intrusive to create an unconstitutional invasion of privacy.

Although it is impossible to create absolute legal immunity in the drug-testing context, policies that sufficiently address the privacy concerns under federal and state law and focus on adequately advancing the employer's legitimate interest in maintaining a safe working environment are upheld where the policy and the evidence demonstrate that reasonable suspicion is established on the basis of objective criteria. Reasonable suspicion requires personal observations of objective facts documented by supervisors and managers trained in recognizing the symptoms of drug/alcohol abuse—"he was drunk" is not adequate, but observations of slurred speech, bloodshot eyes, odor of alcohol, etc. are. It is also important that the employer implement the necessary safeguards for maintaining the confidentiality of records, select a laboratory that is qualified and experienced, and ensure that transportation is secured unless refused. In this context, the employee should not be told to drive to a medical clinic to provide a specimen; but instead, arrangements should be made for transportation. Furthermore, even if the employee refuses to consent to the drug test, the employer should require that transportation still be arranged for the employee.

It is unclear whether a post-accident testing policy would survive a judicial challenge under federal and some states' laws. At least in the context of a train wreck, the U.S. Supreme Court has endorsed automatic post-accident drug testing. In *Skinner v. Railroad Labor Executives' Association*, (489 U.S. 602, 634 [1989]) the Federal Railroad Administration (FRA) promulgated a regulation that required railroads to see that blood and urine tests of covered employees were conducted following certain major train accidents. The U.S. Supreme Court found that the tests posed only limited threats to the employees' justifiable privacy interests even though individualized suspicion was not prerequisite, observing that the FRA's interest was compelling because the positions were safety sensitive and the risk of human loss was great. Because of this language, some courts have narrowly applied the holding in *Skinner* to situations wherein human loss or environmental damage occur.

Due to the privacy interests involved, employers must proceed with extreme caution in deciding whether to implement any drug testing program. For instance, it is likely that courts might still require that the program be announced substantially before its implementation and that employees be allowed to receive counseling or treatment without fear of discharge before the program is enforced. It is also probable that the court might consider limiting such testing to employees in safety sensitive positions where there has been a fatality or serious accident. There is also no evidence that the traditional requirement that the least intrusive manner of drug testing be utilized would be changed.

Random drug testing is not likely to be legal without establishing a record of the safety sensitive positions to which its application is limited. In other instances wherein the propriety of drug testing was upheld in court, the employer maintained a written policy, communicated to employees in advance of testing and receipt of the policy was expressly acknowledged in writing, and the employer also maintained adequate safeguards. In the case of screening applicants, the employer must disclose in or at the time of the application that testing is required and that an offer of employment is conditional upon passing a drug or drug and alcohol screen.

Due to the complex and evolving law in this area, including increased focus on personal privacy rights, employers should consult an experienced labor and employment law attorney before implementing any pre-hire medical inquiry or drug test.

Conclusion

The concept of a "background check" is as broad as the employer (legally) wants to make it. It can include reference checks, employment verification, criminal history, and pre-hire drug screen (especially for safety-sensitive and government jobs). But if you're going to undertake the investment of a thorough, job-related background check, it is important to do it right and legally. In light of increased privacy and identity theft laws, employers should consult an experienced employment law attorney in this area.

Privacy and Workplace Communication Issues

Rapid advances in information technology have dramatically affected workplace communication, presenting a host of new legal and practical challenges for employees and employers. The cost effectiveness, speed, and convenience of e-mail allows immediate, wide dissemination of large amounts of all kinds of information—all in one keystroke. But increased e-mail, blogging, and internet usage by employees bring the usual labor and employment law suspects: unlawful harassment and discrimination claims, hostile work environments, invasion of privacy claims, defamation, misappropriation of trade secrets and unfair competition, and unfair labor practice charges.

This chapter discusses the some of these emerging legal issues surrounding the increasing and already widespread use of e-mail, blogs, and other forms of electronic communication in the modern workplace. It reviews the recent legal developments affecting these new forms of electronic communication and offers some guidance to employers in this increasingly complex area. We will consider the following:

- Can employers monitor employees' e-mail and internet usage (for example, to prevent sexual harassment)?
- What should employers do to prevent identity theft and/or trade secret theft, or misappropriation, by hackers, competitors, former employees, and disgruntled current employees?
- Should employers attempt to regulate web logs, i.e., "blogging," by employees in cyberspace?
- To what extent can employers regulate consensual romantic relationships between supervisors and subordinates, or between coworkers? Which questions are off-limits in a workplace investigation, as potential invasions of the right of employees to individual privacy, or based on other legally designated prohibitions?
- Under what circumstances may employers inquire about applicants' and employees' medical conditions, and what must employers do to safeguard the privacy of such information?

In addition to these recurring issues, as employers increasingly rely on e-mail to provide employees information (such as handbooks, at-will statements, and arbitration agreements) on workplace policies, they face legal questions relating to the validity of an employee's electronically transmitted consent and agreement to (or acknowledgment of) such policies or changes in policies. There are still many conflicting ideas about the circumstances and policies that are appropriate for electronic consent by employees.

Monitoring of Workplace E-Mail

According to the American Management Association's 2003 E-mail Rules, Policies, and Practices Survey, 75 percent of those surveyed had written e-mail policies and over 50 percent of those surveyed monitored employee e-mail. One of the reasons that over 50 percent of U.S. companies monitor employee e-mail is because monitoring has become easy and inexpensive.

For less than $100, an employer can purchase software such as eBlaster 3.0 (www.eblaster.com) and Spector Pro 4.0 (www.spectorsoft.com) to monitor e-mails, chat rooms, instant messaging, key strokes, web sites visited, and passwords.

Hostile e-mails are disrupting company operations with an increasing frequency. Company managers may feel powerless to stop such communications, which sometimes come from disgruntled former employees. For example, in *eBay, Inc. v. Bidder's Edge, Inc.*, (100 F. Supp. 2d 1058 [N.D. Cal. 2000]), eBay sought an injunction to stop Bidder's Edge from using an automated querying program to obtain information from eBay's web site. The court granted the injunction on the ground that Bidder's Edge was trespassing. The court concluded that Bidder's Edge consumed eBay's processing and storage resources, thus committing a "trespass to chattels." The court worried that without an injunction, other auction aggregators would converge on eBay's site, draining computing resources. A more recent decision by the California Supreme Court, (*Hamidi v. Intel Corp.*, 30 Cal. 4th 1342 [2003]), resulted from a former Intel employee sending tens of thousands of e-mail messages to current Intel employees. The California Supreme Court held that Intel could not seek relief under a "trespass to chattels" cause of action. The Court suggested, however, that internet service providers suffering actual harm to their computer servers might be able to state a trespass claim. The Intel decision also suggested that Intel might recover under "defamation, publication of private facts, or other speech-based torts," or an interference with contract claim. In yet another recent case, *Franklin v. Dynamic Details, Inc.*, (04 C.D.O.S. 1850 [March 3, 2004]), e-mails accusing the plaintiffs of misuse of copyrighted materials, violation of nondisclosure agreements, and misrepresentation were held not to support claims for libel or interference with contract—the very claims suggested by the California Supreme Court in *Hamidi*. The Franklin court assessed the e-mails in exactly the same manner as other speech, confirming the conclusion in *Hamidi* that e-mail does not enjoy "unique immunity."

Yes, We're Watching You!

Employers monitor employees' e-mail for three primary reasons:

1. To prevent/address workplace harassment and discrimination;

2. To prevent disclosure of trade secrets and unfair competition;

3. To improve employees' performance and productivity.

Employers have a duty to prevent and remedy instances of workplace harassment to ensure that they do not create or allow a "hostile work environment" (29 C.F.R. § 1604.11). Some states also have similar antidiscrimination statutes that go beyond the requirements of federal law in this area. For example, California Government Code section 12940(j) states that employers "shall take all reasonable steps to *prevent* harassment from occurring" (emphasis added). Harassment claims are often based upon unwanted e-mail attachments or photographs, or inappropriate communications by phone or e-mail. An employer's effort to monitor its employees will be a factor in determining whether an employer met its duty to protect its work environment; see, for example, *Yamaguchi v. United States Dept. of Air Force* (109 F.3d 1475, 1483 [9th Cir. 1997]). Furthermore, inappropriate e-mail messages and internet surfing in the workplace may expose an employer to a host of other tort claims, including defamation, invasion of privacy, and interference claims.

Because trade secrets derive their value and legal significance from not being known to competitors, employers must establish reasonable steps to maintain their secrecy. Employees who have been exposed to trade secrets pose a risk of misappropriation of trade secrets or unfair competition. Consequently, employers must be able to show their reasonable efforts to maintain the confidentiality of their trade secrets or other sensitive information.

With inexpensive software such as eBlaster 3.0 and Spector Pro 4.0, employers can monitor employee performance and productivity for any of the following reasons:

- *Curb employee misuse of the internet.* Employers monitor an employee's amount of time spent on the internet (decreased productivity), as well as visiting web sites unrelated to work, or downloading inappropriate or unlawful material.

- *Assess employee's contact with customers and the public.* This is especially relevant in the telemarketing industry, and sales and customer service departments.
- *Evaluate an employee's communications* (telephone, e-mail, chat rooms) with customers, clients, or co-workers for professionalism.
- *Evaluate the amount of time employees spend on the phone with customers.*
- *Monitor keystrokes per hour and average the amount of keystrokes among a range of employees.*
- *View what is on an employee's computer screen, monitor internet use, and even monitor a computer's idle time.* Networking hardware and software allow an employer to view an employee's computer hard drive.

The ECPA and Related Federal and State Statutes and Case Law Relating to Them

In e-mail and internet monitoring cases, the courts typically balance the employee's reasonable expectation of privacy against the employer's legitimate business interests. Although the federal wiretap law forbids eavesdropping unless one of the parties to the conversation consents, another law, the Electronic Communications Privacy Act of 1986, (U.S. Code 18 § 2510[5][a]) allows employers to monitor job-related telephone conversations. *Briggs v. Am. Air Filter Co.* (630 F.2d 414, 420[(5th Cir. 1980]) holds that an employer can intercept business communications; *Watkins v. L.M. Berry & Co.* (704 F.2d 577, 583-84 [11th Cir. 1983]) states that "We hold that a personal call may not be intercepted in the ordinary course of business . . . except to the extent necessary to guard against unauthorized use of the telephone or to determine whether a call is personal or not. In other words, a personal call may be intercepted in the ordinary course of business to determine its nature but never its contents."

Not surprisingly, there have been many legislative developments in this contentious area.

Title I and II of the Electronic Communications Privacy Act of 1986 (ECPA)

Under Title I of the ECPA (U.S. Code 18 sects. 2510-2521), it is unlawful for anyone, including an employer, to intentionally intercept an electronic communication. Several exceptions to this statute include:

- interception incident to rendering the communications service;
- protection of the service provider's rights;
- consent (law varies whether one or both parties to a transmission must consent); and
- interception in the ordinary course of business.

Under Title II of the ECPA, (U.S. Code 18 sect. 2701-2711), it is unlawful for anyone to intentionally access a facility providing wire or electronic communication service without authorization and thereby gaining access to a wire or electronic communication while in electronic storage. This section has two main exceptions: consent by the sender or receiver of a communication, and authorization by the wire or electronic communication service provider.

How Employers May Access Employee E-Mails without Violating the ECPA

In one recent appellate court decision, *Fraser v. Nationwide Mutual Insurance Co.* (352 F.3d 107 [3d Cir. 2003]) an employee sued his employer for accessing his e-mails without his permission, alleging a violation of his privacy rights under Titles I and II of the ECPA. Because the employer was concerned that the employee might be revealing company trade secrets to its competitors, it had searched its main file server for any e-mails that exposed the employee's improper behavior. The employer found e-mails confirming the employee's disloyalty and terminated his employment. The court held that by searching its electronic storage files for the e-mail, the employer did not intercept the transmission, as prohibited by Title I of the ECPA. Furthermore, the court held that since the e-mail was located on the employer's server, and the employer administered that server system, the employer was acting within its legal bounds under the communications service provider exception to Title II.

Despite this decision, employers should be aware that a federal wiretap statute prevents unauthorized retrieval of e-mails stored temporarily on a computer or server as they make their way to their intended recipients. Because the law governing employer monitoring of employee e-mail is evolving quickly and often due to individual state law developments, it is important for employers to have a lawyer periodically review their e-mail monitoring practices.

"Ordinary Course of Business" Exception to Title I of the ECPA

To come within the "ordinary course of business" exception to Title I of the ECPA, an employer without a communicated privacy policy must have a particular reason for intercepting a particular communication, and take reasonable steps to intercept nothing beyond that initial reason, particularly with respect to personal e-mail communications. In *Watkins v. L. M. Berry & Co.* (704 F.2d 577, 583-84 [11th Cir. 1983]), the court held that once the employer learned of the personal nature of a legitimately intercepted personal call, the employer was obligated to stop the interception. In *Deal v. Spears* (980 F.2d 1153, 1158 [8th Cir. 1992]), the court found that although initially entitled to listen due to legitimate business reasons, the employer exceeded the ordinary course of business exception by monitoring 22 hours of the employee's personal calls.

Employers also should continue to monitor state law developments, as many states have civil and criminal statutes regulating the use and interception of electronic communications. See, for example, Cal. Penal Code §§ 631 et seq. prohibiting electronic eavesdropping. *TBG Ins. Servs. Corp. v. Superior Court* (96 Cal. App. 4th 443, 455 [2002]) ruled that an employee had no reasonable expectation of privacy in the use of an employer-provided computer for personal matters where the employee signed an acknowledgment of the employer's computer use policy that included the employer's right to monitor internet usage.

National Labor Relations Board (U.S. Code 29 § 157, 158[a])

Under federal law, employees have the right to "engage in other concerted activities for the purpose of collective bargaining or other mutual aid or protection," which includes being able to communicate with one another while at work regarding unionization and other matters of common concern. Employers cannot interfere with, restrain, or coerce employees in the exercise of their communication rights for this purpose. When monitoring employees, an employer must be cautious to avoid intercepting or interfering with any communication attempts between employees or employees and their union representatives regarding matters of unionization or common concern, such as wage and hour issues or workplace conditions.

Effective Employer E-mail and Internet Monitoring Policies

An effective e-mail and internet monitoring policy should cover a number of elements, including:

- *Monitoring use of proprietary assets.* The employer's published policy should contain statements to the effect that company computing systems are provided as tools for business, and all information created, accessed, or stored using these systems is the property of the company and subject to monitoring, auditing, or review.
- *Establishing no expectation of privacy.* This entails statements about the extent or limitations of privacy protections for employee use of e-mail, the internet, and computer files.
- *Improper employee use.* Make clear statements regarding which uses of company computers are inappropriate, including specific notice banning offensive material (for example, obscenity, sexual content, racial slurs, derogation of people's personal characteristics), and language relating e-mail and internet use to general prohibitions of harassment.
- *Allowable employee uses.* These statements should explain proper or acceptable uses of the company systems, including whether or not the company permits personal use.
- *Protecting sensitive company information.* Provide clear instructions for handling proprietary information on company systems.
- *Disciplinary action.* Explain that there are penalties and disciplinary actions for violations of company usage policy, up to and including termination.

- *Employee acknowledgment of policy.* Include a statement requiring that employees demonstrate that they understand the company policy and acknowledge their responsibility to adhere to the policy.

If applicable, an employer should also consider disclaiming any privacy rights created by passwords; explaining employee liability for and employer disclaimer of, liability created by e-mail and internet usage; and advising employees that deletion of messages locally will not delete messages on the system server; addressing the "consent" and "communication service provider" exceptions to the ECPA. In practice, employee monitoring should use the least intrusive means available to monitor, and should occur only when necessary. (See the Appendix for a sample Computer E-mail and Internet Use Policy.)

Other Practical Steps Including Mandatory Employee Training

Based on some of the recent case law discussed below, employers should consider training all supervisors—and in some cases, all employees—regarding the employer's electronic communications policies and practices. It is safest to take a "lowest-common-denominator" approach to such employee training, explaining what should be common sense and good judgment to its employees, such as no visiting pornographic web sites, no transferring proprietary and/or confidential information owned by the employer to outsiders without a carefully drafted and signed nondisclosure agreement in place, and so forth, depending on the nature of the employer's business.

Common mistakes that employers need to avoid include:

- Improper disposal of computer files or records (e.g., resale of computer disks or drives);
- Improper disclosure of private information through inadvertent mistakes (e.g., disclosure of medical information without required notice and consent, sending faxes to the wrong number);
- Improper access to customer or consumer information (e.g., allowing non-employees to use computer system or insufficient firewall and/or encryption protection).

> ### Web Logs:
> ### The New Employee Medium
>
> As the electronic frontiers keep expanding, employers are beginning to confront practical and legal concerns raised by more modern forms of employee communication, including blogs and instant messaging. Employers should train all employees on appropriate use of such media for workplace communications. It may come as a surprise to some employees that their every key stroke, even on IMs, is recorded for possible future collection and use in legal proceedings. See S. Swanson and P. Sherman, "What Employers Should Know (and Do) About Blogs," in *Bender's California Labor & Employment Bulletin 10*, p. 354 (Oct. 2005).

The legal risks in connection with monitoring employee e-mail apply equally to the increased use of web logs or "blogs" by both employers and employees; harassment and discrimination, identity and trade secret theft, and performance and productivity.

Given the proliferation of such workplace blogs, and their potential to disseminate a lot of information to a mass audience very quickly, courts will likely be deciding more disputes concerning blogging by employees and employers in the future. For these reasons, most employers, and particularly those in the technology industry where blogging has become more prevalent, should consider adopting a written policy regarding blogs.

Protection of Employer Data, Including Trade Secrets

Electronic communications, coupled with the ever-increasing use of the internet, has greatly complicated the ability to ensure that both private employee data and employer trade secret information remain private and secure. Unfortunately, the prevalence of hackers and rogue employees has led to disturbing incidents of identity theft. In addition, business competitors poach each other's valuable employees and engage in high-stakes trade secret battles, with expensive forensic searches of computer records, electronic discovery, and elaborate internet searches. Companies committed to protecting their trade secrets thus must develop, implement, and enforce policies restricting the use and dissemination of their most valuable information.

Most cases of misappropriation of trade secrets now concern stolen electronic information including customer lists, company databases, and technical information. Such information can be sent to another e-mail address or copied onto a disk or CD. Proving such misappropriation may require forensic computer searches, review of server logs, or subpoenas to third parties, including internet service providers. The surge in employee use of cellular telephones, pagers, Blackberries, and other personal device assistants (PDAs) means that employers must be even more vigilant about protecting their trade secrets and other confidential or proprietary data. For example, an employee-acknowledged procedure to examine company-provided devices is helpful for employers to have in place, but nowadays disloyal employees can easily download vast amounts of company data onto PDAs, external disk drives, and other portable electronic storage devices.

Under the Uniform Trade Secrets Act, which 44 states have now adopted, information will only retain trade secret status if the owner undertakes "efforts that are reasonable under the circumstances to maintain its secrecy." Such efforts can include:

- Employee agreements requiring that all confidential and propriety information of the company not be disclosed;
- Exit interviews for all departing employees;
- Use of personal identification codes and password protection for computer access;
- Disclosure of valuable information on a need-to-know basis;
- Requirements for footers or headers designating qualifying information as confidential or proprietary;
- Restrictions on access to facilities;
- Use of locked files for hard-copy materials;
- Execution and collection of nondisclosure agreements with all third parties, including customers and consultants;
- Use of on-site security and/or guard dogs.

Ideally, employers would consistently enforce the above preventive policies. Policies that employees ignore or circumvent can cause valuable information to lose its otherwise trade secret status. In responding to an application for a temporary restraining order or a preliminary injunction, a defense lawyer will likely search the internet for evidence that the alleged trade secret is nothing of the sort. A case can be lost when opposing counsel can show the court the results of a single Google search on a so-called trade secret.

Companies should adopt formal policies to govern the posting of sales, marketing, and technological information on their web sites and carefully review the content of "webinars" (web-based interactive seminars) and other avenues for releasing company information. If a company outsources its web site development to a third party, confidentiality agreements must be in place. Companies also should ensure that confidential information posted on its intranet (internal web site) is not available to the public. For example, if employees regularly download intranet information and send it to customers, none of the information posted on the intranet may attain trade secret status, including customer names, internal financial information, the results of sales contests, or technical product information. An intranet protected by a firewall that limits transmission of sensitive information, however, should be sufficient for protecting trade secrets. See, for example, *United States v. Keystone Sanitation Co.* (903 F. Supp. 803 [M.D. Pa. 1995]).

Consumer and Business-to-Business Issues

Employers also must ensure compliance with numerous consumer protection statutes that make certain employee communications actionable. For example, in December 2003, Congress passed the Controlling the Assault of Non-Solicited Pornography and Marketing (CAN SPAM) Act, which contains several ambiguous provisions that businesses need to accommodate before sending an e-mail to customers. The CAN SPAM Act requires commercial e-mail (the primary purpose of which is the "commercial advertisement or promotion of a commercial product or service") to include:

- Clear and conspicuous identification that the message is an advertisement or solicitation;
- Clear and conspicuous notice of the opportunity to decline to receive further commercial e-mail from the sender;
- The valid physical postal address of the sender.

The CAN SPAM Act prohibits predatory and abusive commercial e-mail, including sending commercial e-mail through another's computer without authorization; using a computer or any internet access service to relay or retransmit multiple commercial e-mail messages with the intent to deceive or mislead recipients as to the origin of such messages; materially falsifying header information and intentionally initiating the transmission of multiple commercial e-mails; registering for five or more e-mail accounts or two or more domain names, using false identity information and sending multiple commercial e-mails from any combination of such accounts or domain names; and falsely representing oneself to be the registrant or the legitimate successor in interest to the registrant of five or more internet protocol addresses, and sending multiple commercial e-mails from such address. The CAN SPAM Act prohibits commercial e-mail and transactional or relationship e-mail messages that contain or are accompanied by header information that is materially false or materially misleading. It is unlawful under the CAN SPAM Act for any person to initiate the transmission of a commercial e-mail if such person has actual knowledge, or knowledge fairly implied on the basis of objective circumstances, that a subject heading of the message would be likely to mislead a recipient, acting reasonably under the circumstances, about a material fact regarding the contents or subject matter of the message.

The CAN SPAM Act provides for aggravated violations for e-mail harvesting and dictionary attacks, automated creation of multiple e-mail accounts, and relays or retransmissions through unauthorized access. State laws that regulate the use of e-mail to send commercial messages are preempted by the CAN SPAM Act except to the extent that any such state law prohibits falsity or deception in any portion of a commercial e-mail message. The Act does not, however, preempt state laws that might apply more generally to e-mail messages including trespass, contract, or tort laws. The Federal Trade Commission (FTC) is primarily responsible for enforcing the CAN SPAM Act, as well as other consumer protection and privacy statutes. Other federal agencies (FDIC, SEC, FCC, etc.), however, are charged with enforcement with respect to the businesses they oversee. State attorneys general, other state agencies, and internet service providers may file actions to recover for violations of the CAN SPAM Act. The Act authorizes criminal and civil penalties for violations, and in most cases, it imposes strict liability on businesses that hire others to send commercial e-mail on their behalf. Damages for such violations can be substantial. Other features are that "opt outs" must be implemented within 10 business days; courts and enforcing authorities can reduce damages for businesses who have established policies for good faith compliance with CAN SPAM; it is not limited by its terms to bulk e-mail; and it obligates businesses, in some cases, to make reports to the FTC or take affirmative action against spammers who mention the business, even when there is no privity with the spammer.

Employers should note that other consumer protection laws—including false advertising and unfair competition laws—regulate employees' communications with outsiders such as customers, consultants, and partners.

Employee Electronic Signatures and the ESIGN Act of 2000

In 2000, recognizing the proliferation of electronic communication, Congress passed The Electronic Signatures in Global and National Commerce Act (cleverly, the ESIGN Act, U.S. Code 15, §§ 7001 et seq.), to facilitate the use of electronic records and signatures in interstate and foreign commerce by ensuring the validity and legal effect of contracts entered into electronically. The general intent of the ESIGN Act is set out simply in its first section: "[A] signature, contract, or other record relating to such transaction may not be denied legal effect, validity, or enforceability solely because it is in electronic form."

The ESIGN Act provides that electronic signatures and records are as valid as their paper equivalents, and thus are subject to the same legal scrutiny of authenticity that applies to paper documents. However, ESIGN does not address the more complex legal issue of the proper form for electronically communicated policies or agreements. A few courts have recently begun to opine on this issue and have collectively held that so long as an employer clearly communicates in the text of an e-mail how an employee's rights are affected by a policy, and the manner of agreeing to the policy is set out in the e-mail, an employee's assent to such a policy is more likely to be held valid, even if such assent is manifested by continued employment.

Emerging Case Law Regarding Enforceability of Electronic Signatures or Consent to Employment Policies

The case law thus far opining on the validity of electronic acknowledgments, consents, and signatures by employees has been a mixed bag. Employers desiring to implement an electronic signature or acknowledgment program can, however, learn some valuable lessons from the emerging case law.

Mass E-Mails with Insufficient Notice to Employees of Jury Trial Waiver Are Invalid

In one recent decision, *Campbell v. General Dynamics Gov't Sys. Corp.* (407 F.3d 546, 548 [1st Cir. 2005]), an appellate court held that a mandatory arbitration agreement, contained in a dispute resolution policy linked to a company-wide e-mail announcement, did not bind an employee who subsequently brought a claim under the Americans with Disabilities Act (ADA), U.S.Code 42, §§ 12101, et seq. The court found that compulsory arbitration was not appropriate under the ADA because the e-mail did not afford the employee "some minimal level of notice" that his continued employment would effect a waiver of his right to pursue his claim in a judicial forum.

In this case, the employer sent a company-wide e-mail regarding a new dispute resolution policy. The e-mail described that the last step of the company's approach to dispute resolution was arbitration by a qualified and independent arbitrator. This e-mail did not describe how the policy would affect an employee's right to access a judicial forum. Nor did it indicate that the disputes covered by the policy included federal statutory claims such as claims arising under the ADA. Also significant was the fact that the e-mail neglected to specify that the arbitration provision of the policy would become binding upon continued employment. The company buried the more substantive aspects of the policy in a summary document and handbook, which were incorporated in the e-mail as embedded links to their electronic files.

After General Dynamics terminated Mr. Campbell on the grounds of persistent absenteeism and tardiness, Mr. Campbell brought a claim under the

ADA, alleging that he suffered from sleep apnea, a medical condition for which the company allegedly did not provide a reasonable accommodation. The company sought to stay proceedings and compel the employee to submit his claims to arbitration, in accordance with the mandatory arbitration agreement. The district court denied General Dynamics' motion, holding that "a mass e-mail message, without more, fails to constitute the minimal level of notice required" to enforce an agreement to arbitrate ADA claims.

Upon review, the court subjected General Dynamics' e-mail communication to close scrutiny and determined that General Dynamics did not provide the employee with sufficient notice for the arbitration agreement to be contractually binding. Of particular significance to the court was that the e-mail did not state directly that the policy contained an arbitration agreement that would waive an employee's right to a judicial forum. The court also took issue with the fact that the company did not require employees to acknowledge that they had received, read, and agreed to the embedded policy. Moreover, the company lacked a tracking system to show whether employees had, at a minimum, clicked on the embedded links to review either the summary or the handbook. The court found the language of the e-mail itself insufficient to give the employee fair warning that "showing up to work the next day would result in a waiver of important rights." Accordingly, the appellate court held that the mandatory arbitration agreement was contractually ineffective.

The court emphasized that its decision "should not be read as a general denunciation of e-mail as a medium for contract formation in the workplace." In fact, despite invalidating the arbitration agreement here, the court provided some guidance to employers seeking to uphold the validity of a work policy communicated to employees electronically. For example, had General Dynamics required employees to acknowledge receipt of the e-mail and their understanding of the contents of the linked materials, the court would have been more likely to enforce the policy. In the alternative, General Dynamics could have clearly and conspicuously stated in the policy itself that, by continuing to show up for work after reading the policy, employees were acknowledging their acceptance. Had General Dynamics emphasized in the e-mail that the links contained important information concerning a new and binding arbitration policy, the court would have been less likely to find a lack of adequate notice.

Only the Arbitration Agreement Itself Need Be in Writing

In another recent court decision (*Caley v. Gulfstream Aerospace Corp.*, 428 F.3d 1359 [(11th Cir. 2005]) the appellants-plaintiffs were employees of defendant Gulfstream Aerospace Corporation. In July 2002, Gulfstream adopted a dispute resolution policy (DRP), requiring arbitration of all employment-related claims. Gulfstream mailed a copy of the DRP to employees at the Savannah facility. In addition, the DRP was placed on Gulfstream's intranet, where it was accessible to the plaintiffs, and was distributed electronically to approximately 1,000 employees through a notice called the "Management Newsletter." Notices relating to the DRP were posted on 13 bulletin boards throughout the Savannah facility. In November 2003, the plaintiffs filed two related complaints against Gulfstream, alleging various claims under the Age Discrimination in Employment Act (ADEA), the Fair Labor Standards Act (FLSA), the Employee Retirement Income Security Act (ERISA), and Title VII. The district court compelled arbitration of the plaintiffs' claims based on the DRP.

On appeal, the plaintiffs argued that the DRP was not an "agreement in writing" for purposes of the Federal Arbitration Act (FAA) because it was not signed by both parties. Citing U.S. Code 9 § 2, wherein the FAA directs that "[a] written provision" to arbitrate shall be enforceable, the plaintiffs also invoked the FAA's requirement that an arbitration agreement be in writing,

> **Don't Rely on Electronic Signatures Yet**
>
> Despite the emerging case law acknowledging the growing importance of electronic communications between employers and employees, the law is not yet settled and each case will be judged on its own facts until the law is clarified. In particular, employers should ensure, at least for now, that all employees personally sign all important employment policies, such as the at-will policy, any arbitration agreement, the nondisclosure and/or nonuse of trade secrets and/or non-compete agreement, and the employee handbook. The bottom line is that employers want to have evidence that each employee voluntarily agreed to each important policy.

and pointed out its use of terms such as "written provision," "agreement in writing," and "written agreement." The appellate court rejected this argument, however, holding that "no signature is needed to satisfy the FAA's written agreement requirement." Rather, the court held that only the arbitration provision itself need be in writing. Gulfstream's DRP was indisputably in writing and clearly set forth the manner of acceptance. Under the terms of the DRP, employees were to accept by continuing their employment. The court held that the DRP was a binding contract because:

1. The DRP constituted an offer;
2. Under Georgia contract law, the plaintiffs' continued employment with Gulfstream after receipt of the DRP constituted an acceptance of the offer and assent to the terms of the DRP;
3. There was sufficient consideration through reciprocal promises from Gulfstream to arbitrate covered claims.

Accordingly, the Eleventh Circuit concluded that the district court properly granted the defendants' motion to compel arbitration.

Moving into the Future and Leaving Paper Behind

In *Mannix v. County of Monroe* (348 F.3d 526 [6th Cir. 2003]), the appellate court considered an employee's wrongful termination claim based on the employer's alleged failure to provide reasonable notice of the employee's at-will employment status. In this case, the employee, Donald Mannix, had accepted an offer of employment from Monroe County, Michigan, by signing an offer letter that expressly provided for employment at will. Moreover, numerous county policies stated that employment could be terminated by either party without cause. The county updated these employment policies and communicated these policies by uploading them on the computer e-mail system "so that all employees would have access to them at any time" and also communicated the policies to department heads and employees. Mr. Mannix admitted that he, as the network administrator, knew about the posting of the policies, but denied reading or understanding them. Mannix claimed that there was one exception to his failure to read and understand the county's electronic employment policies: Mannix claimed to have read and understood one policy that set specific levels of discipline for specific infractions. Mannix used his alleged understanding of this one policy to argue that he had a legitimate expectation that the county needed just cause to terminate his employment.

The appellate court held that Mannix's employment, on the terms expressed in the county's offer letter, was expressly at will and that Mannix was bound by the at-will language regardless of whether he knew its legal meaning. With regard to the updated policies, the court ruled that since the revised policies made clear that county employees could be terminated without cause and that the county posted these revised policies on an internal database available to employees, Mannix did not have a reasonable expectation that the county needed "just cause" to terminate his employment. The court added that even if the policies had in fact created legitimate expectations in the employee of discharge for just cause only, the employer can unilaterally modify such policies.

Significantly for employers considering an employee electronic signature policy, Mr. Mannix also argued that he never received notice of certain policies and that, unlike hardcopy distribution of employment policies, the electronic distribution system did not include a mechanism where the county collected proof of actual receipt of the policies by its employees. Mannix claimed that this situation created a material issue of fact as to whether he actually received notice of his at-will status. Nonetheless, the court held that an employer's distribution of a new employee handbook constitutes reasonable notice, regardless of whether the affected employee actually reads it. Moreover, the court ruled that reasonable notice should be considered in light of the workforce in general rather than as to an individual employee. In conclusion, the appellate court ruled that the county undertook steps reasonably calculated to reach the affected employees and that "[c]onsidering the advancement and ubiquity of electronic corporate communications, we will not induce a return to older practices by imposing a paper receipt requirement."

Enforcing Employee Electronic Signatures
These recent court decisions provide a few useful lessons for the ever-increasing number of employers who rely on e-mail to communicate changes in poli-

cies at the workplace. First, employers should carefully draft descriptions of how a certain policy will affect an employee's rights. This means, for example, that if the employer intends for a new arbitration policy to cover all disputes between employees and the employer, then the policy should state clearly that the policy applies to, but is not limited to, those claims that are expressly listed in the policy. In devising this list, the employer should be mindful to address and exclude certain causes of action such as labor practice charges that may be filed under the National Labor Relations Act, and unemployment and workers' compensation claims that may not be subject to mandatory arbitration under the relevant state substantive law (U-Haul Co. of California and Machinist District Lodge 190, 347 NLRB No. 34 [2006]).

Second, if an employer intends for the method of acceptance of (and consideration for) such a policy to be continued employment, then the employer must very clearly communicate this intention to the affected employees.

Finally, employers should specifically seek an electronic acknowledgment that the affected employees have read, understood, and agree to abide by the electronic policy. Employers may utilize a "click-on" tool that asks employees to mark a box to indicate that they have read, understood, and accepted the policy. However, if employers use a click-on agreement method, employers should maintain records of these click-on acknowledgments and follow up with employees who have not taken any affirmative step to acknowledge the new employment policy.

These recent court decisions also show that the more widely communicated a policy or change in policy is, the more likely employees will be placed on notice. Thus, for example, if an employer chooses to communicate an arbitration policy electronically, the employer should consider communicating the policy more than once via e-mail, and, in addition, perhaps circulate a paper copy of the policy to employees or post the policy in various common areas. Furthermore, the terms of the policy itself should leave little room for interpretation or debate as to how the employees' rights are being changed or affected. Also, if the employer sends the policy in an e-mail, the material terms will be more clear to an employee if they are not hidden in a series of links. Finally, the policy should clearly establish the means of accepting the terms. In the Caley case, for example, the policy at issue clearly stated that by continuing to work, employees of Gulfstream were binding themselves to the terms of the arbitration agreement. However, some employers may prefer to have employees sign a written agreement, as a "belt-and-suspenders" approach, particularly with respect to important policies such as arbitration and at-will agreements. An electronic acceptance of a policy also is more likely be held valid if it is abundantly clear from the language of the policy itself that electronically agreeing, or "click-acknowledging," constitutes acceptance of the policy.

Although the Mannix court decision dealt exclusively with Michigan law and only involved some elements of electronic communications between employers and employees, it is important because the appellate court recognized and supported the common use of e-mail by employers to communicate updates in employment policies even where the employer provides no proof of actual receipt by the affected employees. However, employers should be mindful that the facts of the Mannix case are somewhat extreme. In Mannix, the complaining employee had expressly signed an at-will offer of employment. The employer had consistently inserted language confirming at-will employment in its subsequently updated employment policies. The employee's best arguments were that he did not understand the meaning of at-will employment, and that his interpretation of the updated policies that he actually did receive created, in his mind, a legitimate expectation that the employer needed just cause for termination of his employment. The employee's last-ditch argument was that even if the policies were clear with respect to his at-will employment status, the employer did not sufficiently communicate these policies to him due to their electronic form. Nonetheless, the court strongly endorsed electronic corporate communications.

Regulating Consensual Relationships in the Workplace and Lawful, Off-Duty Conduct

Another emerging workplace communication issue involves the extent to which employers can regulate consensual intimate relationships between employees. In *Miller v. Dept. of Corrections*, the California Supreme Court held that office romance can lead to hostile environment sexual harassment claims by nonparticipating coworkers. (2005 Cal. LEXIS 7606, 05 C.D.O.S. 6268 [Cal. July 18, 2005]). The Court held that male and female employees may under certain circumstances have viable claims for "hostile environment" sexual harassment under the state's Fair Employment and Housing Act (FEHA) when their supervisor gives preferential treatment to their co-worker(s) with whom the supervisor is involved in a sexual relationship. The Miller court stated:

> Although an isolated instance of favoritism on the part of a supervisor toward a female employee with whom the supervisor is conducting a consensual sexual affair ordinarily would not constitute sexual harassment, when such sexual favoritism in a workplace is sufficiently widespread, it may create an actionable hostile work environment in which the demeaning message is conveyed to female employees that they are viewed by management as "sexual playthings" or that the way required for women to get ahead in the workplace is by engaging in sexual conduct with their supervisors or the management.

The Miller case involved two female California Department of Corrections employees who claimed, among other things, sexual harassment due to the hostile work environment created by their supervising warden and at least three female co-workers with whom he was having extramarital affairs. In addition to the plaintiffs allegedly having to witness arguments at work between the warden and his paramours about their relationships, the warden allegedly passed the plaintiffs over for promotions in favor of his paramours and denied them valuable work experience that they needed to advance. The warden, along with his paramours, allegedly gave them unpleasant assignments, and the paramours verbally and, in the case of one plaintiff, physically, assaulted them, making their work environment intolerable to the point that they eventually quit after having worked for the department 15 years and 25 years, respectively. In one instance, a plaintiff and one of the paramours were vying for the same promotion. The paramour allegedly told the plaintiff that the warden would have to give her the job or she would "take him down" by describing "every scar on his body." The warden then promoted his paramour, even though the plaintiff allegedly had a higher rank, superior education, and more experience.

The court responded to concerns regarding the intrusiveness of regulating personal relationships by distinguishing between the relationship itself, which it was not regulating, and the effect that the relationship has on the workplace. The court noted that it had not considered any interactions between the warden and the paramours that were truly private.

Employers should consider implementing antifraternization and anti-nepotism policies, regulating even consensual relationships between employees that could lead to favoritism, or perceived favoritism, and create a hostile environment for other employees. A transfer to another department or supervisor may eliminate most of these problems.

Confidentiality of Employee Medical Information

The Health Insurance Portability and Accountability Act or HIPAA (Federal Regulations Code 45 § 160, 164 [1996]) mandates that a company that collects its employees' protected health information (PHI) for purposes of heath care group plans (including flexible spending arrangement and cafeteria plans), comply with complicated privacy, security, and electronic data interchange rules. HIPAA prohibits employers from using an employee's PHI for employment related purposes. If HIPAA applies to an employer, the employer only may disclose PHI either directly to the employee or subject to that individual's express authorization. Many state laws regulate the use and disclosure of employees' medical information. For example, the California Confidentiality of Medical Information Act (Cal. Civ. Code §§ 56-56.37) covers "any individually identifiable information in possession of or derived from a provider of health care regarding a patient's medical history, mental or physical condition, or treatment." In *Pettus v. Cole* (49 Cal. App. 4th 402, 425 [1996]) the court found that an employer's use, as a basis for adverse personnel action, of a patient's communications with a psychiatrist in an employment-related exam violated law. See Appendix for a sample HIPAA policy for employees and a disclosure form.

According to the Americans with Disabilities Act (ADA), an employer must collect information relating to the medical condition or history of an applicant or employee on separate forms, in separate medicals files, and treated the information as confidential. However, an employer may:

- inform supervisors and managers regarding necessary restrictions on the employee's work or duties and necessary accommodations;
- inform first aid and safety personnel, when appropriate, if the disability might require emergency treatment; and
- provide relevant information to government officials investigating compliance with this chapter on request.

In the case of *Norman-Bloodsaw v. Lawrence Berkeley Laboratory* (135 F.3d 1260 [9th Cir. 1998]), for example, the court held that the ADA does not restrict employee applicant medical examinations, but it does guarantee the confidentiality and restricted use of information.

Telecommuting Risks

Employees enjoy the privilege, convenience, and flexibility of telecommuting. Employers who allow telecommuting are likely to see improvements in employee morale. There are many reasons for this trend, including employee retention issues, technological advances that have made working from home more feasible, increased efficiency and reduced costs of telecommuting, crowded freeways and the lack of suitable parking near work sites, and the increasing numbers of parents who require more flexible work arrangements. By virtue of technology alone, employers may be swept into telecommuting arrangements without thoroughly assessing the business and legal implications, including potential liability issues that arise primarily in the context of employee work hours, and home safety and accommodations.

To minimize liability, employers should conduct periodic home office inspections. Employers should also consider requiring telecommuters to complete a self-certification safety checklist. In addition to liability under labor and employment laws, telecommuting raises other legal issues. For example, telecommuting may involve the use of employer-owned equipment and the storage of the employer's proprietary information at home offices. These circumstances may require review of employer and employee insurance policies to confirm whether the insurance covers employer-owned equipment and other information in case of loss or damage. Such confidential information use and storage also makes it difficult to protect the employer's trade secrets, such as customer lists, billing history, key contacts, data, and preferences. Furthermore, employers should ensure that employees will return equipment and information upon demand by having employees sign written agreements with provisions for such returns (see the sample Telecommuting Agreement in the Appendix).

Employers can minimize the potential liability associated with telecommuting arrangements by creating a telecommuting agreement or adding telecommuting provisions to an existing employee handbook. Such agreements should clearly set forth the terms of any telecommuting arrangement and should include the following provisions:

- Define telecommuting and make it clear telecommuters are still subject to all of the employer's policies and procedures even though they will be working off site.
- Agreement by the employee to return any employer-provided equipment upon demand by the employer or termination of the telecommuting arrangement or the employment.
- Agreement by the employee to return all of employer's proprietary information upon the employer's demand or termination of the telecommuting arrangement or the employment.
- Acknowledgment by the employee that he or she received a home office checklist to ensure that the home working environment is safe.
- Any safety checklist for the home office should comply with current OSHA guidelines and should indicate that it complies with those guidelines.

- Set out the work days and hours for telecommuters.
- Advise telecommuters that the employer retains the right to terminate the telecommuting arrangement at any time, without cause or advance notice.
- Grant the employer the right to inspect the telecommuter's home office and state when such inspections can occur.
- Agreement by non-exempt employees to work no more than 40 hours per week without the express permission of a supervisor and to keep accurate time records.
- Nondiscriminatory standards for a telecommuting arrangement to protect employers from claims that telecommuting was denied to particular employees for discriminatory reasons.
- Agreement by the employee to promptly report any accidents that occur while he or she is working in the home office.
- Specific guidelines regarding reimbursement for expenses related to the home office.
- Detail what equipment the telecommuter will be using, who will provide it, who is responsible for maintenance, damage, loss, etc.
- Consider confidentiality and protection of trade secrets policies.
- Agreement as to liability insurance for accidents that occur at an employee's home office.
- Consider defining/limiting work space for which employer will assume some responsibility; for example, no employer liability if someone drowns in the employee's home swimming pool.

Every employer who allows employees to perform work from a home office, during or after normal business hours, should be aware of the legal issues raised by telecommuting. Employers should adjust the telecommuting arrangement with these issues in mind so that they may minimize potential liability while allowing employees to take advantage of the benefits of telecommuting. The International Telework Association and Council (ITAC) provides information for employers who are considering implementing some form of telecommuting in their workforce, and their web site (www.workingfromanywhere.org) is devoted to researching telecommuting efficiency and implementation. The ITAC recently released "Telework America Survey 2002," which looks at the advances in telecommuting stemming from the increased availability of high-speed internet access. Employers can purchase a copy of the study, or view the executive summary at www.workingfromanywhere.org/pdf/TWA2003_Executive_Summary.pdf.

Compliance Suggestions

As discussed above, an increasingly complex patchwork of privacy and other laws continue to evolve rapidly to regulate workplace communication. Making matters even more complicated, many of the emerging privacy issues (e.g., monitoring employees' e-mails and computer usage) have resulted in inconsistent interpretations and applications by the courts. Many traps for the unwary employer exist, and many employers recently have been subjected to costly and time-consuming government audits and civil liability arising from their handling of workplace communications.

Therefore, the first and most important lesson for all employers is to learn to spot privacy and related legal issues in the workplace, and consult with experienced legal counsel before inadvertently taking action that could result in an employee claim. A privacy and workplace communication audit, in which the employer examines its existing policies designed to protect employees and applicants' privacy rights, and a privacy risk assessment, may be advisable for many employers. In particular, due to the highly fact-specific nature of each workplace policy and the complexity of the applicable federal and state laws, employers should consult with counsel knowledgeable in this area and proceed with caution.

Employers should be proactive in responding to the increased legal risks of workplace communication with well-conceived policies and procedures concerning conducting background checks; guarding against identity and trade secret theft; conducting workplace investigations; collecting, handling, and transferring personal information about applicants and employees, including medical information and personal background information that tends to identify applicants and employees; monitoring employees' e-mail, computer, and telephone usage; adopting antifraternization policies and regulating relationships at work; taking any adverse action based on an employee's activities away from the workplace; and providing information in response to reference requests (employees and former employees have sued employers for invasion of privacy, defamation, intentional interference with prospective economic advantage, and on related theories based on employers' policies and responses to former employee reference requests); handling applicant and employee medical information, including in making reasonable accommodations for disabled employees and responding to requests from employees out on medical leaves (workers' compensation, FMLA, etc.).

Employers should exercise extreme care in handling applicant and employee medical and other private information, and take precautions to minimize the risk of compromising the confidentiality of such information. By developing systems to handle private and confidential information about applicants and employees, including plans for transfer and disposal of such data, employers can fulfill their obligation to keep such personal information separate from other employment records. Employers also should thoughtfully limit access to personal information related to applicants and employees to those who have a true need to know; these and other special precautions in handling electronic records relating to applicants and employees can be taken to combat the recent surge in identity theft. Although cost is always a concern, employers should consider encrypting certain electronic data such as applicants' and employees' personal information, and installing firewalls, password-protected sites, and the like. Employers may wish to consult with a computer forensics expert to determine the most efficient methods of protecting private information about applicants and employees.

With respect to identity theft, one of the simplest ways for a company to avoid compliance problems is to encrypt the personal information of its customers (or employees), as the law only applies when an individual's "unencrypted data" is at issue. However, encryption is a costly and time-consuming measure, and given the many ambiguities in the law, it cannot prevent all possible liability. Even if a company were to encrypt its data, it would still be vulnerable if its

> ## Some Helpful Web Sites
>
> California Department of Consumer Affairs: www.privacy.ca.gov
>
> FTC's Identity Theft Affidavit: www.ftc.gov/bcp/conline/pubs/credit/affidavit.pdf
>
> Identity Theft Resource Center: www.idtheftcenter.org/index.shtml
>
> California Civil Code: www.leginfo.ca.gov/cgi-bin/calawquery?codesection=civ&codebody=&hits=20
>
> Thomas-U.S. Congress on the internet: http://thomas.loc.gov/
>
> Legal Information Institute-United States Code: www.law.cornell.edu/uscode

data were unencrypted or if it did not keep up the maintenance of the encryption (which itself is costly). Companies might also wish to consider installing firewalls and other software applications to guard their computer databases, and particularly those containing "personal information" of consumers or employees. Another step a company could take to avoid the specific problem of rogue employees is to thoroughly check the backgrounds, and particularly the criminal backgrounds, of its applicants and employees. This will help minimize the risk of liability under the new law, as well as liability for tort claims such as negligent hiring, supervision, and retention. However, employers should seek legal advice when conducting such background checks to ensure compliance with applicable (and evolving) federal and state law. (See the section on the Federal Credit Reporting Act in Chapter 5.)

The recent legal developments with regard to workplace communication also underscore the critical need for employers to take immediate and effective steps to deny departing employees' access to company computers. For instance, employers should quickly cancel or revoke a departing employee's passwords, and not allow a departing employee continuing access to computer databases that include personal information of customers, clients, other employees, etc. Yet another preventive step companies could take is to separate the names of customers from their corresponding personal data (such as

Social Security numbers). This would make it more difficult for a hacker to gain unauthorized access to both the individual's name and personal data. Because the new law requires notice only when the company reasonably suspects unauthorized access to both the individual's name and personal data, keeping these two items separate will decrease the risk of a security breach.

Clearly, electronic communications in the workplace are going to increase, not decrease. By paying attention to some of the mistakes made by the employer in the *Campbell v. General Dynamics* case, and guidance provided by the courts in the Caley and Mannix decisions discussed previously, employers seeking to enforce electronic employee signatures and click-on acknowledgments can improve their chances in litigation over enforcement of such electronic agreements.

Keeping
Your Secrets

Developing and protecting intellectual property are critical to the success of many businesses, particularly given an increasingly mobile work force. Although most employers recognize the need to protect their valuable intellectual property, confusion exists both as to what can be protected and how to protect it. "Intellectual property" encompasses all manner of ideas, creations, designs, inventions, improvements, and unique plans by individuals. The law has long recognized and protected employers' intellectual property. Today, "IP" encompasses trademarks, patents, copyrights, trade secrets, and other forms of ideas and developments. Increasingly, the courts protect intellectual property just as they have protected personal property for centuries. Liability can attach for theft (sometimes referred to as "infringement" or "misappropriation") of intellectual property.

This chapter will look at different legal aspects of intellectual property and provide some practical guidance for employers to protect their assets, including information such as customer lists and negative know-how (what not to do) that qualify for statutory trade secret protection under most states' laws. Given the rapidly evolving law in this area and the value of intellectual property to most businesses, it makes sense to adopt a proactive approach to defining and protecting an employer's assets, including trade secrets. Indeed, given that one of the statutory requirements for trade secret status is whether the information sought to be protected was/is the subject of reasonable efforts to maintain its secrecy, employers can take specific steps now to both define and protect their invaluable trade secrets.

This chapter will also discuss restrictive covenants in employment agreements, such as non-compete agreements, to protect employer assets. Because the law varies from state to state regarding the enforceability of such restrictive covenants, employers are strongly encouraged to discuss such options with an experienced employment attorney before implementing them.

Defining Trade Secrets

Currently, 44 of the 50 United States have adopted some version of the Uniform Trade Secrets Act (UTSA). It is important to recognize at the outset just how broadly the law protects trade secrets. Under the UTSA, a trade secret is any information that:

- has independent economic value, whether actual or potential, by being generally unknown in the industry, to the public, or to others who can realize economic value from its disclosure or use, and
- is the subject of efforts that are reasonable under the circumstances to maintain its secrecy.

Given this broad definition, employers can and should focus on specific steps to both define and protect the secrecy of their trade secrets.

FIGURE 7–1. **What Makes a Trade Secret?**

Courts evaluate trade secret claims on a case-by-case basis in light of the UTSA's requirements of value and secrecy. Among the questions a court is likely to consider are the following:

- Is the information common knowledge?
- How valuable is the information in this particular industry?
- Could the information be easily/independently recreated (such as looking for names of potential customers in the telephone book)?
- Was the information created through substantial time, effort, and expense?
- Does the information include qualitative research (such as which were the best or most valuable customers)?
- Is the information sophisticated (such as billing information, key managerial contacts, and specific customer requirements)?
- Is the information limited to identities of customers and potential customers or does it include customers' preferences, purchasing patterns, key contacts, decision makers, etc.?
- Did the competitor who took the information enjoy much success in a relatively short period of time (suggesting the information had independent value, other factors being equal)?
- Could the information be valuable in the hands of a competitor (or is the information the kind that gives the employer a competitive advantage)?

Common Types of Trade Secrets

The courts have recognized that the following types of information may constitute a trade secret in appropriate cases:

- *Customer and supplier lists.* Courts have noted that fundamental to the preservation of our free market economic system is everyone's concomitant right to have his or her ingenuity and sweat equity invested in the success of the business or occupation protected from gratuitous use by others. As a result of this policy, customer lists and other sophisticated customer information such as billing rates, key contacts, specialized requirements, and mark-up rates can be commercially valuable and not readily ascertainable to other competitors, particularly if the information was developed by screening a large number of prospects at considerable time, effort, and expense. For example, an employer's customer database may have potential economic value because it allows a competitor to direct its sales efforts to those potential customers that are already using the employer's products and/or services. On the other hand, if the information is generally known to the public or is not sophisticated, difficult, or particularly time-consuming to acquire, it probably will not qualify for trade secret protection. One important point for employers to recognize is that former employees cannot be required to "wipe clean the slate of their memories" to erase customers' names and addresses that are easily obtainable through normal resources such as the telephone directory. But, to afford protection to the employer, the information need not be in writing but may be in the employee's memory.

Generally, the identity of customers is not a trade secret, but information about them usually is. An employer may be able to obtain an injunction (an order from a court prohibiting use or disclosure of customer lists and customer data) against the subsequent use by a former employee of knowledge of the "peculiar likes and fancies and other characteristics" of the former employer's customers where such knowledge will aid in securing and retaining their business. As a general principle, the more difficult information is to obtain, and the more time and resources expended by an employer in gathering it, the more likely a court will find such information constitutes a trade secret. Thus, a customer list can be found to have economic value because its disclosure would allow a competitor to direct its sales efforts to those customers who have already shown a willingness to use a unique type of service or product as opposed to a list of people who only might be interested. Its use enables the former employee to solicit both more selectively and more effectively.

- *Pricing, cost, and profit margin information.* Armed with detailed information about your business's prices (wholesale, retail, and special), costs, and profit margins, a departing salesperson could have a devastating effect on your business. Such competitively sensitive information would help your former employee (and his new employer and your competitor!) to solicit your customers more selectively and more effectively. For example, the former employee might solicit your customers directly and barely underbid your prices to get the business in the short term. Particularly where margins are thin, such anti-competitive conduct can have disastrous consequences to your business.
- *Key contacts, customer, preferences, and purchasing history.* By itself, knowledge of the identities of the businesses that buy from a particular provider of goods or services is of no particular value to that provider's competitors unless it indicates to them a fact that they previously did not know—that those businesses use the goods or services that the competitors sell.
- *Employee compensation data and special skills.* Courts have recognized that employee lists for temporary employment agencies may derive some independent economic value by containing special information such as the employees' skills and preferences that cannot be obtained through public sources. However, such information may not qualify for trade secret protection where it is developed through former employees' own efforts and temporary employees listed with several different temporary employment agencies.
- *Specialized techniques, methods of operation.* This includes specifications for material and manufacturing processes, tolerances for mass-produced items, portions of which were patented.
- *Negative know how.* Lengthy efforts that, from a negative viewpoint, indicate what does not work or which potential customers are unlikely to become actual customers. The definition of trade secret includes information that has commercial value from a negative viewpoint; for example, the results of lengthy and expensive research that proves that a certain process will not work could be of great value to a competitor.

One may also have a trade secret in information obtained by reverse engineering another's trade secret.

- *Contract expiration dates.* Client preferences and requirements.
- *Computer source-coded and related information.*
- *Mere ideas if parties agree to maintain confidentiality.*
- *Unique combination of information partly in the public domain.* A trade secret can exist in a combination of characteristics and components, each of which by itself is in the public domain, but a unique combination of process, design, and operation can afford a competitive advantage and is a protectable secret.

The "Inevitable Misappropriation of Trade Secrets" Doctrine

The "inevitable misappropriation" doctrine was first articulated in *PepsiCo, Inc. v. Redmond* (54 F.3d 1262 [7th Cir. 1995]), in which a high-level executive of Pepsi left the company to assume essentially the same position for archrival Quaker Oats. Pepsi claimed that in his new employment, Mr. Redmond would "inevitably" use or disclose Pepsi's trade secrets, including marketing plans and marketing research. The Seventh Circuit Court of Appeals agreed, prohibiting Mr. Redmond from working for Quaker Oats for a one-year period.

The Uniform Trade Secrets Act (UTSA) allows relief for actual or *threatened* trade secret misappropriation. Many courts have endorsed the inevitable disclosure doctrine, which allows a court to actually prohibit or restrict the employment of the employee by a competitor where there is a threat that the employee will disclose trade secrets and/or the competitor may benefit from such conduct.

Inevitable disclosure by a former employee may arise in a variety of circumstances, including:

- The employee in fact had access to confidential information while he or she worked for you.
- The employee now works for another company in the same business as yours, and in a job substantially similar to the job he or she held with your company.

- The new employer fails to or cannot effectively enforce an articulated plan for making sure employees do not use or disclose the confidential information of their former employers.
- The frequency of pirating information (or employees) in your industry.
- The employee's ease of duplicating your confidential information.

Practical Steps to Protect Your Trade Secrets and Other Valuable Intellectual Property

Here are some practical steps that employers can and should take to protect their trade secrets and other intellectual property:

- *Employee acknowledgments.* Insist that all employees who will learn about the trade secret acknowledge in writing that the employee understands that certain defined information is confidential, the employer owns the trade secret, the trade secret is in fact secret, the employer has taken reasonable measures under the circumstances to protect its confidentiality, and the trade secret has independent economic value because of its secrecy; that is, the trade secret is not generally known to the employer's competitors or the public. The acknowledgment should state that the employee has *read, understands, and agrees to abide by* the employer's trade secret policies, including the definition of the trade secret.
- *Nondisclosure agreements.* Also include a provision in the employment contract in which the employee expressly agrees not to disclose to others (including customers, suppliers, and distributors) or use the trade secret during or after the employment, at least until the trade secret becomes generally known through lawful means.
- *Employee handbooks and manuals.* In addition to individual employment contracts, consider including a trade secret policy in the employee handbook distributed to all employees. Also include an acknowledgment signed by each employee, expressing his or her understanding and agreement to abide by the policies in the handbook, including the employer's trade secret policy.

- *New employee orientation.* Discuss in standard new employee orientation sessions the importance of the employer's trade secret to the success of the business, and of nondisclosure to those outside the company. Inform employees that their nondisclosure obligation extends to all third parties, including customers, business partners, suppliers, distributors, and agents, and not merely to the employer's direct competitors.

- *Continuing education of employees.* Continue to educate the workforce about the need to protect trade secrets, including how to look for signs of trade secret theft. Periodic meetings, seminars, newsletters, and memoranda can serve to protect an employer's trade secrets, as an employer's own educated and vigilant work force is the first line of defense against trade secret theft. In one recent California case, for example, vigilant employees reportedly tipped off the local district attorney about suspected trade secret theft by one of their employer's competitors.

- *Internal controls.* Restrict access internally by disseminating such confidential information only to those employees who truly have a need to know. Implement appropriate monitoring procedures. Limit computer access through passwords. Stamp confidential documents with a legend, such as "trade secret - document contains confidential and proprietary information - strictly limit circulation."

- *Require all third parties to execute nondisclosure agreements.* If the business requires disclosure of the trade secret to third parties such as business partners, insist that the third party sign a nondisclosure and non-use contract similar to the one signed by its employees.

- *Return of all company property.* Include an express policy in the employee handbook and in employment contracts requiring the departing employee to return all company property before leaving, including confidential information stored on the employee's home and/or laptop computer.

- *Exit interviews.* Arrange exit interviews with departing employees to remind them of their contractual obligation not to disclose or use the employer's trade secrets in the employee's new endeavor.

- *Follow-up with new employer.* Consider sending a follow-up letter to the departing employee and his new employer to notify them of their nondisclosure/nonuse obligations.
- *Monitor the risk of disclosure or unauthorized use.* Consider internally auditing efforts to define trade secrets and the specific measures implemented to protect them. Monitor a departing employee's activity with the new employer, such as dramatically decreased sales in the former employee's sales territory that could be attributable to the former employee's misappropriation of trade secrets.

See the Appendix for sample forms for screening new employees, protecting trade secrets, ensuring nondisclosure, and conducting exit interviews.

Avoiding Unfair Competition/Misappropriation Claims By Competitors

On the other side of intellectual property protection, here are five techniques employers should adopt to avoid being accused of unfair competition or misappropriation of trade secrets when hiring competitor's employees:

1. Employment contracts should state that the employer does not want the new employee to use or disclose any trade secrets owned by any prior employer, and that the employee agrees not to use or disclose such trade secrets.

2. Review new employee's nondisclosure and/or employment contracts carefully to determine risks of inadvertent misappropriation.

3. Counsel new employees on employer's trade secret policy, including admonition not to use or disclose any trade secrets owned by former employers.

4. Can the new employee perform the job without using a former employer's trade secrets? This addresses the inevitable disclosure doctrine.

5. Consider talking to former employers about what kind of information they consider to be a protected trade secret.

Screening New Employees

Those hiring employees from a competitor now should take extra care to ensure—and be able to demonstrate in court—that the incoming employees will not use or disclose the former employer's trade secrets. Those companies should consider putting into place a preventive program to minimize the risk that incoming employees will use their former employer's trade secrets.

Similar to an exit interview, employers can screen applicants to determine whether they will use their former employer's trade secrets while performing their employment duties. Among other things, the employer should review all of the candidate's contracts and policies with the former employer; review the candidate's educational background and work experience (without revealing confidential information), and all secrecy warnings given the candidate; and determine whether the candidate has ever been involved in trade secret litigation in the past.

Avoiding Unfair Competition Claims

For those employers unwilling to screen new employees and enforce reasonable trade secret policies, consider the enormous expense of trade secret or unfair competition litigation. A competitor can aggressively seek both immediate injunctive relief (for example, a temporary restraining order barring your new employee from working for you) and depositions of the key team members who made the hiring decision and (possibly) your customers and vendors. The costs of such litigation far exceed preventative policies and agreements at the outset of employment.

Employment Contracts

Employers should consider including provisions in offer letters and contracts expressly precluding the employees' use or disclosure of the former employers' trade secrets, and affirming that the employer does not want the employee to use or disclose any former employer's trade secrets.

Communications with Former Employers/Competitors

In situations where employers anticipate litigation with a competitor over a hiring decision (under, for example, inevitable disclosure of trade secrets), employers should consider sending a letter to the competitor to inform it of the employer's internal controls to prevent the use or disclosure of the former employer's trade secrets.

Monitoring the Risk

To ensure that all incoming high-risk employees understand their obligations to their former employers, consider conducting trade secrets education sessions for them and establishing an ongoing "trade secret mentor" program. This will enable the highest-risk employees to consult with a trade secrets mentor whenever they have questions regarding their obligations.

Restrictive Covenants in Employment Contracts

In states that permit them, many employers use restrictive covenants, such as noncompete, nonsolicitation of customers, and nonsolicitation of employees provisions in their employment contracts. Employers seeking to use such restrictive covenants should be aware that the governing law varies from state to state. Indeed, in some states noncompete agreements are not only illegal, but their mere inclusion may constitute unfair competition under the applicable law. (See, for example, California Business & Professions Code § 17200; *Application Group, Inc. v. Hunter Group, Inc.*, 61 Cal. App. 4th 881, 905 [1998].)

In addition, many states have laws regulating the assignment of inventions to the employer, and prohibit such assignments where the employee has developed it on his or her own time. In such states, an employer may not require the employee to assign rights in any invention that the employee develops on his or her own time without using the employer's equipment, technology, etc., unless the invention relates, at the time of conception or reduction to practice, to the employer's business or to actual or demonstrably anticipated research or development by them; or results from any work performed by the employee for the employer.

Adding to the complexity in this area, in states such as California that prohibit noncompetes, there are various statutory exceptions, including for the sale of goodwill of a business, or the sale or other disposition of all of the former employee/executive's shares in a corporation.

Other methods that employers should consider to prevent unfair competition and theft of trade secrets by former employees include:

- Nonsolicitation of customers' provisions
- More limited noncompete agreements. For example, limiting solicitation of one or two key customers
- Severance payment coupled with a noncompete agreement during the period of the severance payment
- Reasonable nonsolicitation of employees ("anti-raiding") provisions
- Duty of loyalty and fiduciary duty provisions—the law imposes a duty of undivided loyalty on current employees, and an even higher fiduciary duty on officers and executives.

Conclusion

No matter how you treasure your technology, your skilled workforce, your secret recipes, your confidential financial information or business plans, a single disgruntled employee can use them to compete against you unfairly after he or she leaves. Accordingly, it is very important for all employers—especially start-up employers—to protect their trade secrets and other competitive secrets with vigilance. Employers must have reasonable policies both to protect their own valuable trade secrets and to avoid unfair competition claims by competitors when hiring their talent.

Retaining and Motivating Great Employees

E mployers recognize that their most prized asset is a productive and efficient workforce, and that they need to invest in their employees, including the use of performance counseling to motivate and train them. In particular, employees, managers, and supervisors need training on employment law and management issues, as well as prevention of sexual harassment and discrimination.

Describing the many legal obligations imposed on employers is beyond the scope of this book, which focuses on hiring and firing issues, considerations, and legal requirements. However, the following is a list of big-picture issues for all employers, and particularly small and start-up businesses, to consider:

- Basic wage and hour rules
- Safety regulations
- Right to work in U.S.
- Essential training
- Postings
- Record-keeping
- Handbooks
- Workers' compensation
- Basic benefits
- Privacy (drug testing, background checks, monitoring of employee e-mail, etc.)
- Leaves of absence
- Duties of nondiscrimination
- Employment tax compliance

Due to the complexities in these areas, and the fact that the legal requirements vary from state to state, it is advisable to consult with an experienced labor and employment law attorney regarding compliance issues. This chapter provides some general guidelines and tips to help small and start-up employers spot potential problems that need to be addressed. When in doubt, ask an experienced labor and employment law attorney who is familiar with the particular requirements in the states where you have employees.

Employee and Supervisor Legal Compliance Training

Given the potential exposure to liability from even routine employment decisions, employers should consider training all employees, and should focus on training managers and supervisors, regarding basic employment law issues and requirements, such as the need to prevent unlawful harassment, discrimination, and retaliation in the workplace. The following list also reminds employers of their legal obligations, such as legal requirements to post certain information in the workplace governing wages and hours, anti-discrimination, workplace safety, workers' compensation insurance, workplace violence, and related issues.

Employee Relations Issues

- The employee, manager, and supervisor's responsibilities, both legal and practical, in regard to employee relations
- How to manage problem employees
- How to rehabilitate personnel files
- How to document performance problems; no termination should come as a surprise to the terminated employee.
- The problem with grade inflation in evaluations. Not all employees are "excellent." Be honest, or it will be difficult to distinguish between employees when later making promotion, demotion, compensation, and termination decisions.
- The legal and practical problems arising from inappropriate or close relationships with subordinate employees
- How to motivate and train employees through careful performance reviews and verbal counseling
- Common discipline and termination issues
- How to write performance evaluations with objective facts, a professional tone, and no name-calling, focusing on improving the employee's performance
- How to provide (and document) verbal counseling
- When to call the human resources department and/or senior management
- How to handle difficult terminations
- Responding to employee complaints
- The importance of fairness and consistency: Say and do things that you will be proud of later.

Unlawful Harassment and Discrimination Issues

- The employee, manager, and supervisor's responsibilities and duties regarding harassment and discrimination
- Responsibilities under federal and state law not only to recognize and stop unlawful harassment, discrimination, and retaliation, but to take reasonable steps to prevent such conduct in the workplace
- How to recognize, stop, and prevent unlawful harassment and discrimination in the workplace
- How to avoid discrimination claims
- How to avoid retaliation claims
- Potential personal liability for unlawful harassment, including but not limited to sexual harassment
- Importance of internal complaint procedures that work
- Importance of workplace investigations and how to conduct them
- When to involve the human resources department and/or upper management
- Sensitive cultural differences in your workforce and how to handle them
- The legal and practical problems arising from romantic relationships with coworkers, and between managers and subordinates
- The use of electronic mail at work

Employers should use well-drafted policies to prevent unlawful harassment, discrimination, and retaliation in the workplace. Some considerations for this documentation include:

- Defining unlawful harassment, discrimination, and retaliation, using examples
- Including an internal complaint process or procedure
- Including legal remedies available through the EEOC and parallel state agencies, and directions on how to contact these agencies
- Protection against retaliation

- Confidentiality to the extent possible
- Human resources hotline or emergency e-mail with quick response time
- Promising to conduct a fair, prompt, and thorough investigation into all complaints of unlawful harassment, no matter how minor, and to take appropriate remedial action
- Writing in clear, understandable, non-lawyerly language
- Centralizing the complaint and investigation process
- Tracking and document all complaints, and calendar follow-up with complainant and alleged harasser as appropriate.

An employer should be prepared to prove to a judge or jury that it has educated and trained its workforce on detecting and preventing unlawful harassment and discrimination.

Recruiting, Interviewing, and Hiring Issues

- The manager and supervisor's responsibilities and duties with respect to interviews and hiring
- Handling "reasonable accommodation" issues under the Americans with Disabilities Act (ADA) and applicable state law
- Background and reference checks
- Avoiding discrimination and unfairness allegations by applicants
- Limiting questions to the purpose of the interview—will this applicant be successful in this position? Ask only questions relevant to the applicant's education, experience, expertise, etc. to perform the job, and when in doubt, don't ask it.
- Defining what is improper to ask prospective employees:
  - Questions about marital and family status
  - Questions about language skills and place of birth (national origin, race discrimination claims)
  - What year the applicant graduated from high school (tends to reveal the applicant's age)

- Questions about religion, ethnic background, etc. and discussions about religion, sex, politics, and other emotionally charged issues
- Legal right to work in the United States; use IRCA and I-9s
- Immigration law compliance (I-9 Forms completion and verification)

Other trouble spots for front-line management depend on employer, industry, legal trends, and ongoing risk assessment.

Overtime Laws, Protected Leaves of Absence, and Miscellaneous Employment Law Issues

- Eligibility for and payment of overtime
- Compliance with other wage-hour laws, such as payment of vacation
- Exempt versus nonexempt classifications
- Docking pay for salaried, exempt employees
- Importance of correctly recording all time worked: off-the-clock work is unlawful and strictly prohibited
- Importance of granting meal and rest breaks: In California, there must be one unpaid, 30-minute meal break for every six-hour shift, during which employee is relieved of all duties (and alternative, on-duty meal periods and written waiver of meal periods)
- Responsibilities and duties of managers, supervisors, and employees to provide for a safe work environment, including reporting reasonably suspected safety concerns or violations and handling workers' compensation and OSHA claims
- Independent contractor versus employee classifications
- Privacy issues and the internet
- Protected and unprotected leave of absence eligibility and potential traps for the unwary
- Preventing and detecting theft and other misconduct in the workplace: the role of the supervisor and the manager

- Handling whistleblower claims
- Prohibition on disclosing pay rates or discussing working conditions
- Posting requirements
- Policy prohibiting improper pay deductions and internal complaint resolution process
- Failure to pay last wages upon termination ("waiting time" penalties)
- Vacation accrual policies
- Commissions
- Bonus plan administration and calculations
- Travel time
- Miscalculation of overtime rate of pay ("regular rate" issues)
- Establish work week, pay day, time keeping, and payroll advance/deduction policies
- Reimbursement of business expenses
- Personnel files, inspection, and copying rights
- Disciplinary meetings and sound practices: practicing the "two-on-one" rule of two supervisors for each employee receiving counseling
- Leaves of absence, by law and by policy
- Workers' compensation
- Family and medical leave
- Jury duty
- Time off to vote
- School leave (parent-teacher conferences)
- Alcohol and drug rehabilitation
- Disability accommodation

Given the high exposure, publicity (and thus increased employee and union awareness), and costs associated with wage-hour litigation (e.g., class actions, penalties, attorneys' fee, to name a few), employers should proactively

The Value of "Self Audits"

In *Niland v. Delta Recycling Corp.* (377 F.3d 1244 [11th Cir. 2004]), it was held that the employer's self-audit and payment of back wages to employees were adequately supervised by the Department of Labor (DOL) and employees' acceptance of payments barred their right to pursue additional compensation where an independent accounting firm had been retained by the employer to calculate the employee's back wages based on formulas, assumptions, and factors approved by the DOL. The lesson for employers: Fix the problem before the government comes knocking!

audit their wage-hour classifications and practices, and make changes if necessary within the business constraints.

In particular, employers should consider the following preventive steps to avoid wage-hour claims:

- *Audit time-recording policies* to ensure all non-exempt employees are properly recording their time worked and all required meal and rest period breaks.

- *Provide and ensure compliance with meal and rest period requirements.* Many states have laws requiring employers to provide timely and sufficient meal and rest breaks. For example, under California law, there can be no more than five hours per day worked without a meal period of not less than 30 minutes, except that if the total work period per day of the employee is no more than six hours, in which case, the meal period may be waived by mutual consent of both the employer and employee. A second meal period of not less than thirty minutes is required if an employee works more than ten hours per day, except that if the total hours worked is no more than 12 hours, the second meal period may be waived by mutual consent of the employer and employee only if the first meal period was not waived.

- *Avoid off-the-clock work claims:* Failure to pay for off-the-clock work (such as company sponsored/required meetings, prep, and closing time) is a major and increased liability for employers. Adopt a clear policy prohibiting off-the-clock work and make sure all employees know about it. The policy may be worded as follows: "The company prohibits any non-exempt employee from working off the clock. All employees are required to keep accurate and up-to-date records of the time that they work. Managers and supervisors are prohibited from allowing any employees to work off the clock. Violations of this policy may result in disciplinary action, up to and including termination of employment." The employer should ensure that the policy is well publicized and accessible to all employees.

- *Instate a policy prohibiting improper salary deductions.* The new Fair Labor Standards Act (FLSA) regulations, which went into effect on August 23, 2004, contain a safe harbor exception for violations of the FLSA's salary basis requirement. Therefore, employers should adopt a well-drafted policy prohibiting improper salary or pay deductions. This is particularly important for exempt employees, who must generally receive a predetermined salary

> ## The Risk of Off-the-Clock Work Claims
>
> More and more wage and hour class actions are being filed, alleging that employees were told to work off the clock to benefit the employer's operations. In various off-the-clock claims, employees have been known to say/testify that they were: told/pressured to do it; the time records are not accurate; the job required unpaid pre-work activities, meetings, uniform changing requirement; they were on restricted on-call duty; they attended unpaid training sessions and/or meetings; supervisors erased hours for employees' time cards to avoid paying overtime; they were locked in after working hours and made to work off the clock; the job required it. A strong, well-known policy against off-the-clock work can prevent these claims from happening.

(the salary basis requirement). The new FLSA regulations provide that if an employer has adopted a policy prohibiting improper salary deductions (for example, for absences of less than one day, for certain disciplinary reasons, because the employer was closed due to inclement weather, a deduction of three days pay because the exempt employee was absent for jury duty, a deduction for a two-day absence due to a minor illness when the employer does not have a bona fide sick leave plan, a policy or practice of providing wage replacement benefits, and a deduction for a partial day absence to attend a parent-teacher conference), then the exemption will not be lost for one-time or even several

Waiting to Be Engaged vs. Engaged to Wait

In *Ballaris v. Wacker Siltronic Corp.* (370 F.3d 901 [9th Cir. 2004]), employees spent 30 minutes per day changing into "bunny suits" before clocking in and entering cleaning rooms; employer must pay for time because it required employees to wear plant outfits (mainly for employer's benefit) and to change at work.

inadvertent salary deductions. Such an internal policy must have three components:

1. The policy must clearly specify that the employer prohibits certain salary or pay deductions, and it must also include an internal complaint procedure

2. A provision to reimburse employees for any improper pay deductions

3. A good faith commitment on the part of the employer to comply with its policy in the future.

Employers must continue to monitor compliance with wage and hour laws, and pay practices, given the increasing numbers of employee claims in these areas.

Workplace Safety

- Occupational Safety and Health Act requirements
- Illness and injury prevention program
- Training
- Medical monitoring
- Reporting injuries/illnesses
- Emergency evacuation and other contingency plans
- Inspections
- How to handle OSHA audits, complaints, and citations
- Recognizing and preventing violence in the workplace

We have looked at some examples of the areas in which to train employees, particularly managers and supervisors, who have primary responsibility for enforcing and implementing labor and employment policies. Every business is different. Small employers may want to start with essential employment law training, and provide periodic training as the employer responds to increased risks. In sum, the content, type and frequency of employee training should be tailored to the employer's business and needs, in addition to complying with all applicable legal requirements (see Figure 8.2, at the end of this chapter, for a comprehensive list of Federal Major Federal Employment Laws, Executive Orders, and Regulations). For example, some states, including California and Massachusetts, now require employers to provide mandatory sexual harassment prevention training to all supervisors. The California law applies to employers with 50 or more employees.

Many employers have begun to reevaluate their security and emergency evacuation plans as a result of the September 11 terrorist attacks and other threats. In one postal workers' lawsuit, for example, the union argued that the U.S. Postal Service responded inadequately to the threat of postal worker contamination following revelations that anthrax-laced letters were mailed to media outlets in New York City. Employers should anticipate that some employees might second-guess their security measures in the event of another terrorist attack or even in response to a natural disaster or workplace violence incident. Among other things, an employer should consider the size of its workforce, the location of its facilities, the possible hazards or security risks within and outside its work environment, and the potential natural disasters in the area. It may be advisable to consult with appropriate and qualified experts in formulating a comprehensive safety, security, and evacuation plan. Employers also should consider possible violence in the workplace and plan accordingly. It is now much easier for employers to obtain injunctive relief to prevent threatened violence in the workplace. Employers may also wish to consider hiring additional, private security guards and notifying law enforcement in appropriate cases.

Numerous web sites provide guidance in this area. The EEOC has posted a "fact sheet" on its web site that describes what employers may and may not do when developing emergency evacuation plans (www.eeoc.gov/facts/evacuation.html). More information on emergency preparedness for employees with disabilities can be found on President Bush's New Freedom Initiative Disability Direct web site (www.disabilities.gov/category/6/51) and on the

Job Accommodation Network's web site (http://janweb.icbi.wvu.edu/media/ emergency.html). The Red Cross' web site (www.redcross.org/services/disaster/keepsafe) contains several articles dealing with traumatic incidents, and the American Psychological Association also has posted several informative articles on coping with the aftermath of a disaster (http://helping.apa.org/ daily/tassey.html) and managing traumatic stress (http://helping.apa.org/daily/ traumaticstress.html). Employers should prominently post their emergency and evacuation plans in the workplace and distribute them for future reference and guidance.

Conducting Legal and Effective Workplace Investigations

Adopting and enforcing internal complaint investigation and resolution policies is an employer's best strategy against future legal challenges brought by unhappy employees. In some cases, an effective internal complaint procedure can provide employers a complete defense to employee lawsuits. As always, thoughtful drafting is essential. Some recent legislation, such as the Sarbanes-Oxley Act, requires public companies to maintain a separate complaint policy for anonymous whistleblowers. Important considerations for all internal complaint policies and procedures are whether they are effective and how they will make the employer look to a jury—and to potential plaintiffs. In this section, we will review the recent and emerging legal requirements for internal complaint resolution policies, and offer suggestions for employer compliance in this increasingly complex and important area.

Sources of Legal Requirements for Internal Complaint Resolution Policies

Many recent and emerging employment laws, including case law, require effective internal complaint resolution policies. For example, in 1998, the U.S. Supreme Court decided *Faragher v. City of Boca Raton*, (524 U.S. 725, 780 [1998]) and *Burlington Industries, Inc., v. Ellerth*, (524 U.S. 742, 747 [1998]). In both cases, the plaintiffs alleged that their supervisors had created hostile work environments in violation of Title VII. The Court ruled that although an employer is responsible for a hostile environment created by a supervisor with authority over the employee, the employer may defend against liability for such harassment if the employer shows it exercised reasonable care to prevent and correct any sexually harassing behavior and the employee unreasonably failed to take advantage of the preventive or corrective opportunities provided by the employer. The Court reasoned that a plaintiff who "unreasonably failed to avail herself of the employer's preventative or remedial apparatus" should not recover damages, since the damages could have been avoided. (This defense, however, is unavailable to an employer if the supervisor's harassment resulted in a tangible employment action, such as a discharge or a demotion.)

One very interesting case, *Holly D. v. California Institute of Technology*, (339 F.3d 1158 [9th Cir. 2003]), demonstrates both the importance of an effective internal complaint policy and the specific features and components that make for a successful Faragher/Ellerth affirmative defense. The plaintiff contended that a professor she worked for coerced her into performing unwanted sexual acts with threats that she would be discharged. For a two- to three-year period, she and her supervisor engaged in repeated sexual acts in the office, until she finally decided that she no longer wanted the relationship. Although Holly D. had collected physical evidence of the affair, the court ruled against her because of the remedial action Cal. Tech took on receiving her complaint. The *Holly D.* court discussed the type of evidence necessary for an employer to establish the "reasonable care to prevent and correct promptly" prong of this affirmative defense:

- A written policy which defined prohibited behavior, identified contact personnel, and established procedures to investigate and resolve any claims;
- Adequate dissemination of the employer's policy; and
- Periodic training on preventing sexual harassment, which the employer publicized by e-mail.

The court in the *Holly D.* case applauded the employer's conduct in "promptly convening an investigatory committee, which impartially interviewed every witness suggested by either Holly D. or [Professor] Wiggins."

The court also rejected the plaintiff's so-called sexual harassment expert's hindsight conclusion that the employer did not do enough: "Even were we to assume that all of these additional steps were advisable, Cal Tech's failure to pursue all possible leads does not undermine the substantial showing in this case that its investigation was, in toto, both prompt and reasonable." As to the second prong of the Faragher defense, the plaintiff's inexplicable delay in pursuing the employer's available internal remedies was fatal to her claim; she sought no relief for two years after the first alleged unwelcome sexual conduct, and for a full year participated in the alleged unwelcome sexual activity before complaining.

In short, to take advantage of this defense to a sexually hostile environment claim, an employer must show:

- It took reasonable steps to prevent and correct workplace sexual harassment;
- The employee unreasonably failed to use the preventative and corrective measures that the employer provided; and
- Reasonable use of the employer's procedures would have prevented at least some of the harm that the employee suffered.

Courts have noted that sexual harassment claims, and particularly hostile environment claims, often manifest over time and accordingly might be prevented or remedied early through effective use of the employer's internal complaint resolution policy. In addition, some courts have recognized as a defense to whistleblower claims an employee's unreasonable failure

---

Protect Your Employees—and Your Business

Employers should disseminate policies that include, at a minimum, the following information:

- The illegality of sexual harassment

- The definition of sexual harassment under applicable state and federal law

- A description of sexual harassment, utilizing examples

- The employer's internal complaint process available to the employee

- The legal remedies and complaint process available through the department and the commission

- Directions on how to contact the federal and/or state agencies responsible for enforcing the sexual harassment legal prohibitions

---

to exhaust an employer's internal complaint procedures. Further, as most employers know, employees are increasingly blowing the whistle on corporate fraud, violations of the law, and fundamental public policies. For example, in the wake of the Enron, Arthur Anderson, and Tyco International scandals, Congress hurriedly passed and President Bush signed into law the Sarbanes-Oxley Act of 2002, (U.S. Code 15 § 78j-1[m][4]), which creates new protections for employees of public companies who reasonably believe that a violation of federal securities law, the rules of the SEC, or "any provision of federal law relating to fraud against shareholders" has occurred or is occurring. In particular, the audit committees of boards of directors of public companies must adopt anonymous internal whistleblower complaint procedures if they have not already done so. Additionally, some state laws protect whistleblowers. These statutes also generally prohibit employers from taking any adverse employment action in retaliation for such a disclosure. To date, seventeen other states have statutes protecting private sector employees. These statutes vary as to the nature of protected conduct, the remedies available, and other provisions.

Another source of the legal obligation to implement an effective internal complaint procedure is the federal Occupational Safety and Health Act (OSHA) of 1970, which gives employees the right to file complaints about workplace safety and health hazards. An employee also may file a discrimination complaint against his/her employer if the employer takes adverse action against the employee for exercising any rights established under OSHA, or for refusing to work when faced with an imminent danger of death or serious injury and there is insufficient time for OSHA to inspect. States with OSHA-approved state plans provide the same protections to workers as federal OSHA, although they may follow slightly different complaint processing procedures. There are currently 22 states and jurisdictions operating OSHA-approved state occupational safety and health programs that cover both the private sector and state and local government authorities (for a complete listing, see www.osha.gov/fso/osp/index.html). Four other states operate approved state plans that cover state and local government employees only.

Further, the August 2004 Fair Labor Standards Act (FLSA) regulations contain a safe harbor exception for violations of the FLSA's salary basis requirement, such as improper deductions from an exempt employee's salary. The new FLSA regulations provide that if an employer has adopted a policy prohibiting improper salary deductions, then the exemption will not be lost for one-time or even several inadvertent salary deductions. Such an internal policy must have the following three components:

1. The policy must clearly specify the employer prohibits certain salary/pay deductions, and must include an internal complaint procedure.

2. The employer's commitment to reimburse employees for any improper pay deductions.

3. The employer's good faith commitment to comply with its policy in the future.

Finally, an employer has a duty to engage in an interactive process with a disabled employee to determine the nature of accommodation necessary to enable the employee to perform the job's essential functions. An employee may start the interactive process by directly asking for an accommodation. In *Bultemeyer v. Fort Wayne Community Schools* (100 F.3d 1281, 1285 [7th Cir. 1996]), the court held that "The employer has to meet the employee halfway, and if it appears that the employee may need an accommodation but does not know how to ask for it, the employer should do what it can to help." Thus, an effective internal complaint policy can help

Improper Salary Deductions

- Absences of less than one day
- For certain disciplinary reasons
- Because the employer was closed due to inclement weather
- Deduction of three days pay because the exempt employee was absent for jury duty
- Deduction for a two-day absence due to a minor illness when the employer does not have a bona fide sick leave plan, or policy or practice of providing wage replacement benefits
- Deduction for a partial day absence to attend a parent-teacher conference.

employers address (and defend) disability discrimination claims and satisfy their reasonable accommodation obligations. Recent case law also suggests that the effective use of an employer's internal complaint resolution policies can serve to avoid or limit damages.

Practical Internal Complaint and Investigation Policy Drafting Considerations

The applicable statutes and case law offer many compliance suggestions for employers preparing or revising their internal complaint resolution procedures. The exhaustive requirements may seem just that, but they serve the welcome function of eliminating or mitigating damages. If an employer is given the opportunity quickly to determine, through the operation of its internal procedures, that it has committed an error, it may be able to minimize, and sometimes eliminate, any monetary injury to the plaintiff by immediately reversing its initial decision and affording the aggrieved party the appropriate remedy. The law rules against individuals who increase damages by foregoing available internal remedies.

Implementing an effective internal complaint resolution policy is critical to remedy workplace misconduct and to help defend future lawsuits. The courts' recent decisions suggest that they will scrutinize how employers' policies have worked in the real world by examining an employer's complaint history to see whether complainants were discouraged, how well investigators were trained, and other indications. On this point, one court noted:

> [T]o take advantage of the avoidable consequences defense, the employer ordinarily should be prepared to show that it has adopted appropriate anti-harassment policies and has communicated essential information about the policies and the implementing procedures to its employees. In a particular case, the trier of fact may appropriately consider whether the employer prohibited retaliation for reporting violations, *whether the employer's reporting and enforcement procedures protect employee confidentiality to the extent practical, and whether the employer consistently and firmly enforced the policy. (McGinnis,* 31 Cal. 4th at 1045 [emphasis added]).

Similarly, the U.S. Supreme Court noted in the Faragher case:

> An employer may, for example, have provided a *proven, effective mechanism for reporting and resolving complaints of sexual harassment,* available to the employee without undue risk or expense. If the plaintiff unreasonably failed to avail herself of the employer's preventive or remedial apparatus, she should not recover damages that could have been avoided if she had done so. If the victim could have avoided harm, no liability should be found against the employer who had taken reasonable care, and if damages could reasonably have been mitigated no award against a liable employer should reward a plaintiff for what her own efforts could have avoided. (*Faragher*, 524 U.S. at 807 [emphasis added]).

The recent court decisions send an important message to employers, both private and public: Careful creation and implementation of internal procedures for resolution of workplace complaints may lead to early and efficient resolution of ubiquitous whistleblower and/or retaliation complaints, litigation avoidance, and a complete defense to whistleblower and retaliation lawsuits. Adoption of effective internal complaint resolution procedures benefits both employees and employers. As the courts have recognized, when an employee utilizes internal complaint procedures, the employer may be able to minimize, and sometimes eliminate, damages by immediately reversing its initial decision.

Such internal procedures provide employers with a quick and efficient way to correct erroneous employment decisions, which can avoid both adverse publicity about the whistleblower's complaints and the expense and uncertainty of litigation.

Courts Recognize the Value of Internal Complaint Policies

"Such 'whistle-blower' provisions are intended to promote a working environment in which employees are relatively free from the debilitating threat of employment reprisals.... They are intended to encourage employees to aid in the enforcement of these statutes by raising substantiated claims through protected procedural channels." *Passaic Valley Sewage Commissioners v. Department of Labor,* 992 F.2d 474, 478 (3d Cir. 1993) cert. denied, 510 U.S. 964 (1993).

By utilizing such internal complaint procedures, employees may be able to blow the whistle and reverse erroneous initial decisions without having to wait years for resolution of the litigation.

For most private employers, no specific law clearly defines the type of internal complaint resolution procedures they must implement to establish an affirmative defense. But private employers may be able to rely on language from some of the recent cases discussed above in drafting such internal complaint resolution processes. It seems clear that an effective internal grievance mechanism should involve more than just a complaint reporting procedure. Employers should design an internal complaint resolution process that affords whistle-blowing employees a full and fair opportunity to present evidence to support their claims.

By disseminating an effective internal complaint policy to all employees, employers can significantly improve employee morale and commitment to the company. Such a policy allows employees to disclose job-related concerns and air complaints or problems before they get more serious and unmanageable. Employees also feel that their opinions matter. For similar reasons, such a policy improves employee productivity, as less time is spent complaining to and discussing such problems with other co-workers. Furthermore, employees can focus on their work instead of on ongoing problems that are not resolved. Employers should draft their internal complaint policies so that they are specific to their particular companies or industry, and should avoid using boilerplate, or form, policies. For example, employers may consider an e-mail complaint procedure, or toll-free hotline for employees to report complaints. In addition, employers should draft internal complaint policies in plain English, using clear, understandable, non-technical, and nonlawyerly language. Such

> **A Sample Whistleblower Complaint Policy**
>
> The company prohibits any retaliation against an applicant or employee, and does not discriminate against any applicant or employee, based on that applicant or employee's whistle-blowing activity against a former employer.
> Any employee who reasonably believes that he or she is a victim of retaliation may also call a whistleblower hotline to report the retaliation: (800) _____.

efforts make it more likely that employees will understand and utilize the employer's internal complaint procedures. If policies are difficult for employees to understand, it is less likely the employer can argue it maintained an effective policy and thus limit its liability and/or damages.

Employers should strive to conduct a fair, prompt, and thorough investigation of all complaints, no matter how minor or trivial. The immediacy of an employer's response to an internal complaint is critical, as many court decisions equate the employer's alacrity with how seriously the employer has taken the complaint. Once an employer receives a complaint, any unnecessary delay in commencing an investigation likely will be viewed as acquiescence on the employer's part to the problem. In one case, for example, *Steiner v. Showboat Operating Co.* (25 F.3d 1459, 1464 [9th Cir. 1994], cert. denied, 115 S. Ct. 733 [1995]), the appellate court reversed the district court's entry of summary judgment for the employer on the employee's Title VII claim where the employee had complained of verbal harassment by her supervisor two or three times, and the employer had simply instructed the supervisor to apologize, but did not initiate an investigation until the plaintiff filed a complaint with the Nevada Equal Rights Commission. Similarly, in *Bennett v. New York City Dep't of Corrections* (705 F. Supp. 979, 987-88 [S.D.N.Y. 1989]), the court denied the employer's motion for summary judgment on the plaintiff's Title VII claim, noting that although the defendants reacted swiftly and decisively on some occasions, the employer did not interview the plaintiff or conduct any investigation into one of her written complaints for four weeks. Few complaints should be considered too trivial to act

---

"Constructive" Termination Based on Employer's Failure to Act Promptly

The theory of "constructive" termination is that the working conditions have become so intolerable that the reasonable employee has no choice except to quit. Courts have recognized that an employee may be "constructively" terminated based on the employer's inaction in response to employee complaints. In *Coley v. Consolidated Rail Corp.* (561 F. Supp. 645, 651 [E.D. Mich. 1982]), the employer was found to have constructively discharged the plaintiff when it failed to act promptly in response to her complaint, causing her resignation. Don't make this mistake. Respond to all employee complaints promptly and fairly.

upon. Generally speaking, it is more prudent for management to overreact than to take less action than may be necessary. Keep in mind that in many instances, such as sexual harassment, real complaints are often understated because of embarrassment or fear of reprisal.

It also is very important for employers to emphasize, both in their written policies and in communications with and training of their employees, that no retaliation will be tolerated against either a complaining employee or any witness. Employers should take other steps to ensure that employees feel comfortable and protected in making complaints of workplace harassment. For example, a written policy that requires reporting harassment to the employee's supervisor is problematic if the supervisor is the individual accused of the harassment. Employers should centralize decision-making regarding harassment complaints, workplace investigations of them, and remedial action taken. In *McGinnis* (31 Cal. 4th at 1045), the court acknowledged that some delay by employees in reporting harassment may be reasonable if employees reasonably fear retaliation.

Confidentiality often becomes an issue, particularly with regard to internal investigations of harassment complaints. Alleged victims and alleged harassers, in addition to co-workers, often request both anonymity and confidentiality as a precondition to their cooperation with the employer's investigation. Many employers very quickly and uncritically grant confidentiality before realizing that they are not in a position to do so. Specifically, it may well be that the employer will need to rely on the information and provide it to state and/or federal investigators. The employer may have legal obligations to take remedial action by disciplining the harasser, which precludes absolute confidentiality. The employer may, indeed, find it necessary to introduce such evidence of appropriate remedial action in court as part of its defense to a lawsuit. Accordingly, the better practice is to promise the employee that the employer will proceed with discretion and will proceed confidentially as to those who do not need to know. It should be noted that absolute confidentiality is not possible. However, the employer should seek to preserve confidentiality to the best extent possible.

After receiving an internal employee complaint, employers must decide whether to perform an investigation in-house or whether to hire an outside investigator, such as a law firm, private investigator, or consultant. If the accused is an executive or senior manager, an internal investigation may be problematic because of potential conflicts of interest or lack of freedom to dispassionately and independently evaluate the facts. Also, small and medium-sized businesses may not have professional staff with the experience, expertise, and time to conduct a legally defensible workplace investigation. Conducting an inadequate investigation may expose the employer to liability.

Thus, if an employer chooses to proceed using internal resources, it must ensure that proper steps are taken to obtain an unbiased and complete investigation. Use of an outside investigator may lessen the risk of an adverse decision based on an inadequate investigation, assuming that they are properly trained and dispassionate. Outside investigators not only often have experience and expertise conducting such investigations, but also may ensure greater confidentiality and objectivity. However, use of an outside investigator means, in certain situations, that the employer must comply with the Fair Credit Reporting Act (FCRA), and any state law equivalent. Employers should consider consulting with an experienced labor and employment law attorney in sensitive cases before proceeding with any workplace investigation.

Having a written internal complaint policy is of no value unless employees are both aware of the policy and trained to use it. Employers should train all managers and supervisors on the importance of, and practical advice for handling, employee complaints. Likewise, the policy must be widely disseminated to all employees and all employees should be trained on the employer's policies regarding the internal complaint procedure and all other employment policies and laws. The employer also should consider conducting diversity training in the workplace, which both demonstrates the employer's commitment to an environment free of discrimination and harassment, and helps educate the employees about appropriate and inappropriate behavior. Employers also must continue to monitor compliance, both with evolving legal requirements and with the company's internal complaint resolution policies.

Another sound, proactive practice is periodically to audit whether the internal complaint resolution policies are effective in practice. For example, do the employees know about and understand the company's internal complaint resolution policy and procedure? Do the employees understand the internal complaint-reporting procedure, and who to call to make the initial complaint? One important component of such an audit is interviews of prior complainants regarding the effectiveness of the company's internal complaint resolution policies. Employers also should continue to monitor all legal requirements, including additional protections for victims of discrimination, unlawful harassment, and retaliation.

Conducting the Workplace Investigation

Some laws require employers to undertake prompt and fair investigations into alleged workplace misconduct. The most obvious example is in response to claims of discrimination, retaliation, or unlawful harassment. But employers need to understand how to conduct workplace investigations even where they are not technically or legally required. Employers should avoid making decisions until they have all the facts and they need to treat all parties—alleged victims, alleged wrongdoers, and alleged witnesses—with dignity, fairness, and respect. Careful workplace investigations can greatly assist employers in avoiding, or at least minimizing, potential liability for violation of labor and employment laws.

This section discusses some basic tips for conducting effective and legal workplace investigations, which employers can apply to all types of workplace investigations, whether legally required or merely prudent.

Plan the investigation before hastily embarking on it. Among other things, employers should consider the goals of the investigation, the timing of the investigation, the scope of the investigation, the budget for the investigation, and the mechanics of the investigation (who to interview, whether to make notes and how detailed the notes should be, whether to involve an attorney, etc.).

Consider using a neutral third party to conduct the investigation, particularly in cases where the investigation may be subject to challenge as biased or where it is possible that the complaining employee may file a claim or a lawsuit. Employers must proceed with caution when choosing the third party—a biased or untrained investigator can doom the entire investigation and the action taken as a result of that investigation. Recognize, however, that not every employee complaint requires the employer to hire a third party investigator; in many cases, the human resources manager or another qualified and uninvolved manager may be able to conduct an adequate and effective investigation.

Be careful about promising absolute confidentiality. In most cases, due to the requirement of an investigation, employees may learn of the complaint by virtue of the fact that the employer will be interviewing witnesses to the alleged wrongdoing. Try to limit information provided on a need-to-know basis. Disciplinary or other remedial action may need to be taken after the investigation, and accordingly, absolute confidentiality is impossible to maintain.

Meet with the complaining employee and gather all facts, names of witnesses, and documents relating to the complaint. It is generally a good idea to have at least two people present to hear the complaint, to avoid the untenable situation where it is the employee's word against the employer's word. Consider asking, but not requiring, the complaining witness to put his or her complaints or concerns in writing—sometimes the story changes and gets worse over time! An early statement by the complaining witness can prove invaluable later, in case of a lawsuit or claim, to show that the employer promptly investigated and addressed what the employee complained about initially, and not what the employee's attorney later adds to the complaint. Try to obtain an exhaustive list of all complaints, all facts, documents, and witnesses supporting each complaint, and the details of each complaint. Instruct the complaining employee, preferably in writing, to inform the employer of any further problems, including while the investigation is being conducted.

Patience is a virtue: Don't make any hasty decisions! Wait until collecting all relevant evidence before making a decision on discipline or other remedial measures. Recognize the risk of false claims, and the rights of the accused.

The investigator should avoid editorializing (for example, "I think she's lying"); instead, try to report the facts in a neutral manner. Remember the line from Sergeant Friday in "Dragnet," the television show: "Just the facts, ma'am."

Remind all parties—the complaining employee, the alleged wrongdoer(s), and all witnesses—that the employer will not tolerate any retaliation against any party for participating in the investigation in good faith and providing truthful information. Recognize that in some situations, perceptions can be different, and be very careful of accusing the complaining employee of lying if you cannot prove it.

Review the personnel records of the complaining employee, the alleged wrongdoer, and all witnesses for evidence of motives and prior complaints or workplace issues. For example, did the complaining employee complain immediately on the heels of receiving a negative performance evaluation? Were the alleged victim and the alleged harasser in a prior consensual intimate relationship, or is there evidence that the alleged conduct was welcomed by the complaining employee by his or her active participation in the conduct at issue?

Review the employer's policies to ensure compliance with what you already said—one of the worst things to allow is a violation of your own policies!

You might want to consider searching (within the legal limits, of course) the affected employees' e-mails for evidence either supporting or disproving the complaint. Consider "freezing" or "imaging" the e-mails and hard drives of the affected employees to preserve evidence for possible use later.

When interviewing the accused employee, remind him or her that no decision has been made yet, that the purpose of the investigation is to gather the facts, that the employer will not tolerate any retaliation, and that maintaining confidentiality during the investigation is of the utmost importance. Inform the accused employee about the nature of the complaint, and ask for a response to each complaint. Ask about witnesses and documents that might corroborate the accused employee's story.

After interviewing all parties, go back to the complaining employee to report on findings, obtain any additional facts, documents, and names of witnesses, and ask the complaining employee what precisely he or she wants to have happen as a result of the complaint. The employer may not necessarily agree with the complaining employee's desired result based on the circumstances and the results of the investigation, but it is generally a good idea to check with the complaining employee to determine whether there may be a misunderstanding, hurt feelings, or reconsideration that might assist in reaching a resolution that is acceptable to all parties. Consider typing up the investigator's notes, particularly where there may be a later claim or a lawsuit. "Sanitize" the notes by removing name-calling and unnecessary editorializing. Number all the pages in the investigator's report to avoid charges later that notes were removed or edited by the employer in a self-serving manner.

Make a decision after reviewing all the relevant facts and documents. Consider asking an experienced labor and employment attorney for guidance in difficult "he said, she said" situations. Consider separating the alleged victim and the alleged harasser even in those situations where the facts are unclear, to avoid even the appearance of favoritism or the risk of subsequent claims of retaliation or further harassment or discrimination. Recognize that not every complaint of wrongdoing, even if the employer concludes that one or more employees acted inappropriately, justifies termination of employment. Consider suspensions, warnings, write-ups, employee training, and other disciplinary measures short of termination.

Go back to the complaining employee and the alleged wrongdoer to inform them of the employer's decision following the conclusion of the investigation. It is very important to reiterate the employer's policy that no retaliation—against any employee—will be tolerated, and that any retaliation will result in disciplinary action up to and including termination of employment. Document the decision carefully, for possible use later in the event of claims.

Periodically monitor the situation to ensure that the complaining employee's concerns have been addressed, and that there has been no repetition of the offending conduct. It is advisable to use a "tickler" system to follow up with the alleged victim at regular intervals to ensure that the situation has not deteriorated and to discover any new complaints.

As with other employment decisions, employers should strive to make decisions and statements that they will be proud of later. Case law suggests that even if an employer reaches the incorrect decision (for example, that no sexual harassment occurred), the quality of the employer's investigation (prompt, thorough, fair, and conducted in good faith) may insulate the employer from liability, or help to minimize liability in the event of a later claim or lawsuit.

Performance Counseling

Although the focus of this book is on the beginning and end of the employ-ment relationship, employee performance appraisals, reviews, and counseling during the employment relationship are extremely important. Although many employers have preserved at-will employment relationships with members of their staff, and thus could end the employment relationship for any or no rea-son, employers typically have good reasons to terminate the employment. In defense of nearly all employment claims and lawsuits by former employees, employers will need to rely on performance reviews to explain the legitimate, non-discriminatory reason(s) for termination decisions.

Many employers successfully use the performance review process to moti-vate and reward their employees. Performance reviews should be as construc-tive as possible. Here are some guidelines to assist employers in conducting performance appraisals.

- *Document, document, document.* You want to avoid a situation in which it is the employee's word against your word. Carefully document all per-formance issues, even verbal counseling sessions.

- *Be very careful with the language that you choose.* Anything you write in the performance review is potential evidence in a lawsuit. Try to avoid col-orful adjectives and just stick to the facts. Describe the performance problem succinctly, without editorial comment.

- *Be candid—in a professional manner—with the employee about performance deficiencies.* Remember that no good termination should come as a sur-prise to the terminated employee. Employees are entitled to know where they stand with the employer. It is only fair to tell employees specifically where their performance needs improvement, and to pro-vide specific timetables, measures for improvement, and the conse-quences of continued deficient performance.

- *Stay on target; the goal is to improve performance.* All performance counsel-ing should be governed by this goal. It is not productive to engage in name-calling or personal attacks on employees in performance counsel-ing sessions or reports. Avoid humiliating or embarrassing the employee.

- *Provide measurable goals and follow through on performance issues identified.* Be realistic about performance improvement and provide concrete suggestions for improvement.

- *Check for precedents and consistency in the treatment of similarly situated employees.* How has the employer disciplined or counseled other employees who have engaged in the same conduct or had the same performance deficiency?

- *Use the "two-on-one" method of performance counseling.* Have two supervisors, or one supervisor and a human resources representative, meet with the employee. This will help avoid the situation of the employee's word against his or her supervisor's word. Remember, however, that an employer should never block or impede an employee who wishes to leave such a meeting, to avoid a potential false imprisonment claim by the employee. In addition, employers with unions must know that union employees are entitled to have their union representative present during any disciplinary interview.

- *Attempt to obtain the affected employee's acknowledgment—in writing—of the performance deficiency and counseling on it.* However, if the employee refuses to sign the performance appraisal or write-up, the employer should simply note that fact in the employee's personnel file and/or on the performance appraisal or write-up itself.

As with other employment decisions, the goal is to take action that employers will be proud of later. Recognize that write-ups and performance appraisals can and will be used as evidence in any subsequent lawsuit or government audit against the employer, so be sure to maintain integrity and professionalism in your documentation and take actions that reflect your highest standards and compliance with the law.

Employee Handbooks and Required Postings in the Workplace

Employers should recognize that, in addition to helping employers comply with applicable labor and employment laws, employee handbooks, manuals, and employment policies may help motivate and counsel employees. Employee handbooks provide a useful checklist and reminders for supervisors and employees regarding common workplace issues. They can also help ensure consistency in the application of employment policies. In addition to employee handbooks, employers should check the labor and employment regulations in the state(s) they have employees to see what notices they are required to post.

Employee Handbooks and Policies

There are some preliminary considerations for employers with regard to employee handbooks. Some labor and employment laws only apply to employers with a threshold number of employees. In addition, if the workforce is unionized, so that the employees in the union have a collective bargaining agreement with the employer, the employer should consider a separate handbook for union employees. Employers with government contracts and others in highly regulated industries should consider the effect of such contracts and government regulation on their business and employees, and use the handbook to communicate those requirements and issues, and make sure employees understand them.

Figure 8.1 (page 124) contains a list of sample topics and policies that employers should consider including in their employee handbooks. In addition, there is a sample Employee Handbook in the Appendix; note that it must be modified depending on the laws of the state in which the employees are working. Many chambers of commerce and other employer organizations have sample employment policies and procedures, including the topics listed above. However, due to the evolving and complex legal requirements, and potential exposure for illegal policies and practices, employers are strongly encouraged to have an experienced labor and employment law attorney review handbooks before employers begin using them.

Posters in the Workplace

Most states require that employers post in a prominent place in the workplace

FIGURE 8–1. **Topics and Policies to Include in an Employee Handbook**

- Handbook General—a general statement about the purpose of the handbook (for example, as a guide for employees).
- Introduction, Welcome, and History of Company
- Application of Handbook and Effective/Revision Dates
- Disclaimer and Right to Revise
- Acknowledgment by Employee
- Employment
- Integrated At-Will Policy
- Equal Employment Opportunity Statement
- Immigration Law Compliance
- Reference and Other Checks
- Outside Employment
- Employment of Relatives (Anti-Nepotism)
- Reasonable Accommodation of Disabilities
- Employment Status and Records
- Employment Categories
- Exempt v. Nonexempt
- Regular v. Temporary
- Full Time v. Part Time
- Independent Contractors
- Probation
- Personnel Files & Right to Inspect
- Medical Information
- Personnel Data Changes
- Performance Evaluations
- Transfer/Promotion (must translate into foreign language if spoken by at least 10 percent)
- Seniority
- Termination of Employment
- Exit Interviews
- Severance Pay
- Rehire
- Reference Requests
- Employee Benefits
- Holidays

- Vacation
- Sick Time (some states' laws require benefits for registered domestic partners of employees)
- Health/Dental/Life Insurance
- 401k
- COBRA (20 or more employees)
- State Disability Insurance
- Workers' Compensation
- Unemployment Insurance
- Educational Assistance
- Employee Assistance Program (EAP)
- Charitable Contribution Match
- Payroll and Work Hours
- Paychecks
- Pay Deductions
- Work Hours and Timesheets
- Meal Periods
- Rest Periods
- Overtime Pay
- Reporting Time Pay
- Make-Up Time
- Expense Reimbursement
- Bonuses
- Recruiting Bonuses
- Uniforms
- Tool & Equipment Restrictions
- Training & Education Programs
- Meal & Lodging Credits
- Work Conditions
- Safety (must mention Illness Injury Prevention Program in handbook)
- Security & Violence Prevention
- Drug Free Workplace (if government contractor)
- No Smoking
- Use of Company Property and Vehicles
- Invention Assignments
- Privacy
- Right to Search Desk, Locker, Packages

- Right to Monitor Telephone, E-mail, and Internet Usage
- Background Checks
- Reference Requests
- Drug Testing
- Employee Conduct and Disciplinary Action
- Standards of Conduct and Ethics
- Sexual and Other Harassment, Discrimination, and Retaliation
- Drug and Alcohol Use
- Conflicts of Interest
- Confidentiality and Nondisclosure
- Punctuality and Attendance
- Dress Code
- Personal Calls and Mail
- Solicitations and Postings
- Problem Resolution
- Discipline Policy
- Leaves of Absence
- Paid Leaves
- Work-Related Disability Leave
- Bereavement Leave
- Jury and Witness Duty Leave
- Voting Time Leave
- Unpaid Leaves
- Disability Leave
- Family and Medical Leave (must translate into foreign language if spoken by at least 10 percent)
- Pregnancy Disability Leave and Transfer (must translate into foreign language if spoken by at least 10 percent)
- Domestic Violence Leave (check state law)
- Military Leave
- Leave for Children's School Activities (check state law)
- Alcohol & Drug Rehabilitation (check state law)
- Volunteer Firefighters
- Personal Leave

(for example, in the lunchroom) information about labor and employment laws, including the following:

- Unlawful harassment (including sexual harassment), discrimination, and retaliation are prohibited
- Minimum wage, overtime, paydays, and other wage-hour law requirements
- Family Medical Leave Act (FMLA) eligibility
- Workers' compensation claims reporting procedures
- Workplace safety policies
- Protected leaves of absence, depends on individual state laws
- Whistleblower Hotlines. Note that public companies must implement an anonymous internal complaint procedure or hotline for employees to complain about fraud and accounting violations, pursuant to the federal Sarbanes-Oxley Act.

It is very important that employers check the legal posting requirements in each state where they have employees. Some states, such as California, will provide posters to employers for a nominal fee, and some chambers of commerce and employer organizations provide such posters and information about required postings. Employers can use the posters to help publicize a culture of legal compliance, and emphasize the employer's desire to inform employees of their legal rights and obligations. They also reinforce the employers' own policies, as many of the posting requirements overlap with handbook provisions and employment policies.

Happy Employees Don't Need a Union

Employees choose to join unions for a variety of reasons. Some of those reasons include:

- A perception that management and supervision are arbitrary and unfair
- The substance abuse policy is not administered fairly or consistently, or the purpose of and reason for the substance abuse policy have not been communicated to the employees

- Compensation and benefits are not commensurate for peers doing similar work
- Employee discipline and grievance systems are not established or are seen as arbitrary and unfair
- There is a lack of attention to employee facilities such as restrooms, eating areas, and parking areas
- Promises that were made or implied have not been kept
- Working conditions and employee safety concerns are viewed as substandard or inadequate
- Management does not make an effort to obtain employee input before making changes that directly affect employees
- After voting against a union in a prior vote, the company has not kept promises
- Promised pay raises have not materialized
- Seniority is ignored in decision making
- Company personnel policies are enforced unfairly
- Employees' complaints are, or have been, ignored

In most cases, the supervisor is the key to preventing employees from choosing to join a union. The best labor relations practices are preventive and address problems before employees seek representation from a union. Indeed, by following the guidelines in this book, employers will go a long way towards avoiding union representation of their employees. Honest and frequent communication with employees is essential. Employers should adopt and enforce in practice an open door policy with regard to employee complaints and concerns.

Conclusion

Once hired, it is important to train, develop, and motivate your employees. By following the practical and legal tips discussed in this chapter, you will go a long way toward keeping your employees happy and highly motivated. Above all, employers must take all employee complaints and concerns seriously, and must respond appropriately.

FIGURE 8–2. **Major Federal Employment Laws, Executive Orders, and Regulations Affecting Personnel Management**

Law, Exec. Order, or Regulation	Coverage	Brief Summary	Post Rqrmt	Enforcement Agency	Primary Penalties
Fair Labor Standards Act, U.S. Code 29 § 201, et seq.	Employers with two employees handling goods that have moved in commerce and annual dollar volume (ADV) of sales of at least $500,000; certain employers have no ADV thresholds; firms covered before March 30, 1990 continue to be subject to overtime pay, child labor, and record-keeping requirements of the act; employees of firms with less than $500,000 annual volume may be covered in any work week when they are individually engaged in interstate commerce	Minimum wage of $5.15; overtime after 40 hrs./week at 1.5 times the regular rate; accurate time records required for all nonexempt employees; child labor restrictions apply; retaliation prohibited; for tipped employees, maximum tip credit of $3.02/hr. after Sept. 19, 1997	Yes	U.S. Department of Labor (DOL), Wage-Hour Division	Civil: Employees (jury trial) or govt. may sue for double back wages for 2–3 years; atty's fees; child labor penalties up to $10,000/child; and penalties up to $1,000 for each employee for repeated or willful minimum wage or overtime violations; compensatory and punitive damages available for retaliation; opt-in class action available; willful violators may also be prosecuted criminally
Migrant and Seasonal-Agricultural Worker Protection Act (MSPA), U.S. Code 29 § 1801, et seq.	Most agricultural employers, including forestry operators; farm labor contractors.	Requires disclosure of job terms, record-keeping, payment of wages when due, housing/vehicle safety standards for migrant and seasonal workers; workers' compensation arrangements; contractor licensing; farm labor contractors must register with the DOL before recruiting, soliciting, hiring, employing, furnishing, or transporting any migrant or seasonal worker; protects workers from retaliation.	Yes	DOL, Wage-Hour Division	Civil money penalties up to $1,000 for each violation, lawsuits by workers for greater of statutory or actual damages; criminal penalties, including imprisonment and fines for willful violations
Temporary Agricultural Workers (H-2A Visas), U.S. Code 8 §§ 1101, 1184, 1188	Agricultural employers seeking to hire temporary agricultural workers under H-2A visas	Employer may not import foreign workers unless they have applied to the Employment and Training Administration (ETA) for certification that there are not sufficient workers who are able, willing, qualified, and available to perform the work; and the employment of foreign workers will not adversely affect the wages and working conditions of similarly employed workers in the U.S.	No	DOL, Wage-Hour Division	NA
Temporary Non-Agricultural Workers (H-2B Visas), U.S. Code 8 §§ 1101, 1184, 1188	Employers seeking to hire temporary nonagricultural workers under H-2B visas.	Employer may not import foreign workers unless they have applied to the Employment and Training Administration (ETA) for certification that there are not sufficient workers who are able, willing, qualified, and available to perform the work; and the employment of foreign workers will not adversely affect the wages and working conditions of similarly employed workers in the U.S.	No	DOL, Wage-Hour Division	NA

Law, Exec. Order, or Regulation	Coverage	Brief Summary	Post Rqmt	Enforcement Agency	Primary Penalties
Workers in Professional and Specialty Occupations (H-1B Visas), U.S. Code 8 §§ 1101, 1182, 1184	Employers seeking to hire nonimmigrant aliens as workers in specialty occupations or as fashion models using the H-1B nonimmigrant visa classification	Immigration and Nationality Act (INA) sets forth procedures for hiring these workers; the employer must file a Labor Condition Application (LCA), and certain forms with the DOL, stating that they will pay the employee at least the local prevailing wage, offer benefits, provide working conditions that will not adversely affect U.S. workers, not employ such workers where there is a strike; there are also notice requirements.	No	DOL, Wage-Hour Division; INS	Civil penalties ranging from $1,000 to $35,000 per violation; payment of back wages; preclusion from future access to the program for a period of at least one year
Family and Medical Leave Act (FMLA), U.S. Code 29 § 2601	Employers engaged in interstate commerce with at least 50 employees within 75 miles; all public employers are also covered whether or not they meet the 50 employee test.	Requires up to 12 weeks (including intermittent leave) of unpaid, job-protected leave annually for certain family and medical reasons; to be protected, employee must have worked at least 12 months for the employer and must have worked at least 1,250 hours during the 12 months immediately before the leave begins	Yes	DOL, Wage-Hour Division	Employees/DOL can sue for back wages and benefits, reinstatement, atty's fees and actual losses sustained; double damages possible for willful violations.
Title VII of the Civil Rights Act of 1964 (1991), U.S. Code 42 § 2000e	Employers engaged in interstate commerce with at least 15 employees each working day in each of 20 weeks in current or preceding calendar year; includes federal, state and local governments (different procedures for claims against the federal government)	Prohibits discrimination based on race, color, national origin, religion, sex, pregnancy (including childbirth or related condition); also bars retaliation against those making the complaint; claims must be filed with the EEOC within 180-300 days after the act of discrimination; employees can sue after the EEOC processes the charge or within 90 days after receipt of notice of termination of proceedings by the EEOC	Yes	Equal Employment Opportunity Commission (EEOC)	Employees/EEOC can sue for back wages, reinstatement or front pay, promotion, atty's fees; for intentional discrimination, employees can sue for capped compensatory and punitive damages with jury trial allowed; Rule 23 class action available
Americans with Disabilities Act of 1990 (ADA), U.S. Code 42 §§ 1201–12213	Employers engaged in interstate commerce with at least 15 employees; includes state and local governments; does not include federal government	Prohibits discrimination in terms, conditions, and privileges of employment against individuals with actual or perceived disabilities who, with or without reasonable accommodation, can perform essential job functions; employer must make reasonable accommodation unless it is shown to be an undue hardship	Yes	Equal Employment Opportunity Commission (EEOC)	Employees/EEOC can sue for back wages, reinstatement or front pay, promotion, atty's fees; for intentional disability discrimination, employees can sue for capped compensatory and punitive damages with jury trial allowed; Rule 23 class action available
Sections 501 and 505 of the Rehabilitation Act of 1973, U.S. Code 29 § 701, et seq	Federal employers	Prohibits discrimination against qualified individuals with disabilities who work in the federal government	Yes	Equal Employment Opportunity Commission (EEOC)	Monetary or equitable relief

Hiring and Firing

Law, Exec. Order, or Regulation	Coverage	Brief Summary	Post Rqrmt	Enforcement Agency	Primary Penalties
Section 1981 (Civil Rights Act of 1866), U.S. Code 42 § 1981	All private employers, including individuals, regardless of size or dollar volume; includes state, local, and certain federal government entities not covered by Title VII	Prohibits racial and ethnic bias in employment; includes all minority and ethnic groups; complaint must be based on race or color—not national origin; employers also forbidden from retaliation; longer statutory period than Title VII; employees do not have to go through an administrative agency	No	Private Lawsuits	In addition to suits for back wages, reinstatement or front-pay, promotion, and atty's fees, allows jury trials and uncapped punitive and compensatory damages
Walsh-Healey Public Contracts Act (PCA), U.S. Code 41 § 35, et seq	Employees of employers w/federal gov't. manufacturing and supply contracts in excess of $10,000 who work on gov't. contracts	Employer must pay covered employees 1.5 times basic rate after 40 hours in a workweek and comply with federal minimum wage requirements; also cannot hire employees under 16 or convicts	Yes	DOL, Wage-Hour Division	Gov't. withholds funds and can collect back wages; $10/day fine for each minor under 16 or convict knowingly employed; debar from future contracts
McNamara-O'Hara Service Contract Act (MOSCA), U.S. Code 41 § 351, et seq	Employers w/federal gov't. service contracts in excess of $2,500 involving use of service employees	Employer must pay specified minimum hourly rates and fringe benefits that prevail in the locality; if contract is less than $2,5000, must meet federal minimum wage and overtime requirements	Yes	DOL, Wage-Hour Division	Gov't. can withhold funds and collect back wages; debar from future contracts
Davis-Bacon Act, U.S. Code 40 § 276a, et seq	Federal public works construction contracts in excess of $2,000	Employer must pay specified minimum hourly rates and specified fringe benefits	Yes	Contracting Agency and/or DOL, Wage-Hour Division	Gov't. can withhold funds and collect back wages; debar from future contracts
Copeland Anti-Kickback Act, U.S. Code 48 § 948	Federal contractors, subcontractors, employers, and foremen with respect to construction or repair of any public building or public work financed in whole or in part by loans or grants from U.S.	Federal contractors, subcontractors, employers, and foremen may not make deductions from pay (except for deductions permitted by CFR 29 Part 3 or pre-approved by Sec. of Labor) by force, threat, or intimidation; requires weekly reports of wages paid each employee on covered contract; employees are entitled to full pay and payments on a weekly basis	No	Contracting Agency and/or DOL, Wage-Hour Division	Fine of up to $5,000 or imprisonment for not more than 5 years; if willful, subject to contract termination and debarment
Contract Work Hours and Safety Standards Act, U.S. Code 40 § 3703, et seq	Federal contracts for $100,000 or more, including construction, requiring employment of laborers and mechanics other than contracts subject to Walsh-Healey Public Contracts Act (PCA)	Employer must pay 1.5 times basic rate for hours over 40 in a week	Yes	DOL, Wage-Hour Division	Gov't. can withhold funds and collect back wages; debar from future contracts; $10/day penalty for each day overtime worked without payment of proper overtime; for intentional violations, fines of up to $1,000 or up to 6 months imprisonment

Law, Exec. Order, or Regulation	Coverage	Brief Summary	Post Mgmt	Enforcement Agency	Primary Penalties
Executive Order 11246	Employers with federal gov't. contract in excess of $10,000 in any 12-month period. Includes manufacturing and supply, service, and construction contracts	Requires antidiscrimination clause in contract plus written affirmative action plan (AAP) for single contract of $50,000 and 50 employees; complaint must be filed within 180 days of violation	Yes	DOL's Office of Federal Contract Compliance Programs (OFCCP)	Terminate contract; debar from contracts; collect back wages; prosecute for false statements
Rehabilitation Act of 1973, Section 503, U.S. Code 29 § 701, et seq	Employers with federal gov't. contracts in excess of $2,500	Requires affirmative action and nondiscrimination in employment of disabled persons; written AAP required if 50 employees and a contract of $50,000	Yes	DOL's Office of Federal Contract Compliance Programs (OFCCP)	Gov't. can withhold funds, collect back wages, and require hiring, reinstatement or promotion; debar from future contracts
Rehabilitation Act of 1973, Section 504, U.S. Code 29 § 701, et seq	Employer programs or activities receiving federal financial assistance	Prohibits discrimination, denying benefits, or exclusion from participation, including employment, regarding any qualified disabled individual	Yes	Federal agency responsible for providing financial assistance, DOJ	Gov't. can withhold funds and collect back wages; debar from future contracts; employee can sue for back wages and reinstatement; compensatory and punitive damages available
Vietnam Era Veteran Readjustment Asst. Act, U.S. Code 38 §§ 3680, 3485, et seq	Employers with gov't. contract of $25,000 or more	Requires affirmative action regarding Vietnam era veterans and disabled veterans; written AAP required if 50 employees and a contract of $50,000	Yes	U.S. DOL's Office of Federal Contract Compliance Programs (OFCCP)	Gov't. can withhold funds, collect back wages, and require hiring, reinstatement, and promotion; debar from future contracts
Executive Order 12989	Federal contractors and subcontractors	Dept. of Justice will receive complaints, investigate federal contractors or subcontractors for compliance with INA's employment provisions	No	Dept. of Justice	Debarment from federal contractors for 1 year for knowingly employing illegal aliens
Drug-Free Workplace Act of 1988, U.S. Code 41 § 701, et seq	Employers with federal contracts of $25,000 or more; all federal grant recipients	Establish drug-free awareness program and make good faith effort to carry out; requires penalties or rehabilitation for employees convicted of workplace drug offenses	Yes	Federal agency that contracts or provides assistance	Termination of the contract; debarment from future contracts/grants if persistent problems
Equal Pay Act of 1963 (EPA), U.S. Code 41 § 701, et seq	Employers with two employees handling goods which have moved in interstate commerce and annual dollar volume of sales of at least $500,000; certain employers have no dollar volume thresholds, includes state, local, and federal governments with exemptions for certain employees	Prohibits pay differentials on basis of sex in substantially equal work requiring equal skill, effort, and responsibility under similar working conditions; also protected against retaliation; no exemption for executive, administrative, professional, and outside sales employees; claim must be brought within 2-3 years; can sue under both the EPA and Title VII, or directly under the EPA	Yes	Equal Employment Opportunity Commission (EEOC)	Employees or EEOC can sue for back wages for two years, or three years if willful violation; jury trial; reinstatement or front pay; atty's fees; opt-in class action available; punitive damages are not available

Hiring and Firing

Law, Exec. Order, or Regulation	Coverage	Brief Summary	Post Rqmt	Enforcement Agency	Primary Penalties
Employee Polygraph Protection Act of 1988 (EPPA), U.S. Code 29 § 2001, et seq	Employers subject to the FLSA; exemptions for state and local governments and certain gov't. contractors and employers in the security and drug industries	Generally prohibits the use of lie detectors and lie detector results in private employment; limited exemptions apply for certain internal investigations; even if exempted, there are extensive notice and administrative requirements	Yes	DOL, Wage-Hour Division	Civil money penalties up to $10,000. Gov't./employee can sue for lost wages, benefits, employment, reinstatement, promotion, compensatory and punitive damages, and atty's fees
Uniformed Services Employment and Re-employment Rights Act, U.S. Code 38 §§ 4301– 4333	All employers	Prohibits discrimination the basis of uniformed service and guarantees the re-employment of veterans and other members of the uniformed services returning to their prior employment	Yes	U.S. DOL's Veterans Employment and Training Service (VETS)	Employees/Atty. Gen. on behalf of employees can sue for loss of wages or benefits and atty's fees; liquidated damages if violation is willful
Immigration Reform and Control Act of 1986 (IRCA), U.S. Code 8 § 1324, et seq	All employers	Prohibits hiring of illegal aliens or keeping them employed if employer later learns the employee is an illegal alien; requires verification and record-keeping of work authorization documents	No	Dept. of Justice's Immigration & Naturalization Service; Wage-Hour Division	$2,000/illegal alien for the first offense; up to $10,000 fine for repeated hiring violations; fines up to $1,000 for record keeping violations
Omnibus Transportation Employee Testing Act of 1991, U.S. Code 49 §§ 102–143	All transportation employers with employees engaging in safety-sensitive transport and service agents	Requires drug and alcohol testing for safety sensitive transportation employees in aviation, trucking, railroad, mass transit, pipeline, and others; employers must get written consent to perform such tests before employees are to be given safety-sensitive duties	No	Office of Drug and Alcohol Policy and Compliance (ODAPC); DOT	Remove employee from work in the safety sensitive position immediately if failed drug or alcohol test
Worker Adjustment and Retraining Notification Act (WARN), U.S. Code 29 § 2101, et seq	Employers with at least 100 employees, not counting those who have worked less than 6 months in the last 12 months and those who work an average of less than 20 hours/week; does not include federal, state, and local government employers	With some exceptions, requires 60-day notice to employees and state and local governments before a plant closing or mass layoff; a plant closing occurs when facility or unit is shut down for more than 6 months, or when 50 or more employees lose their jobs during any 30-day period at a single site; mass layoff occurs when a layoff of 6 months or longer affects either 500 or more workers or at least 33% of the workforce if it affects between 50 and 499 workers	No	DOL issues regulations, but WARN is enforced only by private suit	Payment of 60 days' wages and benefits to employees; newly-hired workers get less. $500/day civil penalty paid to local government for up to 60 days

Law, Exec. Order, or Regulation	Coverage	Brief Summary	Post Rqrmt	Enforcement Agency	Primary Penalties
Protection of Juror's Employment, U.S. Code 29 § 1875; Jury Systems Improvement Act, U.S. Code 28 § 1875	All employers	Employer may not discharge, threaten to discharge, intimidate, or coerce any permanent employee solely because of federal jury service; jurors are treated as if they are on leave	No	United States District Court	Civil penalties up to $1,000 for each violation; court-appointed counsel may sue on behalf of employee for lost wages or benefits in accordance with employer's policy, reinstatement, and atty's fees. No compensatory or punitive damages
Social Security Act (FICA), U.S. Code 42 § 301, et seq	Employers who pay over $50 per quarter in wages	Employer and employee each must contribute 7.65% of wages up to $68,400 and 1.45% over $68,400 for 1998; wage base subject to annual adjustment	No	U.S. Social Security Admin. and Internal Revenue Service (IRS)	Back taxes plus interest and penalties collectible by IRS
Federal Unemployment Tax Act (FUTA), U.S. Code 26 §§ 3301–3307, 3311	Employers who employ 1 or more persons 20 or more weeks/year; also, any person who paid cash wages of at least $1,000 for domestic service during any calendar quarter in current or preceding calendar year	Must contribute 0.8% (varies with credits for participation in state unemployment programs) of up to $7,000 of each employee's wages	No	Internal Revenue Service (IRS)	Back taxes plus interest and penalties collectible by IRS
Employee Retirement Income Security Act of 1974 (ERISA), U.S. Code 29 § 1001, et seq	Employers in interstate commerce; does not include government entities or churches	Requires extensive pension and welfare plan reporting, plus disclosure to plan participants and beneficiaries; minimum participation, vesting, and funding standards for pension plans, including profit-sharing plans; plan termination insurance for pension plans	No	DOL, Office of Pension and Welfare Benefits and Pension Benefit Guaranty Corp; Employee Benefits Security Administration	Employees, beneficiaries, or gov't. can sue for benefits and to enforce rights; administrative fines up to $1,000/day for failure to file annual report; personal liability of up to $100/day for failure to provide timely information to participant
Consolidated Omnibus Budget Reconciliation Act of 1985 (COBRA), U.S. Code 7 § 1314, et seq	Employers involved in interstate commerce and claiming tax deduction for group health plan expenses or who have highly compensated employees participating in group health plans; exception if fewer than 20 employees for over 50 percent of the work days in preceding year.	Requires the election of continuation of coverage at the employee's expense for a limited amount of time under employer's group health plan to employees, spouses, and/or dependent children upon the occurrence of specified events, including termination of employment or reduction in hours	No	DOL and Internal Revenue Service; EBSA	Same as ERISA, plus personal liability up to $100/day for failure to provide timely employee or dependent notice of commencement of coverage or election form
Health Maintenance Organization Act (HMO), U.S. Code 42 § 300	Employers subject to the FLSA's minimum wage provision with at least 25 employees, offering a health benefits plan, and with at least 25 employees in HMO service area	Since October 24, 1995, employer may offer membership in qualified HMOs voluntarily, but covered employers no longer can be required to offer an HMO option; however, an employer who voluntarily offers an HMO option (or who was obligated to offer an HMO option before October 24, 1995) may not discriminate financially against those employees who enroll in an HMO	No	Dept. of Health & Human Services' Office of Health Maintenance Organization	Fines of up to $10,000 for every 30-day period when employer is out of compliance

Law, Exec. Order, or Regulation	Coverage	Brief Summary	Post Rqmt	Enforcement Agency	Primary Penalties
Health Insurance Portability and Accountability Act (HIPAA) of 1996, U.S. Code 29 § 1181, et seq	Employers subject to ERISA, Internal Revenue Code (IRC) or Public Health Service Act (PHSA) and who employ two or more employees; excludes governmental plans	Prohibits discrimination based on health-related factors in providing group health insurance benefits; requires certification of participant's periods of group health coverage; limits pre-existing condition exclusion periods; expands and clarifies COBRA coverage.	No	U.S. Dept of Labor (DOL), Department of Health and Human Services (HHS) and Internal Revenue Service (IRS)	Employees or beneficiaries can sue for benefits and to enforce rights to benefits; tax of up to $1,000/day for violations of the law, minimum penalty $2,500 if discovered through IRS audit, maximum penalty $500,000; government can take civil action; criminal penalty if willful violation
Occupational Safety and Health Act (OSHA), U.S. Code 29 § 651, et seq	Employers in interstate commerce; private industries only	Employer must furnish safe employment according to designated workplace standards; record keeping; subject to inspections and investigations; no retaliation against employees for exercising rights; employee must file complaint for retaliation within 30 days; employers have a general duty to keep the workplace free from recognized, serious hazards	Yes	Occupational Safety and Heath Administration (OSHA), DOL	Civil penalties for violations of standards; gov't./employee can sue for reinstatement and back pay; possible criminal action
Federal Mine Safety and Health Act, U.S. Code 30 § 801, et seq	Employers with mine property	Holds operators of mines responsible for the health and safety of their employees; sets up safety standards and inspections each year; employer may not retaliate for exercising rights under this act	No	Mines Safety and Health Administration (MSHA)	$55,000 maximum violation; $55 single penalty for nonserious violations; civil or criminal sanctions for willful or knowing violations; special penalty assessment for serious problems
Consumer Credit Protection Act, Title III (Federal Wage Garnishment Law), U.S. Code 15 § 1601, et seq	Employers under the federal Wage-Hour Law who receive earnings for personal services	Restricts garnishment withholding to 25 percent or less of disposable income; allows larger deductions for support/alimony garnishments and tax liens; no discharge for one or more garnishments of single debt	No	DOL, Wage-Hour Division	Govt. can sue for excess withholding, reinstatement, and back pay; fines of up to $1,000 and/or imprisonment for up to 1 year for willful violations
Debt Collection Improvement Act of 1996, U.S. Code 31 § 3720	All employers	No more than 15 percent of employees' disposable pay may be deducted to collect student loan payments without consent; employer may not discharge, refuse to hire, or discipline because of student loan garnishments	No	Dept. of Education	Employer can be held liable for amount it should have withheld; employee can sue for reinstatement, back pay, punitive damages, atty's fees
Fair Credit Reporting Act (FCRA), U.S. Code 15 § 1681	Employers in interstate commerce	Requires separate notification of intent to use consumer report, signed authorization, and disclosures to applicant/employee before and after adverse action related to report	No	Federal Trade Commission (FTC)	Civil suit for noncompliance (actual, compensatory, liquidated, and punitive damages); criminal liability for obtaining report under false pretenses (fines between $100 and $1,000 and up to 2 years in prison)
Electronic Communication Privacy Act (ECPA), U.S. Code 18 §§ 3117, 2521, 2701, et seq	All employers	Employer cannot use electronic or mechanical device to intercept the conversations of employees, except if the employees have no reasonable expectation of privacy	No	DOJ	Employers subject to fines for violations, imprisonment for 1 year for first offense, and not more than than 5 years if repeated offenses; gov't. can sue for injunctive relief or civil fines

Hiring and Firing

CHAPTER
9

Leaves
of Absence

Required and Voluntary Time Off for Employees

Another essential ingredient in effectively and legally managing employees is ensuring a clear understanding of the legally protected types of leave of absence, which you will learn about in this chapter. Employers should note, however, that many types of legally protected leaves of absence vary from state to state, and sometimes the applicable state law requirements are different from the federal laws. Some types of leave are included more than once to illustrate conflicts and overlaps in the various provisions. In addition, some state legislatures are very active in amending and supplementing the types of protected leaves of absence available to eligible employees.

Accordingly, employers must consult state and even local laws before making decisions regarding whether to grant employees particular leaves of absence.

Family and Medical Leaves

The federal Family and Medical Leave Act (FMLA), signed into law by President Clinton in 1993, is the primary federal statute requiring employers with 50 or more employees within a 75 mile radius to provide unpaid leave of up to 12 weeks to eligible employees. Importantly, the FMLA states that whenever the family and medical leave requirements under federal and state law differ, the employer must comply with whatever provision provides the greater family leave rights to the employee (U.S. Code 29 § 2651[b]). The FMLA provides up to 12 weeks per year of leave for either the birth, adoption, or foster care placement of a child; the care of a family member with a serious health condition; or the employee's own serious health condition. The leave is unpaid (except when vacation, sick leave, or paid time off is used), but employers are required to continue group health benefits during the leave. The employee has the right to return to the same or a comparable position upon the termination of the leave.

The FMLA applies to employers with at least 50 employees. Eligible employees are those who have worked for the employer for more than 12 months before the leave starts, have worked at least 1,250 hours in the 12 months before the leave starts, and work at a location where the employer employs at least 50 employees within 75 miles of that location. The FMLA covers an employee's own pregnancy-related disabilities. Specifically, the FMLA's definition of a "serious health condition" includes "any period of incapacity due to pregnancy or pre-natal care." (29 C.F.R. § 825.114[a][2][ii]). Employers should note that some states, such as California, have separate statutes that require pregnancy disability leave. The effect of this structure is discussed in the section on pregnancy disability leaves, beginning on page 139. The FMLA also covers a pregnancy-related disability of an employee's family member.

Under the FMLA, both the employer and the employee have the right to demand that accrued vacation time or paid time off be substituted during any

FMLA leave (29 C.F.R. § 825.207). Under the FMLA, employees may take intermittent leaves or reduced schedules to care for a family member with a serious health condition, or the employee's own serious health condition when medically necessary. Under the FMLA, intermittent leave for the birth, adoption, or foster care placement of a child is entirely at the discretion of the employer (29 C.F.R. § 825.203[b]).

There are medical certification requirements under the FMLA for employers to ask for a health care provider's certification of the need for the employee's leave of absence. The FMLA has a procedure for requesting a second medical opinion, and allows the employer to request subsequent medical re-certifications under certain circumstances. An employer may ask if leave is being taken for an FMLA-qualifying reason and may ask for information necessary to confirm whether the reason qualifies under FMLA. When an employer employs both spouses, the employer may limit the family leave taken by both spouses for the birth, adoption, or foster care placement of a child to a combined total of 12 weeks. In addition, the FMLA allows the same combined 12-week cap when family care leave is taken to care for a sick parent. (29 C.F.R. § 825.202).

The FMLA requires employees to give certain amounts of advance notice and provides for the employer's remedies if the employee fails to do so. The law also provides that the employer may impose its own customary notice and procedural requirements. However, the FMLA provides that as long as the employee complied with the FMLA's notice requirements, the employer cannot deny or delay FMLA leave (29 C.F.R. § 825.302[d]). The FMLA requires that the

Retroactive Designation of Leave of Absence as FMLA Leave

In *Ragsdale v. Wolverine Worldwide, Inc.,* (535 U.S. 81, 122 S. Ct. 1155, 152 L. Ed. 2d 167 [2002]), the U.S. Supreme Court struck down a regulation promulgated by the U.S. Department of Labor that purported to require employers to designate leave as FMLA leave at the outset of an eligible employee's 12 weeks of leave entitlement. The regulation also provided that leave taken by an employee does not count against that employee's 12-week FMLA entitlement if the employer fails to designate the leave as FMLA leave. The Court ruled that the regulation was contrary to the FMLA and beyond the authority of the Secretary of Labor.

employer designate a particular leave of absence as FMLA leave; however, the FMLA contains a two-day timeline for doing so, and has specific requirements about what must be included in the notice designating leave (29 C.F.R. § 825.208).

The FMLA provides an exception for salaried employees whose pay is in the highest 10 percent bracket at the employer. Under this exception, employers can deny reinstatement to the key employee if necessary to prevent substantial and grievous economic injury to the employer's operation. The law requires the employer to notify the key employee, but the notice requirements in the FMLA are very specific and employers must follow them closely. The FMLA provides another exception to the right of reinstatement. The regulations issued by the U.S. Department of Labor (DOL) specifically address this issue, and (29 C.F.R. section 825.16[a]) states:

> An employee has no greater right to reinstatement or to other benefits and conditions of employment than if the employee had been continuously employed during the FMLA leave period. *An employer must be able to show that an employee would not otherwise have been employed at the time reinstatement is requested in order to deny restoration to employment.* For example: If an employee is laid off during the course of taking FMLA leave and employment is terminated, the employer's responsibility to continue FMLA leave, maintain group health plan benefits, and restore the employee cease at the time the employee is laid off, provided the employer has no continuing obligations under a collective bargaining agreement or otherwise. *An employer would have the burden of proving that an employee would have been laid off during the FMLA leave period and, therefore, would not be entitled to restoration* [emphasis added].

According to this regulation, an employer should be able to terminate its relationship with an employee on FMLA leave, as long as the termination was for a nondiscriminatory reason, such as a reduction in force. However, the employer should note that under the applicable federal regulation the burden falls on it to establish a nondiscriminatory reason for the employment action.

Federal Pregnancy Discrimination Act

Pregnancy is also covered by the Pregnancy Discrimination Act, which is part of Title VII of the Civil Rights Act of 1964, as amended. Both federal and many state statutes require employers to treat pregnancy as they treat other disabilities. Consequently, under some state laws, eligible employees may be entitled to both pregnancy disability leave under the applicable state law while the employee is disabled by pregnancy, and leave to care for the newborn under the applicable state law, which means that an employee may be able to take longer leaves of absence. Under federal law, the employee is entitled to FMLA leave (up to a maximum of 12 weeks) both during the pregnancy disability and when the employee wants to care for the newborn. The effect of this structure is that the pregnancy disability leave will be covered by both the state law and the FMLA for up to 12 weeks, and the employer must comply with both statutes during this period. Any additional pregnancy disability leave will be covered by the state law but not the FMLA, and the employer can comply with the state law only. After the pregnancy disability leave, an employee may then take leave under the state law to care for the newborn for up to 12 weeks, and the employer must comply with the applicable state law (and the FMLA to the extent the employee has any FMLA leave left).

Small (and new or start-up) employers also should note that employees who are not eligible for a family and/or medical leave under the FMLA may be eligible under more stringent state laws. These employees may still be entitled to pregnancy disability leave, but the employer can comply with the state statute and not the FMLA. The FMLA does require continued group health benefits during any pregnancy disability leave that is covered by the FMLA, and employers must comply with the FMLA.

The FMLA gives both the employer and the employee the right to demand that accrued sick leave be substituted during a pregnancy disability leave, but an employee who is receiving temporary disability benefits cannot substitute paid leave (29 C.F.R. § 825.207, 29 C.F.R. § 825.219). The FMLA allows an employer to get a second medical opinion if the employer has reason to doubt the employee's health care provider. The FMLA requires reinstatement of the employee following pregnancy disability leave. Furthermore, the employer is required under the FMLA to reinstate the employee to the same or an equivalent position. The FMLA allows the employer to deny reinstatement if the employee's employment would have been terminated even if he/she had not taken the leave. As discussed in the previous section, the FMLA contains a "key employee" exception.

Leave of Absence as a Reasonable Accommodation for a Disability: Americans with Disabilities Act

The federal Americans with Disabilities Act of 1990 (ADA) requires an employer to make reasonable accommodation for a known physical or mental disability of an employee unless the employer can show that doing so produces undue hardship for its operations. An unpaid leave of absence can constitute a form of reasonable accommodation. The ADA also prohibits an employer from discriminating against an employee in the terms, conditions, and privileges of employment based on a physical or mental disability. Refusing a disabled employee a leave of absence when leaves have been provided to other employees might constitute discrimination.

Under the ADA, unpaid leaves that are used for treatment, recovery, or some other remedy for the disability (e.g., training a guide dog) may be reasonable when the employee expects to return to work, able to perform the essential functions of the job. The ADA requires an individualized inquiry into the needs of the specific individual and the specific job.

Employers also should note that although the ADA and similar state statutes exclude the current use of illegal drugs from their definitions of protected disabilities, some states have laws requiring employers to reasonably accommodate employees who voluntarily enter into a drug or alcohol rehabilitation program. For example, California Labor Code section 1025 requires employers with 25 or more employees to reasonably accommodate an employee who voluntarily enters into a drug or alcohol rehabilitation program, unless to do so would impose an undue hardship. On the other hand, an employer is not prohibited by any law from refusing to hire or from terminating an employee who is unable to perform his or her duties or who cannot perform the duties in safe manner because of current drug or alcohol use. The law is designed to make it easier for people availing themselves of help to become healthy and productive citizens, not to protect a drug or alcohol addiction. Many court decisions have ruled that employers may discharge employees whose alcohol abuse continues despite reasonable but unsuccessful attempts by the employer to accommodate recovery programs. In short, an employer must accommodate an employee's rehabilitation, but not the effects of drugs or alcohol when it comes to work performance. An employer is also obligated to make reasonable efforts to safeguard an employee's privacy with regard to his or her enrollment in a rehabilitation program.

Current Alcohol Abuse Not Protected

Fuller v. Frank, (916 F.2d 558 [1990]) is a case in which the Ninth Circuit affirmed an order granting summary judgment against the claims of a California postal employee who persisted in the abuse of alcohol. The employer attempted to accommodate his problem and bring about a recovery, but the programs were unsuccessful despite repeated attempts, and as a result the employee was discharged. The court reasoned that if this approach were not the law, an employee could conceivably forestall dismissal indefinitely by repeatedly entering treatment whenever dismissal became imminent due to a relapse. In Newland v. Dalton, 81 F. 3d 904 (1996), the Ninth Circuit rejected the claims of a civilian Navy employee based in California who contended that he could not be fired for a "drunken rampage" because the misconduct was a result of his alcohol problem.

Workers' Compensation Coverage and Leave of Absence Requirements

Most states have workers' compensation laws that provide benefits to employees who are injured on the job. Generally, the law requires all employers to maintain workers' compensation insurance to cover such work-related injuries. An employee who is recovering from a workers' compensation injury will be on a leave of absence. The workers' compensation laws generally limit an employer's ability to terminate an employee who is absent due to a workers' compensation injury. An employee is covered by workers' compensation insurance if the employee's injuries arise out of his or her employment and occur within the course of his or her employment.

While on leave, the employee may be paid temporary disability benefits (as well as other benefits) by the workers' compensation insurer (which may be an insurance company or the employer if the employer is self-insured) during the leave. The temporary disability benefits continue until the employee returns to work or the employee is determined to be "permanent and stationary" by the workers' compensation system. "Permanent and stationary" generally means that the employee is expected to get neither better nor worse. Depending upon the injury, the leave can last far longer than 12 weeks under the FMLA.

Although workers' compensation laws generally preempt or displace most other remedies, they generally do not preempt the federal or state family leave statutes or the federal or state disability discrimination laws. In other words, employers must comply with workers' compensation laws, as well as the other requirements discussed above when applicable.

Under the FMLA, the employer and employee both have the right to substitute accrued paid leaves (including vacation, paid time off, or sick leave) under certain circumstances when the FMLA leave is otherwise unpaid. However, workers' compensation leave is not unpaid if the employee accepts workers' compensation benefits. Consequently, the employee must choose to receive either workers' compensation benefits or paid leave provided by the employer. The employee cannot receive both, and the employer cannot force the employee to use any accrued paid leave while the employee is receiving workers' compensation benefits (29 C.F.R. § 825.207[d][2]). Under the FMLA, the employee is entitled to up to 12 weeks of leave and is entitled to be returned to the same or an equivalent position. However, under the workers' compensation laws, an employee may be required to return to a "light duty" position during the 12-week period. The employee has the right to refuse the light duty position under the FMLA, in which case the employee would lose workers' compensation benefits but would retain the right to return to the same or an equivalent position at the end of the FMLA leave. The employee also has the right to take the light duty position, in which case the employee still has the right to return to the same or an equivalent position during the 12-week period, including the period the employee is in the light duty position (29 C.F.R. §§ 825.220[d], 702[d][2]).

The FMLA limits an employee's leave entitlement to 12 weeks in a 12-month period. However, the workers' compensation laws do not include any specific limit on the leave an employee can take. As a result, an employee who has used up his or her 12 weeks of FMLA leave will no longer be protected by the FMLA, but may have rights under the workers' compensation statutes, as well as the ADA and similar state disability laws (29 C.F.R. § 825.216[d]). The workers' compensation laws allow the employer to contact and work directly with the workers' compensation health care provider under certain circumstances. Although the FMLA restricts when an employer may contact the employee's health care provider (even with the employee's permission), the FMLA regulations specifically allow the employer to follow the workers' compensation rules regarding contact with the employee's health care provider when the serious health condition is also covered by the workers' compensation statutes (29 C.F.R. § 825.307[a][1]).

Under the FMLA, the employee must make arrangements with the employer to pay the employee's portion of the employer's group health plan benefits during any unpaid portion of the FMLA leave. The same requirements apply to any FMLA leave when the employee is also receiving workers' compensation benefits (29 C.F.R. § 825.210[f]).

Other Protected Leaves of Absence

Numerous other protected leaves of absence exist under federal and state laws. It is critical for employers to check the requirements in each state where they employ individuals. The following discusses the most common types of protected leaves of absence.

Military Leave of Absence and the USERRA

American employees are playing a vital role in supporting America's efforts against terrorism as an increasing number of them are, as military reservists, subject to a call to active duty. By understanding the rights of employees called to active military duty, employers are poised to alleviate some of the anxieties of leaving the private work force as well as assuring a smooth integration back into the work force. The federal legislation on military leaves of absence from private jobs is fairly comprehensive and is codified at U.S. Code 38 §§ 4301 *et seq.*, the Employment and Reemployment Rights of Members of the Uniformed Services Act (USERRA). Employers should note, however, that some states have their own laws regarding military leaves of absence from the private work force that differ from the federal laws, enabling employers to give departing, or returning employees, a smooth transition.

The USERRA protects all branches of the uniformed services, including the Army, Navy, Air Force, Marines, Coast Guard, Army National Guard, Air National Guard, the Public Health Service's commissioned corps, and any other category of persons designated as such by the president in time of war or national emergency. The USERRA prohibits discrimination against employees based on their past, present, or future application for or service in the U.S. Armed Forces, Public Health Service, National Guard, and Reservists. The USERRA, an updated version of the Veterans Reemployment Rights Act from post-World War II, also requires employers to provide leaves of absence to employees serving in the uniformed services and grants reemployment and job protection rights to such employees. The USERRA defines "service" to include the performance of voluntary or involuntary duties in the uniformed services. Affected employees are entitled to reemployment if they: give proper advance verbal or written notice of such service to their employer; are not on leave for more than five years except under limited exceptions such as where the service is required for a national emergency; and apply for reemployment within the periods prescribed by USERRA. If the military service lasts less than 31 days, the employee must report to work by the beginning of the first full regularly scheduled work period on the first calendar day following completion of his or her service, following the expiration of eight hours after a time for the safe transportation back to the employee's residence. If the military service lasts between 31 and 180 days, the employee must submit an application to his employer within 14 days following completion of such service. For those whose military service lasts longer than 180 days, the employee must submit an application for reemployment within 90 days after the completion of such service. If the employee is hospitalized or convalescing from an injury caused or aggravated by active duty, the above time limits are extended until such time as the employee is incapacitated, up to a maximum of two years.

When an employee returns from military service, the individual must be placed in the position he or she would have attained had the service not occurred. If the employee is not qualified for this position upon return, the employer must make reasonable efforts to qualify the returning employee to the new position. If the employee remains unqualified for the position after the employer has attempted reasonable accommodation efforts, the employee may be placed in the same position he or she occupied before the military leave began.

There are several exceptions to the USERRA's reemployment rights. An employer need not reemploy an individual returning from military service where: the employer has experienced a change in its circumstances that makes reemployment impossible or unreasonable; reemployment would impose an undue hardship on the employer; or the individual's employment prior to military service was for a brief, nonrecurring period and there was no reasonable expectation that it would continue indefinitely for a significant period. The employer bears the burden of proving the above exceptions to reemployment. The USERRA defines "undue hardship" as:

> [A]ctions requiring significant difficulty or expense, when considered in light of: (A) the nature and cost of the action needed under this chapter; (B) the overall financial resources of the facility or facilities involved in the provision of the action; the number of persons employed at such facility; the effect on expenses and resources, or the impact otherwise of such action upon the operation of the facility; (C) the overall financial resources of the employer; the overall size of the business of an employer with respect to the number of its employees; the number, type, and location of its facilities; and (D) the type of operation or operations of the employer, including the composition, structure, and functions of the work force of such employer; the

geographic separateness, administrative, or fiscal relationship of the facility or facilities in question to the employer (U.S. Code 38 § 4303 [15]).

In addition, to be eligible for reemployment, the employee must have been honorably discharged and must have left his or her job for the purpose of performing military service. Under the USERRA, employers also must reasonably accommodate veterans who return to work with disabilities incurred during their military service. After an accommodation, if an employee still cannot perform the job, an employer is obligated to place that individual in an equivalent position that he or she is able to perform. Service members are entitled to seniority and any rights or benefits based on seniority that they would have attained had they remained continuously employed. They must be allowed to participate in all rights and benefits as if they were on any other leave of absence.

The USERRA defines "benefits" broadly to include "any advantage, profit, privilege, gain, status, account, or interest (other than wages or salary for work performed) that accrues by reason of an employment contract or agreement or an employer policy, plan, or practice and includes rights and benefits under a pension plan, a health plan, an employee stock ownership plan, insurance coverage and awards, bonuses, severance pay, supplemental unemployment benefits, vacations, and the opportunity to select work hours or location of employment" (U.S. Code 38 § 4303 [2]). The employee is responsible for any costs that he or she would have normally paid while employed or to the extent that other employees on a leave of absence are responsible for such costs. Military service must also be considered service with the employer for vesting and benefits accrual purposes. While service members may use paid leave time that they accrued before taking military leave, they may not be forced to use it. An individual may elect to continue health plan coverage for up to 18 months after military leave begins or for the period of service, whichever is shorter. For military service of less than 31 days, the individual may only be required to pay the usual employee share of the premium. The individual may be required to pay up to 102 percent of the full premium if military service is longer than 31 days. Reservists' dependents are automatically eligible for government-provided health care through military hospitals and the Civilian Health and Medical Program for Uniformed Services (CHAMPUS) once service exceeds 30 days. Military personnel remain responsible for their personal debts and obligations such as child support and, if necessary, their wages may be garnished.

The USERRA also limits employers' discretion to terminate the employment of individuals on their return from military service: If the service exceeds 180 days, employment may not be terminated for one year after the date of reemployment, except for cause; if service was between 31 and 180 days, employment may not be terminated for 180 days after the date of reemployment, except for cause.

Other Personal Leaves of Absence

Many states require employers to offer sick leave to employees, or regulate the conditions under which it may be taken if an employer provides it. Some state laws prohibit employers from discharging or discriminating against an employee from taking time off from work to serve as a juror or witness where the employee has given reasonable advance notice to the employer that he or she is required to appear in court. These laws also require employers to allow employees to use vacation, personal leave, or other compensatory time off that is otherwise available to the employee for jury or witness duty. Other state laws require employers to provide unpaid leave for victims of domestic violence or sexual assault. These laws generally require an employee taking leave for such reasons to give reasonable advance notice to the employer that he or she is required to appear in court. There are exceptions for emergencies, so long as the employee later certifies the need for leave, such as providing a police report; a court order; documentation of a medical professional, domestic violence, or sexual assault victim's advocate; or other evidence from the court or prosecuting attorney that the employee has appeared in court. Furthermore, some laws prohibit an employer from terminating or in any manner discriminating or retaliating against an employee who is a victim of domestic violence or of sexual assault for taking time off of work to seek medical attention; obtain services from a shelter, program, or crisis center; obtain psychological counseling; or participate in safety training or planning.

Bereavement leave (due to a death in the immediate family) is codified and mandatory for some government employers, but not for private employers. However, many employers offer some form of bereavement leave as part of the benefits package to regular employees, and in some cases, to part-time and long-term temporary workers. Most policies allow this leave for the passing of spouses, children, parents, and siblings but not aunts, uncles, cousins, and grandparents. The trend has also been to grant time off for bereavement for unmarried live-in couples, as some courts have been extending the definition of immediate family to live-in companions. Brief personal leaves taken due to the death of a family member are usually paid, while longer leaves are generally unpaid. Paid funeral leaves are most commonly three days, though some companies opt to extend the paid leave in case of a death of spouse or child, or for funerals held far away. Alternatively, some employers handle bereavement requests on a case-by-case basis to give consideration to such things as the employee's relationship to the deceased, length of travel to the funeral, etc.

Some state laws require employers—public and private—to allow employees time off to vote in statewide elections. Certain limitations may apply, such as: the employee not having enough time outside of work hours to vote; and taking the leave the beginning or end of the regular work hours, whichever gives the employee the most time to vote. The time off, coupled with time available outside of work hours, must be sufficient to enable the employee to vote, and up to two hours of the time off work must be paid. In turn, the employee must give the employer at least two working days' notice that time off for voting is desired if the employee knows in advance that such time will be needed. Additionally, under some state laws, employers must conspicuously post, in the workplace, a notice of the voting leave provisions. If such posting is impracticable, an employer may post the notice where employees can see it as they come and go from their places of work. The notice must be posted at least 10 days before every statewide election. An employee cannot waive the entitlement under this statute in a collective bargaining agreement or by contract. The penalty for violating these provisions is not set forth in the statute. Presumably, an employee who is discharged for taking time off to vote pursuant to these provisions could bring a wrongful termination suit against the employer based on violation of public policy as set forth in the applicable state statute.

Under some state laws, employers are prohibited from discharging or discriminating against an employee for taking time off to perform emergency duty as a volunteer firefighter, reserve peace officer, or emergency rescue personnel. An employee qualifies as a volunteer firefighter if the employee is registered as a volunteer member of an organized fire department officially recognized by the city, county, or district in which the department is situated. Emergency personnel include officers, employees, or members of a fire department, fire protection or firefighting agency, sheriff's department, police department, or a private fire department, regardless of pay. This provision does not apply to any public safety agency or provider of emergency services when, as determined by the employer, the employee's absence would hinder the availability of public safety or emergency medical services. An employer who violates this statute by discharging, threatening to discharge, suspending, or in any manner discriminating against the employee for taking leave must reinstate the employee and reimburse the employee for lost time and benefits arising from the violation. Although an employer is required to allow some employees to take leave to perform emergency duty, an employer may establish reasonable procedures for the employees to follow in taking the leave.

Some state laws prohibit employers from disciplining, discharging, demoting, suspending, or discriminating against an employee who is the parent or guardian of a pupil for taking time off to attend a school conference involving the child's suspension. Related state statutes prohibit certain employers from discharging or discriminating against an employee who is a parent, guardian, or grandparent having custody of one or more children in kindergarten, grades 1 to 12, or a licensed day care facility, for taking time off to participate in activities of the school or day care facility. Some state laws provide that certain private employers make reasonable accommodations for employees with literacy problems who request employer assistance with enrolling in an adult literacy education program.

In light of the variety of protected and voluntary leaves of absence available to employees, employers should carefully check the state requirements in each state where they have employees.

Avoiding Disability Discrimination and Satisfying Reasonable Accommodation Obligations

As discussed above, the ADA prohibits discrimination in the workplace based on an employee or applicant's disability. Employers therefore also must provide disability accommodation to qualified individuals, but the process of disability accommodation can be confusing, as employers may experience difficulty distinguishing between real and illegitimate requests. Nevertheless, it is important for employers to understand both when the disability/reasonable accommodation interactive process is triggered and how best to engage in it. To determine whether a particular medical condition qualifies as a protected mental or physical disability under the ADA, employers must rely, at least initially, on information provided by the employee's health care provider obtained at the initial stages of the interactive process. Nevertheless, certain conditions are specifically excluded from the definitions. Mental and physical disabilities do not include:

- Sexual behavior disorders
- Compulsive gambling
- Kleptomania
- Pyromania
- Psychoactive substance use disorders resulting from the current unlawful use of controlled substances or other drugs

Under the EEOC's guidance and case law, the following also are not medical impairments: mere stress, poor judgment, irritability, chronic lateness, irresponsibility, and normal deviations in weight and height.

It is unlawful for employers to fail to engage in a timely, good faith, interactive process to determine reasonable accommodations at the request of an employee with a known disability, whether or not the interactive process would have resulted in an obligation on the employer's part to provide a reasonable accommodation. The courts and the EEOC have found that the ADA imposes a duty to engage in the interactive process—but the ADA does not make failure meet that duty an explicit violation of the law, in the absence of a showing that accommodation was possible. An employee may start the interactive process by directly asking for an accommodation. The employer also must start the interactive process if it is aware of the need for an accommodation. The employer is responsible for acting in response to statements made to managers and superiors at all levels, and therefore manager and supervisor training is essential. Employers must learn and know that a request for reasonable accommodation—whether it is made orally by the individual it concerns, made on that individual's behalf by a third party, or made in writing by the employee or his or her representative (such as a spouse)—is a statement that an individual needs an adjustment or change in their workplace for a reason related to a mental or physical condition. Employers do not have an obligation to initiate an interactive process if an employee does not request a reasonable accommodation and the employer neither knows nor has reason to know of the disability.

The employer, once on notice from the supervisor or manager who received the information, is then obliged to set a series of actions into motion. These steps should lead, as efficiently as possible, to determining whether reasonable accommodation can be made; and if so, what should be done. The employer should carefully document all steps of the interactive process. The better prepared the employer, the less work disruption—such as preventable lost work time, negative morale influences, or even open dissatisfaction leading to conflict—is likely to follow. A well-prepared employer will better recognize when the interactive process is required and will be able to respond appropriately, without delay. This will save direct costs attributable to lost productivity, indirect costs associated with employee morale, and will minimize the possibility of any party in the matter resorting to litigation.

In sum, once an employer is given notice of a disability, they should immediately:

- Realize that an employee may have a special need

- Recognize that this need may affect: the employee's productivity, work attendance, or absences; ergonomic needs; an existing or concurrent workers' compensation claim; eligibility for Employee Assistance Program (EAP) or other behavioral health benefits
- Ready itself to respond to the request with an invitation to begin a step-by-step process for assessing reasonable accommodation
- Assure timeliness of the process by setting a date and time for the first meeting to go over the process.

The employer should identify which people are necessary participants for the interactive process to be effective. In general, those individuals should include the employee, executive-level support within the company (decision-making authority), and the employee's health care provider (by his or her conveyed opinion or specific recommendations).

The interactive process is the process by which employers and applicants or employees engage in a dialogue about the employee's functional work limitations due to a covered disability, and any accommodations that can be made that would allow the applicant or employee to perform the essential functions of the position. The six practical steps of the interactive process are as follows:

1. Analyze the job, identifying and distinguishing between essential and non-essential tasks.

2. Consult with the employee and his health care provider to identify job related limitations.

3. Identify possible accommodations.

4. Assess the reasonableness of each accommodation, in terms of effectiveness and equal opportunity, with the employee.

5. Consider the preferences of the employee and implement the accommodation that is most appropriate both for the employee and the employer under all the circumstances.

6. Follow up with the employee to ensure the accommodation, if one is made, is working.

An important resource for identifying possible accommodations is the Job Accommodation Network, a service of the U.S. Department of Labor, located on the web at http://janweb.icdi.wvu.edu/. Possible accommodations include, but are not limited to:

- Transfer of marginal job functions to another employee
- A leave of absence, beyond any required under the Family and Medical Leave Act (FMLA)
- Flexible start times
- Ergonomic adjustments
- Telecommuting
- Time off for medical visits
- Limitation on work hours
- Modification of work tools or equipment
- Provision of qualified readers or interpreters
- Adjustment or modification of examination or training materials
- Reassignment to an open position for which the employee is qualified

Given the complexities in this area, employers should consider consulting an experienced labor and employment attorney to determine whether and how best to engage in the interactive process with a disabled employee.

The End
of the Road

Termination Issues

U nfortunately, it sometimes becomes necessary to
end the employment relationship, for many different reasons. Employers need to retain maximum
flexibility to respond to continued poor performance
by employees, economics and business pressures, and
other factors affecting the employment relationship.
As discussed in Chapter 2, employers can avoid and
defend implied contract claims by former employees
(a claim by the employee that the former employer
made promises to the effect that good cause was
required for termination) through integrated at-will
employment statements in applications, offer letters,
employment contracts, and employee handbooks.

Given the potential for claims by terminated employees, employers should proceed with caution and plan all terminations carefully. Employers should avoid making rash decisions to terminate employees. If necessary, an employer should consider sending the employee home on a paid leave of absence while the employer gathers the information necessary to justify a termination decision.

Legal and Practical Considerations

Even at-will employers need to pay attention to the importance of a paper trail, or progressive discipline of an employee before termination. "Progressive discipline" means that the employer will impose lesser discipline for a first offense (for example, a verbal warning), and more severe discipline (for example, a written warning, suspension, unpaid leave, termination) for repeat offenses. In addition, if an employer's termination decision is challenged as based on illegal criteria (for example, because of the employee's protected status, or because the employee filed a prior claim against the employer, or because the employee was a whistleblower), a good paper trail, consistency in the enforcement of an employer's policies, and careful planning and execution are invaluable in defending the employer's termination decision.

Employers should carefully consider what information to provide to terminated employees concerning the reasons for the termination, even if both the employer and employee are fully aware of those reasons due to the nature of progressive discipline or the offense(s). In some cases, it may be advisable to state the bare minimum, even if the employer has a good paper trail documenting the repeat performance deficiencies. Other employers may choose to be candid and upfront with terminated employees about the reasons for their decision. Employers should be mindful, however, that they may be bound and unable to change their articulated reasons for termination decisions, even if they subsequently discover other, independent grounds for the termination decisions.

Some of the same tips discussed in Chapter 8 regarding performance reviews also apply to the termination of employment:

- *Document, document, document:* Remember, if it is not in writing, it will be easier for the employee to contend it never happened!

- *Do not argue with the employee*, and do not allow the employee to have the last word.
- *Do not debate the reasons for the termination decision*, or reconsider it unless there is evidence that you made a mistake.
- *Don't humiliate the employee*—end the employment relationship as professionally as possible.
- *Carefully plan and monitor all communications to the employee* to achieve desired goals and to avoid inadvertent violations of the law.
- *Remember the two-on-one rule:* Have a witness present during the termination meeting.

Special Considerations for Termination

Standardize the termination procedure to the extent feasible, including reviews of the entire situation by senior management, human resources, and/or an attorney experienced in labor and employment law matters. Consistency and uniformity are very important in all aspects of the employment relationship, including termination of employment.

Review the terminated employee's personnel file and any applicable employment policies for warnings of problems. For example, check the employee's personnel file and with supervisors for evidence of prior complaints, whistle-blowing activity, or other red flags for possible claims. Interview the employee's supervisors and managers to ensure that the employer has the entire picture and that the reasons for termination are supportable, supported, credible, and defensible.

Attempt to arrange an exit interview with the terminated employee to discuss, among other issues, the following:

- Unemployment claims and benefits
- Return of all company property (keys, credit card, laptop, etc.), and reminder to terminated employee regarding contractual obligations (for example, not to use or disclose the former employer's trade secrets)
- Avoiding wrongful termination, discrimination, retaliation, and unlawful harassment claims; if the employee fails to mention any such

complaints or concerns during his or her exit interview, it will be less credible if he or she raises them for the first time after the termination of his or her employment.

Consider allowing an internal complaint or grievance process to correct mistakes. It is of course possible that even the best-intentioned employer may make a mistake in managing its employees. Further, an former employee's unreasonable failure to use the employer's internal complaint process before going to court may be a defense to the former employee's claim(s). Accordingly, employers may wish to consider adopting a mediation or arbitration procedure to try to resolve complaints by all employees, including terminated employees.

Arrange for timely payment of terminated employee's last wages, including all accrued and unused vacation in states where required. Decide about responses to reference inquiries, and centralize the response with one person at the company, such as the human resources director.

Severance and Release of Claims Agreements

Employers may wish to consider offering a severance payment (or payments) to terminated employees in exchange for a waiver and release of any actual or potential claims by the employee against the employer. The law governing such agreements is technical and evolving. For example, to obtain a valid release of a claim under the federal Age Discrimination in Employment Act (ADEA), and its amendment, the Older Workers Benefits Protection Act (OWBPA), employers must provide employees who are aged 40 and over with 21 days to review the release agreement and another seven days to revoke the agreement after the employee signs, along with other mandatory disclosures. Therefore, employers are strongly encouraged to consult with an experienced labor and employment attorney regarding the use of severance and release agreements with terminated employees. See the Appendix for a sample "Confidential Severance and Release of All Claims Agreement."

Employers who wish to offer severance payments in exchange for a release of claims should comply with the OWBPA and the ADEA (U.S. Code 29 § 626 [f][1]). Specifically, OWBPA requires that an age discrimination waiver be "knowing and voluntary" and the language of the release must: specifically refer to ADEA claims; provide for consideration beyond that which the employee is already entitled; expressly advise the employee to consult with an attorney before signing; provide adequate time for the employee to consider the agreement before signing it, including a minimum of 21 days in case of an individual termination (which can be waived in writing), or at least 45 days in case of a group termination; and provide the employee 7 days within which to revoke the agreement, which cannot be waived. Significantly, one of the consequences of a defective age discrimination waiver is that the employee can sue for age discrimination and keep the severance payment (see EEOC Regulation, 29 C.F.R. Part 1625). Finally, employers may wish to consider including a "nondisparagement" provision, a provision protecting their trade secrets (including customer lists, customer data, and employees in appropriate cases), a mandatory arbitration provision, and a provision requiring the losing party to pay the other side's attorneys' fees in the event of a dispute over the enforceability of the release agreement.

In deciding whether to offer terminated employees severance, employers should be mindful of the need for consistent treatment of terminated employees. For example, employers should be careful to avoid offering severance to male but not to female employees who are terminated. Such decisions are subject to legal challenge, either on an intentional discrimination or adverse impact (unintentional discrimination, discussed in the next section) theory. Also, employers should be careful lest the mere offer of severance benefits be interpreted as any admission of liability or wrongdoing.

Layoffs and Group Terminations (WARN Act, ADEA)

Finally, employers should avoid potential adverse impact claims and claims by laid off employees under the federal Worker Adjustment and Retraining Notification (WARN) Act, (U.S. Code 29 §§ 2101-2109 [1988]), when making layoff decisions. A disparate impact claim may be based on a disproportionate effect of the employer's layoff decision; that is, even if there is no evidence that the employer *intended* to discriminate against a protected group in making the layoff, but a disproportionately large number of employees in a protected group (age, sex, race) will be affected. The federal WARN Act (and some state counterparts) requires employers to provide 60 days advance notice of a plant closing or mass layoff to affected employees or their union representatives, and to state and government agencies. There are some statutory exceptions, such as unforeseen business circumstances, but they are narrowly construed against the employer. Either claim exposes an employer to substantial penalties and damages, in addition to employees' attorneys' fees if they prevail on either claim. An employer considering a group or mass layoff should therefore consult an experienced labor and employment law attorney.

To qualify as a mass layoff under WARN, the layoff must involve an employment loss at a single site of employment of at least 50 employees (excluding part-time employees), assuming such a layoff involves at least 33 percent of the employees at the employment site. Employment losses of 500 or more employees—again excluding any part-time employees—automatically trigger WARN Act requirements, regardless of how many other employees a company employs at the site. Under the WARN Act, part-time employees mean those who are employed for an average of fewer than 20 hours a week, or those employees who work less than 6 of the 12 months preceding the date WARN notification is required.

Employers also may seek to relocate or consolidate part or all of their business to another facility. Under the WARN Act, employers must notify their employees of such a relocation or consolidation unless the employer offers to transfer the employee to a different site of employment within reasonable commuting distance or the employer offers to transfer the employee to any other employment site—regardless of distance—provided the employee accepts within 30 days of the offer, or within 30 days of the closing or layoff, whichever is later. Under either scenario, however, the offer of transfer cannot result in more than a six-month break in employment. If the transfer would involve such an extended period of nonemployment, the WARN Act notification requirements apply.

Generally, in the acquisition context, WARN notice is not required where the buyer or successor employer offers reemployment to affected employees of the seller. For example, in *International Alliances Theatrical & Stage Employees v. Compact Video Servs.*, 50 F.3d 1461, 1468 (9th Cir. 1995), it was decided that WARN is not triggered even where the buyer of a company modifies terms and conditions to make them less favorable to its employees than prior terms and conditions under the seller. In *Alter v. SCM Office Supplies Inc.*, 906 F. Supp. 1243, 1249 (N.D. Ind. 1995), employees who submitted applications and interviewed with acquiring company did not suffer "employment loss" as defined in the WARN Act. *See also Wiltz v. M/G Transport Services, Inc.*, 128 F.3d 957 (6th Cir. 1997); *Headrick v. Rockwell International Corp.*, 24 F.3d 1272 (10th Cir. 1994); *Rifkin v. McDonnell Douglas Corp.*, 78 F.3d 1277, 1282-83 (8th Cir. 1996) (same); and U.S. Code 29 § 2101 (b)(1)].

There also are several narrow statutory exceptions to the obligation to provide employees with 60 days advance notice of a mass layoff or plant closing under the WARN Act. One such exception is the "unforeseen business circumstances" doctrine, which applies when unexpected events prevent a business from being able to provide 60 days advance notice of a plant shutdown or significant layoff. Employers seeking to come within this exception must bear the burden of proof. In *Hotel Employees and Restaurant Employees Local 54 v. Elsinore Shore Associates* (173 F.3d. 175 [3rd Cir. 1999]), the court decided to apply the WARN Act exception for unforeseen business circumstances, which occurred when the New Jersey Casino Control Commission ordered a casino closing. Once an employer foresees such a layoff or plant closing, however, it must notify its employees.

Another exception to the WARN Act's 60-day notice requirement is the "faltering company exception," which applies when the employer is actively seeking additional capital, which would avoid or postpone a shut down or a mass layoff if obtained. An employer must show that it believed in good faith that had it given such notice it would not have been able to obtain the capital.

Employers may also be relieved from providing 60 days advance notice if the plant closing or mass layoff is due to any form of natural disaster, including floods, earthquakes, or droughts. Employers falling within these statutory exceptions must still provide as much notice as practicable. In addition, employers also must provide a brief statement of the basis for the reduced notification period once any notice is provided.

Remedies for failure to comply with the WARN Act's 60-day notice requirement include back pay (for up to 60 days) and benefits under all ERISA-covered employee benefit plans, including the costs of medical expenses incurred during the employment loss. There also is a civil penalty of $500 for each day of the violation, plus attorneys' fees, but no punitive damages.

Other Legal Issues Arising in Termination Situations

Employers should exercise caution in responding to government inquiries and charges filed by former employees with government agencies–for example, charges filed with the U.S. Equal Employment Opportunity Commission, unemployment insurance, workers' compensation, and the Department of Labor. In many cases, the government or former employees have relied on such employer statements in later litigation against the employer. Furthermore, sometimes what an employer says in one forum (e.g., state disability and workers' compensation claims) can come back to haunt it in another forum (e.g., disability discrimination claim). Accordingly, employers should exercise caution in responding even to "form" or "routine" claims by former employees, such as unemployment and workers' compensation claims. For example, even if an employer decides not to contest a terminated employee's unemployment benefits claim, it may be advisable to respond in writing to such unemployment claims as follows: "Although the employer disagrees with the employee's stated reasons for termination of employment, the employer will not oppose the employee's claim for unemployment benefits."

Another legal and practical issue, discussed in Chapter 5 and mentioned again above, is whether and to what degree to respond to requests from former employees and their prospective employers for employment references. It is important for employers to adopt and enforce consistent policies and practices with regard to the provision of employment references for former employees. For example, if the employer's standard practice is to provide limited information regarding dates of employment and positions held, it will appear unusual to provide more detailed information concerning reasons for termination with regard to individual, former employees. Remember that in most situations, a former employer is not legally required to say anything about former employees. If an employer decides to provide any information, it should consider obtaining a release of liability from the former employee for any information provided, and provide accurate, true, and fair statements or information concerning the former employee.

Conclusion

By paying attention to the legal and practical issues addressed in this book, employers should be able to navigate most employment laws and requirements. Spotting the lurking and sometimes hidden legal issues is first and foremost. But labor and employment law is constantly changing and evolving, and new or different issues often arise in the modern workplace. If an employer is in doubt as to the legality or wisdom of certain employment decisions, policies, or practices, it should promptly consult an experienced labor and employment law attorney.

Appendix
Sample Policies and Forms

We have enclosed the following forms to help you with your hiring, employment, and termination processes. Square brackets [—] indicate where employers should enter company-specific information.

SAMPLE APPLICATION FOR EMPLOYMENT

[Company Logo]

It is the policy of [COMPANY] ("COMPANY") to afford Equal Employment Opportunity ("EEO") to all employees and applicants regardless of their race, creed, color, religion, sex, age, national origin, disability or veteran status, and to conform to all applicable laws and regulations affecting all protected classes. [COMPANY] promotes a drug-free, tobacco and smoke-free work environment. [COMPANY] does not tolerate unlawful discrimination, harassment, or retaliation.

Please fill out the application completely. (If a section is not applicable to the job for which you are applying, please write "N/A.") [COMPANY] is relying on the accuracy of all of the information that you submit. All applicants must read and sign the certification on the last page.

You may attach to this application additional information that you feel will be helpful in evaluating your qualifications. This completed application (and accompanying resume and/or other accompanying documents, if any) will become part of your personnel file if you are subsequently employed by [COMPANY]. In order for the application to be considered, it must be completed in full even if you are providing a resume. " [COMPANY]," as used in this application, includes subsidiaries and affiliates of [COMPANY].

Section 1: Personal Data

Name _____
　　　　　Last　　　　　　　　　　　　　First　　　　　　　　　　　　　MI

Address _____
　　　　Street　　　　　　City　　　　　　State　　　Zip　　　Country

Daytime Phone (_____) _____　Evening Phone (_____) _____

Email Address _____

Section 2: Position Information

Position (s) applied for_____　Desired salary $_____

Willing to work　❑　Full-time　❑　Part-time　❑　Shift work

If position requires, are you available for overtime?　❑　Yes　　❑　No

Section 3: Education

HIGH SCHOOL

Name of High School or GED School _____　City _____ State _____

❑　Diploma　❑　GED　　　If no diploma or GED, years completed _____

COLLEGE/UNIVERSITY

1) School Name _____　City _____ State _____

Degree Earned? ❑ Yes　Type of Degree:　AA　BA　Other _____　Major _____　Year Received _____

　　　　　　❑ No　If no, years completed _____　Start Date _____　End Date _____

2) School Name _____ City _____ State _____

Degree Earned? ❑ Yes   Type of Degree: AA   BA   Other _____   Major _____   Year Received _____

❑ No   If no, years completed _____   Start Date _____   End Date _____

GRADUATE STUDIES

1) School Name _____ City _____ State _____

Degree Earned? ❑ Yes   Type of Degree: AA   BA   Other _____   Major _____   Year Received _____

❑ No   If no, years completed _____   Start Date _____   End Date _____

Section 4: Special Skills or Training

List those skills that are applicable for the job you are applying for, including any additional licenses or certificates that may be job-related.

Keyboarding: _____ WPM

Microsoft Office Skills   _____

Wireless or Telecommunications Experience   _____

Other Special Skills   _____

Hardware and Software Used   _____

Section 5: Employment History

Are you currently employed? ❑ Yes ❑ No   If yes, may we contact your current employer? ❑ Yes ❑ No

Please complete the following section in detail with the most recent/current employer listed first (include exact month and year of employment). If you worked for an employer multiple times, such as with seasonal work, please list each term of employment separately. Please also list service in the armed forces of the United States. Part-time, summer employment, volunteer, or temporary employment should also be indicated if applicable.

If any employment was through a temporary staffing service, please list the name, address, and phone number for that agency (not the company name of your temporary assignment).

Previous Employer _____ Dates Employed _____ to _____
                                                                   (month & yr.)   (month & yr.)

Your Position _____ Supervisor's Name _____

Position Description _____

Starting Salary/Hourly Rate $ _____ Ending Salary/Hourly Rate $ _____ Reason for Leaving _____

Address _____ City _____

State _____ Zip _____ Phone Number _____

Previous Employer _____ Dates Employed _____ to _____
  (month & yr.) (month & yr.)

Your Position _____ Supervisor's Name _____

Position Description _____

Starting Salary/Hourly Rate $ _____ Ending Salary/Hourly Rate $ _____ Reason for Leaving _____

Address _____ City _____

State _____ Zip _____ Phone Number _____

Previous Employer _____ Dates Employed _____ to _____
  (month & yr.) (month & yr.)

Your Position _____ Supervisor's Name _____

Position Description _____

Starting Salary/Hourly Rate $ _____ Ending Salary/Hourly Rate $ _____ Reason for Leaving _____

Address _____ City _____

State _____ Zip _____ Phone Number _____

Previous Employer _____ Dates Employed _____ to _____
  (month & yr.) (month & yr.)

Your Position _____ Supervisor's Name _____

Position Description _____

Starting Salary/Hourly Rate $ _____ Ending Salary/Hourly Rate $ _____ Reason for Leaving _____

Address _____ City _____

State _____ Zip _____ Phone Number _____

List any job-related professional, trade, business, civic, or volunteer activities, and any offices held. (Please exclude memberships or affiliations that would reveal gender, race, religion, national origin, age, ancestry, disability, or any other protected status.)

_____

_____

_____

_____

_____

Hiring and Firing

Section 6: General Information

Have you ever filed an employment application with [COMPANY] under the name on this application or under any other name?

❑ Yes ❑ No If yes, under what name and when?

Have you ever been employed, whether temporary, part or full-time with [COMPANY] or its subsidiaries or affiliates?

❑ Yes ❑ No If yes, list date(s)

Are you currently on "lay-off" status with another employer and subject to recall? ❑ Yes ❑ No

Are you legally authorized to work in the U.S.? ❑ Yes ❑ No

Will you now or in the future require sponsorship for employment visa status (e.g., H-1B visa)? ❑ Yes ❑ No

Within the last five years, have you been convicted of, plead guilty to, or plead "no contest" to a crime (crime means felonies and misdemeanors, including vehicular misdemeanors and felonies) or been released from prison? (Applicants for employment in Hawaii should not answer this question at this time. Applicants in California should not answer this question as it relates to marijuana-related convictions more than two years old under California Health and Safety Code Sections 11357 (b) and (c), 11360 (c), 11364, 11365 or 11550, convictions that have been sealed, expunged or legally eradicated, misdemeanor convictions for which probation was completed and the case was judicially dismissed, or any information concerning a referral to and participation in any pre-trial or post-trial diversion program.)

If yes, please briefly describe the nature of the crime(s), the date and place of conviction, and the legal disposition of the case. [COMPANY] will not deny employment to any applicant solely because the person has been convicted of a crime. [COMPANY] may, however, consider the nature, date, and circumstances of the offense as well as whether the offense is relevant to the duties of the position for which the applicant is being considered.

_____

_____

Are you under the age of 18? ❑ Yes ❑ No

Section 7: Professional References

Please provide the names and business telephone numbers of supervisors for whom you have worked. By providing reference information, you are giving [COMPANY] permission to contact these people. Do not list personal references.

Name _____ Title _____
Business Telephone _____ Employer _____
Professional Relationship _____ Total Years Associated _____

Name _____ Title _____
Business Telephone _____ Employer _____
Professional Relationship _____ Total Years Associated _____

Section 8: Position Advertisement

How did you learn about this position? _____

❑ Walk-in   ❑ [COMPANY] Website   Employee Referral _____ [COMPANY] Recruiter _____

Internet Posting _____   Print Advertisement _____   Job Fair/Open House _____

College _____   College Intern/Co-Op _____   Event _____

Professional Association _____ Agency _____

List any relatives employed by [COMPANY] or its subsidiaries or affiliates

Name _____ Relationship _____ Location _____

Section 9: Certification

Please read the following carefully before signing this application:

- The statements set forth above are true and complete. I authorize [COMPANY] to obtain information about me from previous employers, including relevant facts and opinions about my work and work habits, and I release from liability or responsibility all persons or entities requesting or supplying such information. I release [COMPANY] from liability for considering, relying on or taking into account information it receives from such persons or entities.

- I expressly authorize any educational institutions that I have attended to provide transcripts and degree status. I release from liability or responsibility all persons or entities requesting or supplying such information. I release [COMPANY] from liability for considering, relying on, or taking into account information it receives from such persons or entities.

- I understand that any false information or significant omissions on this application may disqualify me from further consideration for employment, and that if employed, false information or significant omissions on this application shall be grounds for immediate termination of employment.

- If employed by [COMPANY], I agree to adhere to company policies and procedures, although I understand that my agreement to do so does not create a contract of employment between myself and [COMPANY]. I further understand that if hired by [COMPANY] my employment is not for a specific duration and may be terminated by me or [COMPANY] at any time, for any reason or for no reason whatsoever, with or without notice and with or without cause to the fullest extent allowed by law.

- All [COMPANY] employees are "at will" employees to the fullest extent allowed by law. No statements made in the Company's handbook or in any other policy or guideline documents creates a contractual promise from [COMPANY] to its employees.

- I further understand that [COMPANY] may change any terms of my employment including but not limited to work assignments, job duties, work schedules, pay levels, commissions earnings and eligibility, bonus amounts and eligibility, and/or locations.

- If employed by [COMPANY], I agree to sign and abide by the Company's Confidentiality, Proprietary Information, and Trade Secrets policies.

- I understand that any offer of employment is contingent upon a satisfactory background check. If hired, I understand that the authorization I will provide to [COMPANY] for an initial background investigation to be conducted, will remain in effect and will serve as an ongoing authorization for [COMPANY] to procure a background report at any time before or during my employment with [COMPANY].

- I understand that if I am offered employment by [COMPANY] it is contingent on my ability to furnish proof of my identity and U.S. citizenship, or to furnish legal authorization for me to work in the U.S., as required by federal law. Failure to do so and/or lack of proper documentation (within 3 days of hire) will result in termination of employment pursuant to the Immigration Reform and Control Act of 1986.

- I understand that nothing contained in this employment application or in the granting of an interview is intended to create an employment offer or contract between the Company and me.

- I understand that no supervisor, manager, or executive of the Company, other than the Chairman, President, or Chief Operating Officer of [COMPANY], has the authority to alter the foregoing and only a written contract signed by the Chairman, President, or Chief Operating Officer may modify [COMPANY]'s at-will employment policy.

By signing this application I indicate my understanding of the all of above factors.

Applicant Signature: _____   Date: _____

Printed Name: _____

SAMPLE INDEPENDENT CONTRACTOR AGREEMENT

This Independent Contractor Agreement is made as of _____ __, 2007 [Effective Date], between [COMPANY] (the "Company") and [Contractor]("Contractor") (collectively the "parties.").

The Company and Contractor agree as follows:

1. Independent Contractor

This Agreement is not an employment agreement between the Company and Contractor. Contractor is for all purposes an independent contractor and shall not receive any wages, benefits, vacation and sick leave, bonuses, stock or stock options that employees might otherwise be entitled to. The Company will therefore not make any wage withholding from the amounts paid to Contractor under this Agreement. Instead, the Company will at the end of the year issue contractor a Form 1099 for the amounts paid to Contractor.

2. Services of Contractor

Contractor agrees to render the following services to the Company: Contractor will have duties both as an individual contributor and will oversee the work of others, working towards the Company's mid-September closed alpha launch. Contractor will be working in the programs _____, and will coordinate the efforts of at least two other contractors in those areas.

Contractor will generally work at her/his own premises and other locations, set her/his own hours, and will not be supervised or directed by the Company in the performance of her/his services. Contractor's services will be rendered in a competent and timely manner. The Company may, from time to time, provide Contractor with office space, as well as computer, e-mail, and telephone access, for the periods of time that Contractor provides services in the Company's offices.

3. Term of Agreement

This Agreement will commenced on _____ _____, 2006, and continue [through _____] unless terminated earlier by Contractor or the Company upon 30 days' written notice to the other party.

4. Payment for Services

For services rendered pursuant to the Contact, the Company will pay Contractor a monthly retainer in the amount of $ _____. Contractor shall be paid monthly following verification by the Company that the service provided by Contractor meets the Company's reasonable satisfaction, which verification will not be unreasonably withheld.

5. Confidential Information

Contractor recognizes and acknowledges that certain assets of the Company constitute "Confidential Information." The term "Confidential Information" as used in this Agreement shall mean all information that is known only to Contractor or the Company, other employees, or others in a confidential relationship with Contractor, and relating to Contractor's business (including, without limitation, information regarding employees, clients, customers, pricing policies, methods of operation, proprietary computer programs, sales, products, costs, markets, key personnel, formulae, product applications, technical processes, and trade secrets), as such information may exist from time to time, which Contractor acquires or obtains by virtue of work performed for the Company, or which Contractor may acquire or may have acquired knowledge of during the performance of said work. Contractor shall not, during or after the period which s/he provides services to the Company, disclose all or any part of the Confidential Information to any person, firm, corporation, association, or any other entity for any reason or purpose whatsoever, directly or indirectly, except as may be required pursuant to the provisions of services hereunder, unless and until such Confidential Information becomes publicly available other than as a consequence of the breach by Contractor of this Agreement. In the event of the termination of her/his services under this Agreement, whether voluntary or involuntary, and whether by Contractor or the Company, Contractor shall deliver to the Company all documents and data pertaining to the Confidential Information and shall not take with her/him any documents or data or any kind or any reproductions, in whole or in part, or extracts of any items relating to the Confidential Information.

6. Non-Solicitation of Employees or Customers

Contractor may have access to proprietary and confidential information of the Company and the activities forbidden by this subsection would necessarily involve the improper use and disclosure of this proprietary and confidential information. Such proprietary information includes, but is not limited to, the identity of employees and customers of the Company. Contractor agrees that for a period of one (1) year after termination of this Agreement, Contractor shall not, directly or indirectly, (i) solicit on behalf of any direct competitor of Company (i.e. [*description of project/product*]) any customer or potential customer of the Company (or any affiliate) known to Contractor during the term of this Agreement to have been a customer or potential customer of Company; or (ii) engage in any efforts to hire or solicit for employment or work as a consultant or independent contractor, any person employed by the Company (or any affiliate), whether for or on behalf of Contractor, or for any entity, in which Contractor has any direct or indirect interest as a proprietor, partner, stockholder, employee, agent, representative, or otherwise.

7. Non-Competing Activities

Contractor will not at any time during the term of this Agreement engage in any business activity or consulting work for a third party that would be in conflict with the Company, or could adversely affect Contractor's ability to carry out her/his services under this Agreement. Contractor shall not engage in any business activity or consulting work that would require her/him to disclose or use information pertaining to the Company's current or anticipated confidential business transactions or trade secret information. Contractor represents that the provision of her/his services to the Company will not conflict with any duties that Contractor has to any present and/or past employers, customers, persons, or business entities.

8. Termination of Agreement

This Agreement may be terminated immediately upon material breach of this Agreement by either party. This Agreement may also be terminated upon 30 days' notice by either party. The parties shall continue to carry out their obligations under this Agreement until the end of the notice period.

9. Entire Agreement; Representations of the Parties

This Agreement constitutes the final, complete, and exclusive statement of the terms of Contractor's relationship with the Company. This agreement constitutes the entire understanding and agreement of the parties pertaining to the subject matter herein, and supersedes all prior and contemporaneous agreements, representations, and understandings of the parties, including any proposals, oral or written, correspondence, negotiations, and discussions between the parties, and all past courses of dealing or industry customs. The parties agree and acknowledge that they may not and are not relying on any representations, warranties, promises, inducements, or statements, whether oral or written and by whomever made, that are not contained expressly herein.

10. Amendments, Waivers

This Agreement may not be modified, amended, or terminated except by an instrument in writing, signed by Contractor and by a duly authorized representative of Company. No failure to exercise and no delay in exercising any right, remedy, or power under this Agreement shall operate as a waiver thereof, nor shall any single or partial exercise of any right, remedy, or power under this Agreement preclude any other or further exercise thereof, or the exercise of any other right, remedy, or power provided herein or by law or in equity.

11. *Severability; Enforcement*

If any provision of this Agreement, or the application thereof to any person, place, or circumstance, shall be held by a court of competent jurisdiction to be invalid, unenforceable, or void, the remainder of this Agreement and such provisions as applied to other persons, places, and circumstances shall remain in full force and effect.

12. *Arbitration of Disputes*

Disputes arising from or relating to this Contract, its interpretation, or the relationship of the parties shall be submitted to final and binding arbitration in [location] under the rules for the resolution of such disputes of the [Arbitration Provider]. The prevailing party in such arbitration shall be awarded its attorneys fees and costs, in addition to such other relief or remedy to which it is entitled.

Date:_____   Contractor _____
                                              [COMPANY]

Date:_____   By _____

                             Title:_____

U.S. FAIR CREDIT REPORTING ACT BACKGROUND CHECKS INFORMATION AND FORMS

Introduction

The following explains your obligations under the federal Fair Credit Reporting Act ("FCRA") in conducting a background check on employees and applicants.

The Fair Credit Reporting Act ("the FCRA") applies to EMPLOYER's use of an outside investigatory firm or consumer reporting agency to compile information on an employee or applicant. EMPLOYER's direct collection of information without the involvement of a consumer reporting agency, however, does not fall within the scope of the FCRA. Thus, conduct by EMPLOYER such as calling former employers or personal references does not trigger regulation by the FCRA. Similarly, EMPLOYER's direct request of an employee to provide criminal records information is not subject to the FCRA, and EMPLOYER's own conducting of drug testing on applicants is not subject to the FCRA.

EMPLOYER's use of an outside investigative firm to do background criminal checks on employees and applicants falls within the scope of the FCRA. Reports obtained from an investigative firm regarding an employee's or applicant's criminal background constitute "investigative consumer reports" under the FCRA, and the procurement of these reports from an outside agency is subject to the FCRA's disclosure and authorization requirements. EMPLOYER is thus required to comply with the FCRA in obtaining criminal background checks from investigative firms for employment purposes.

EMPLOYER's use of an outside investigative firm to provide drug testing results is also a consumer report under the FCRA. Since a consumer reporting agency is providing the reports, they are "consumer reports" under the FCRA and must be treated the same as all other aspects of the consumer reports EMPLOYER receives.

Under the FCRA, EMPLOYER must make a disclosure in writing to an employee or applicant before obtaining an investigative report (i.e., a criminal background check). This disclosure must stand alone; the document containing the disclosure must consist of nothing more. For example, the disclosure may not be contained among other releases within an employment application. The employee must authorize EMPLOYER's procurement of the consumer report in writing. EMPLOYER must state its intention to obtain an investigative report, describe what the report may contain, and provide this written disclosure no more than three days after the report is requested from the investigative firm.

Enclosed is a sample disclosure and authorization statement, which meets all of the requirements for obtaining consumer reports and investigative consumer reports under the FCRA. **(Encl. A)**. This disclosure and authorization statement should be presented to the applicant before EMPLOYER calls to obtain a background check from its investigative firm.

I also enclose a summary of rights under the FCRA. **(Encl. B)**. This summary of rights must be included with the disclosure and authorization statement in order to satisfy the requirements of the FCRA.

Under the FCRA, EMPLOYER must also certify to the investigative firm that it has made the appropriate disclosure to the employee or applicant, and will comply with any further disclosure requirements of the FCRA. I enclose a sample certification, which should be sent by EMPLOYER to its investigative firm in requesting background checks. **(Encl. C)**.

After an employee or applicant receives EMPLOYER's disclosure and authorization statement, he or she may request additional disclosures under the FCRA. EMPLOYER must provide him or her with information regarding the nature and scope of the investigation, including the name and address of the firm preparing the report. I enclose a sample letter providing this required information to the employee. **(Encl. D)**. EMPLOYER must provide the employee or applicant with this information upon the employee or applicant's request, via the letter, within five days of the request, or within five days of EMPLOYER's request of the investigative firm for the report, whichever is later.

If EMPLOYER decides to take any adverse action against the employee or applicant based upon a background check, or any other investigative report, it must comply with further requirements under the FCRA. "Adverse action" under the FCRA includes denial of employment, promotion, reassignment, retention, any other decision for employment purposes, or any other action based on the consumer report that is adverse to the interests of the consumer. Before EMPLOYER takes any such action, it must provide the employee or applicant with a copy of the consumer report and a written description of the employee or applicant's rights under the FCRA. I enclose a sample letter informing an employee or applicant of possible adverse action. **(Encl. E)**. EMPLOYER must provide this information to the employee or applicant **before** it takes adverse action. The summary of rights under the FCRA **(Encl. B)** should also be included with the letter, as should a copy of the investigative firm's report.

Once EMPLOYER decides to take adverse action, it must provide the employee or applicant with the following information: notice of the adverse action, the name, address, and telephone number of the investigative firm that supplied the report, a statement that the firm did not make the decision to take the adverse action, and notice of the right of the employee or applicant to obtain a free copy of the report. We have enclosed a sample letter to be sent by EMPLOYER to the employee or applicant to notify him or her that adverse action is being taken. **(Encl. F)**. The letter contains all the required information mentioned above.

In addition to imposing its own requirements, the FCRA mandates that EMPLOYER comply with state law, although some states do not have independent fair credit reporting laws.

Enclosure A

Employer and Applicant: Do not attach this page to Employment Application

Consumer Report/Investigative Consumer Report

Disclosure and Release of Information Authorization

I authorize EMPLOYER and [name of reporting agency], a consumer-reporting agency, and/or its agents, to retrieve information from all personnel, educational institutions, government agencies, companies, corporations, credit reporting agencies, law enforcement agencies at the international, federal, state, or county level, relating to my past activities, and I authorize these entities to supply any and all information concerning my background for employment purposes. The information received may include, but is not limited to, academic, residential, achievement, job performance, attendance, litigation, personal history, credit reports, driving records, and criminal history records. I understand and authorize that some or all of this information about me may be transmitted electronically and, when required, may be transferred across international boundaries.

Through this document, it is being disclosed to me and I understand that a Consumer Report or Investigative Consumer Report ("Consumer Report" or "Investigative Report") may be prepared summarizing this information. If my prior employers and/or references are contacted, the report may include information obtained through personal interviews regarding my character, general reputation, personal characteristics, and mode of living. I have the right to request disclosure of the nature and scope of the investigation by making a written request within 60 days of the background investigation. I understand I have the right to inspect those files with reasonable notice during regular business hours and I may be accompanied by one other person. The consumer-reporting agency is required to provide someone to explain the contents of my file. I understand proper identification will be required and I should direct my request to: [name of reporting agency], [INSERT ADDRESS AND PHONE]. I further acknowledge that a "A Summary of Your Rights under the Fair Credit Reporting Act" has been provided to me.

I understand substance-abuse testing/drug testing may be a requirement of the position for which I am applying, or the position I wish to retain. I consent to this testing and understand I must pass the substance abuse testing/drug test and cooperate with all aspects of the testing process as a condition of employment or continued employment. I hereby authorize any physician, laboratory, hospital, or medical professional to conduct such testing and release the results to authorized representative/s of EMPLOYER and/or [name of reporting agency]. I understand some or all of this information may be transmitted electronically and authorize such transmission.

May your current employer be contacted? ❑ Yes ❑ No ❑ Not Currently Employed ❑ Post Hire Only _____ Initial here

Is employment/prospective employment in the US State of California? ___Yes ___No   Please Note: if you are applying for employment in California, a new Disclosure and Release of Information Authorization is required for any subsequent Consumer Report.

Are you applying for employment in California, Minnesota, or Oklahoma: ___Yes ___No

If so, would you like a copy of any Consumer Report prepared on you? ___Yes ___No

I hereby certify all the statements and answers set forth on the application form and/or my resume are true and complete to the best of my knowledge, and I understand that if subsequent to employment any such statements and/or answers are found false or information has been omitted, such false statements or omissions will be just cause of the termination of my employment. Further, I understand that by requesting this information, no promise of employment is being made. I am willing that a photocopy of this authorization to be accepted with the same authority as the original; and that if employed by the above-named company (except if employed in the US State of California), this authorization will remain in effect throughout such employment.

Signature _____ Social Security Number _____ Date _____

NOTE: The following should not be provided until you have read and signed the Disclosure and Release of Information Authorization above. The information requested below is needed to conduct your background investigation and IS NOT considered as part of your application. It is used only for identification purposes. Other than its use in conducting your background investigation and its inclusion in the report, this information will not be shared unless required by law or you specifically authorize. PLEASE PRINT CLEARLY.

| Last Name | First | Middle | Date of Birth (mm/dd/yyyy) |

| Street Address | City | State/Province | County | Zip Code/Postal Code |

| Driver's License Number | County/State of License | Expires On |

List any other COUNTRIES, CITIES, and STATES in which you have lived during the previous 7 years. _____

List any other LAST NAMES you have used in the previous 7 years. _____

List any other LAST NAMES under which you received your GED, high school diploma, or other academic credentials. _____

FOR APPLICANTS WITH INTERNATIONAL HISTORY ONLY

| Mother's Maiden Name | Father's First Name (s) |

| Identification Number or National Insurance Number if Issued Outside USA | Country of Issuance |

Enclosure B

Para informacion en espanol, visite www.ftc.gov/credit o escribe a la FTC Consumer Response Center, Room 130-A 600 Pennsylvania Ave. N.W., Washington D.C. 20580.

A Summary of Your Rights Under the Fair Credit Reporting Act

The federal Fair Credit Report Act ("FCRA") promotes the accuracy, fairness, and privacy of information in the files of consumer reporting agencies. There are many types of consumer reporting agencies, including credit bureaus and specialty agencies (such as agencies that sell information about check writing histories, medical records, and rental history records). Here is a summary of your major rights under the FCRA. **For more information, including information about additional rights, go to www.ftc.gov/credit or write to: Consumer Response Center, Room 130-A, Federal Trade Commission, 600 Pennsylvania Ave. N.W., Washington, D.C. 20580.**

You must be told if information in your file has been used against you. Anyone who uses a credit report or another type of c consumer report to deny your application for credit, insurance, or employment—or to take another adverse action against you—must tell you, and must give you the name, address, and phone number of the agency that provided the information.

You have the right to know what is in your file. You may request and obtain all the information about you in the files of a consumer reporting agency (your "file disclosure"). You will be required to provide proper identification, which may include your Social Security number. In many cases, the disclosure will be free. You are entitled to a free file disclosure if:

- a person has taken adverse action against you because of information in your credit report;
- you are the victim of identify theft and place a fraud alert in your file;
- your file contains inaccurate information as a result of fraud;
- you are on public assistance;
- you are unemployed but expect to apply for employment within 60 days.

In addition, all consumers are entitled to one free disclosure every 12 months upon request from each nationwide credit bureau and from nationwide specialty consumer reporting agencies. See www.ftc.gov/credit for additional information.

You have the right to ask for a credit score. Credit scores are numerical summaries of your credit-worthiness based on information from credit bureaus. You may request a credit score from consumer reporting agencies that create scores or distribute scores used in residential real property loans, but you will have to pay for it. In some mortgage transactions, you will receive credit score information for free from the mortgage lender.

You have the right to dispute incomplete or inaccurate information. If you identify information in your file that is incomplete or inaccurate, and report it to the consumer reporting agency, the agency must investigate unless your dispute is frivolous. See www.ftc.gov/credit for an explanation of dispute procedures.

Consumer reporting agencies must correct or delete inaccurate, incomplete, or unverifiable information. Inaccurate, incomplete, or unverifiable information must be removed or corrected, usually within 30 days. However, a consumer reporting agency may continue to report information it has verified as accurate.

Consumer reporting agencies may not report outdated negative information. In most cases, a consumer reporting agency may not report negative information that is more than seven years old, or bankruptcies that are more than 10 years old.

Access to your file is limited. A consumer reporting agency may provide information about you only to people with a valid need—usually to consider an application with a creditor, insurer, employer, landlord, or other business. The FCRA specifies those with a valid need for access.

You must give your consent for reports to be provided to employers. A consumer reporting agency may not give out information about you to your employer, or a potential employer, without your written consent given to the employer. Written consent generally is not required in the trucking industry. For more information, go to www.ftc.gov/credit.

You may limit "prescreened" offers of credit and insurance you get based on information in your credit report. Unsolicited "prescreened" offers for credit and insurance must include a toll-free phone number you can call if you choose to remove your name and address from the lists these offers are based on. You may opt-out with the nationwide credit bureaus at 1-888-5-OPTOUT (1-888-567-8688).

You may seek damages from violators. If a consumer reporting agency, or, in some cases, a user of consumer reports or a furnisher of information to a consumer reporting agency violates the FCRA, you may be able to sue in state or federal court.

Identity theft victims and active duty military personnel have additional rights. For more information, visit www.ftc.gov/credit.

States may enforce the FCRA, and many states have their own consumer reporting laws. In some cases, you may have more rights under state law. For more information, contact your state or local consumer protection agency or your state Attorney General.

Enclosure C

CLIENT CERTIFICATION OF COMPLIANCE WITH THE FAIR CREDIT REPORTING ACT

In compliance with the Fair Credit Reporting Act, as amended, EMPLOYER (hereinafter, the "Client") certifies to [Name of reporting company] that it:

1. Will use the requested consumer report solely for employment purposes as permitted by the Fair Credit Reporting Act, as amended;
2. Has clearly and conspicuously disclosed to the consumer that a consumer report may be made for employment purposes which includes information as to his/her criminal record, credit background, references, past employment, work habits, education, character, general reputation, personal characteristics, and mode of living, whichever are applicable;
3. Has obtained written authorization from the consumer prior to procuring the consumer report;
4. Will provide to a consumer, upon written request, disclosure concerning the scope and nature of the investigation requested where an investigative consumer report is procured. The disclosure will be made in writing and mailed, or otherwise delivered, to the consumer no later than five (5) days after the date on which the request for such disclosure was received from the consumer or such report was first requested, whichever is later;
5. Will, prior to taking an adverse action against the consumer based in whole or in part on the consumer report, provide to the consumer a copy of the consumer report and a description of the rights of the consumer, as required by § 1681(g) of the Fair Credit Reporting Act, as amended;
6. Will provide the consumer with oral, written, or electronic notice of any adverse action based in whole or in part on the consumer report, and, in the case of an investigative consumer report, provide notice to the consumer no later than 3 days after the adverse action of his/her right to obtain 1) obtain a copy of the investigative report from [Name of reporting company], 2) a summary of the consumer's rights under the FCRA, and 3) information regarding how to dispute the accuracy and completeness of the investigative consumer report;
7. Will not use any information from the consumer report in violation of any applicable Federal or State equal employment opportunity law or regulation.

EMPLOYER

By: _____
                  [Name]

Title: _____

Enclosure D

EMPLOYER
Disclosure of Investigative Consumer Report

Dear [Applicant]:

This is to advise you that on [date], EMPLOYER requested an investigative consumer report for employment-related purposes. Pursuant to your prior request, we are providing you with the nature and scope of the investigation as follows:

[Be Specific]

Previously, we provided you with a summary in writing of your rights under the Fair Credit Reporting Act. For your convenience we have enclosed another copy.

EMPLOYER

By: _____
　　　　　　　Name

Title: _____

Candidate's Name (Please Print)　_____

Social Security Number　_____

Candidate's Signature　_____

Date　_____

Enclosure E

Sample Written Pre-Adverse Action Notice to Applicants

Dear [Applicant]:

In connection with your application for employment, you consented to an independent investigation conducted by a consumer reporting agency and authorized EMPLOYER to obtain a consumer report and/or investigative consumer report for employment purposes. EMPLOYER contracted with [name of reporting company], whose address and telephone number are as follows:

ADDRESS   _____

PHONE   _____

We are enclosing a copy of the report provided by [reporting company] and a copy of your rights under the Fair Credit Reporting Act. You have the right to dispute with [Name of reporting company] the accuracy or completeness of any information provided in the report. If you wish to do so, please contact the agency at the above address/telephone number.

Sincerely,
EMPLOYER

By: _____
                     Name

Title: _____

Enclosure F

Sample Written Adverse Action Notice to Applicants

Dear [Applicant]:

We wish to advise you that we cannot give you any further consideration for employment. This action was influenced in whole or in part by information contained in a consumer report, made at our request and provided by:

[Name of reporting company]

ADDRESS   _____

PHONE   _____

Please understand that the consumer reporting agency that furnished us with the report did not make the decision to take this adverse action, and thus cannot provide you with specific reasons why the adverse action was taken.

Under the Fair Credit Reporting Act, you have the right to obtain a free copy of your file from the consumer reporting agency if you make a request with the agency within 60 days. Enclosed with our letter to you dated _____, you were provided with a copy of the report we received from [Name of reporting company] You also have the right to obtain from the consumer reporting agency, free of cost, an additional copy of the report.

You also must be provided with a copy of the Federal Trade Commission's summary of Consumer Rights, which is attached to this letter. The summary was also included with our letter to you dated _____. You have the right to dispute directly with the consumer reporting agency the accuracy or completeness of any information provided by the consumer reporting agency.

Sincerely,

EMPLOYER

By: _____
               Name

Title: _____

EMPLOYMENT DISCRIMINATION LAWS BY STATE

Jurisdiction	Covered Employers	Enforcement Agency	Categories Protected/ Relevant Statute
Alabama	Employers with 20 or more employees; employment agencies and labor organizations.	Alabama Dept. of Industrial Relations 649 Monroe St. Montgomery, AL 36131	Age (40+) ALA. CODE§§ 21-7-8; 25-1-20 et seq.
Alaska	All public and private employers, employment agencies, labor organizations, and communications media other than social clubs and nonprofit religious, fraternal, charitable, or educational organizations.	Alaska State Commission on Human Rights 800 A, Ste. 204 Anchorage, AK 99501 (907) 276-4692 or (800) 478-4692 www.gov.state.ak.us/aschr/aschr.htm	Race, religion, color, national origin, ancestry, age, physical or mental disability, sex, martial status (and changes thereto), pregnancy, and parenthood. ALASKA STAT.§§ 18.80.220; 18.80.300(10)
Arizona	The state and its agencies, private employers with 15 or more employees, employment agencies and labor organizations, but not the United States, Native American tribes, and bona fide tax-exempt private membership clubs. For sexual harassment actions, employer means a person who has one or more employees in the current or preceding calendar year.	Arizona Attorney General Civil Rights Division 1275 W. Washington Phoenix, AZ 85007 (602) 542-5263 or (877) 491-5742 Tucson Office: 400 West Congress, Ste. 5215 Tucson, AZ 85701 (520) 628-6500 or (877) 491-5740 www.attorneygeneral.state.az. us/civil_rights	Race, color, religion, sex, pregnancy, age (40+), disability, AIDS, and national origin. ARIZ. REV. STAT. ANN. §§ 23341; 41-1463. Government contractors are prohibited from discriminating based on race, color, religion, sex, national origin, or age. ARIZ. EXEC. OR. 75-5
Arkansas	Applies to all public and private employers that employ nine or more employees in the state, but does not apply to employment by religious entities. ARK. CODE ANN. § 16-123-102(5).	No state agency. Rights under the Arkansas Civil Rights Act are enforced by private lawsuit.	Race, religion, national origin, age (40-70), pregnancy, gender, or the presence of any sensory, mental, or physical disability. ARK. CODE ANN. §§ 11-4-601; 16-102(6); 16-123-107; 21-3-203 (public employees)
California	Employers with five or more full or part-time employees within the state. The harassment provisions of the Fair Employment and Housing Act (FEHA) apply to all public and private employers, employment agencies, labor organizations and government contractors, but not nonprofit religious organizations. Last updated: 10/20/03.	Dept. of Fair Employment & Housing 2000 O St., Ste. 120 Sacramento , CA 95814 (916) 445-9918 or (800) 884-1684 Los Angeles: 611 West Sixth St., Ste. 1500 Los Angeles, CA 90017 (213) 439-6799 or (800) 700-2320 San Francisco: 455 Golden Gate Ave., Ste. 7600 San Francisco, CA 94102 (415) 703-4175 or (800) 700-2320 www.dfeh.ca.gov	Race, religious creed, color, national origin, ancestry, physical disability (including HIV and AIDS), mental disability, medical condition (cancer and genetic characteristics), marital status, sex (including pregnancy, childbirth, or related medical conditions), age (40+), sexual orientation, gender (including gender-identity); denial of family and medical care leave; alcohol and drug abuse; political affiliation. Government contractors are also required to have affirmative action provisions under FEHA. CAL. GOV'T CODE§ 12940(a), (j); CAL. LAB. CODE§§ 1025, 1101 et seq.

Jurisdiction	Covered Employers	Enforcement Agency	Categories Protected/ Relevant Statute
Colorado	All public and private employers, employment agencies, labor organizations, and government contractors, other than religious organizations not supported in whole or part by taxation or public borrowing.	Colorado Civil Rights Division 1560 Broadway, Ste. 1050 Denver, CO 80202 (303) 894-2997 www.dora.state.co.us/civil-rights	Disability, race, creed, color, sex, age (40-70), national origin, ancestry, marriage or engagement to current employees, religion, tobacco use, and other lawful activities. COLO. REV. STAT. ANN. §§ 24-34-301, 24-34-402. The public works statute applies to government contractors with respect to race, color, religion, sex, and age. COLO. REV. STAT. 8-17-101
Connecticut	Public employers, private employers with three or more employees, employment agencies, labor organizations, Native American tribes, licensing agencies, and government contractors.	Connecticut Commission on Human Rights and Opportunities 21 Grand St. Hartford, CT 06106 (800) 477-5737 www.ct.us/state.chro	Race, color, religious creed, age, marital status, national origin, sex, ancestry, present or past history of mental disability, mental retardation, pregnancy, genetic information, learning or physical disabilities, and tobacco use. CONN. GEN. STAT. ANN. §§ 31-40s; 31-57e; 46a-51; 46a-60; 46a-81c
Delaware	Public employers, private employers with four or more employees, employment agencies, labor organizations, joint labor-management committees, and government contractors, but not certain religious organizations. The handicap discrimination statute applies only to employers with 15 or more employees.	Delaware Department of Labor, Division of Industrial Affairs Office of Labor Law Enforcement 4425 North Market St. Wilmington, DE 19802 (302) 761-8200 (2 other locations) www.delawareworks.com/ industrialaffairs/services/ LaborLawEnforcement.shtm/	Race, marital status, genetic information, color, age (40-70), religion, creed, sex, national origin, ancestry, disability, and handicap (i.e., mental or physical impairment). DEL. CODE, ANN. tit. 19, § 711-724
District of Columbia	All public and private employers, professional associations, employment agencies, labor organizations, and government contractors.	Office of Human Rights 441 4th St. NW, Ste. 570 N. Washington, DC 20001 (202) 727-4559 ohr.dc.gov/	Race, color, religion, national origin, sex (including pregnancy, childbirth, and related medical conditions), age (actual or perceived), disability and handicap, marital status, personal appearance, sexual orientation, gender identity or expression, family responsibilities (actual or perceived), matriculation (actual or perceived), political affiliation (actual or perceived), genetic information, and tobacco use. D.C. CODE ANN. §§ 1-615.51 et seq.; 2-1402.11; 7-1703.03; 4

Jurisdiction	Covered Employers	Enforcement Agency	Categories Protected/ Relevant Statute
Florida	All public and private employers with 15 or more employees, employment agencies, labor organizations, and government contractors.	Florida Commission on Human Relation 325 John Knox Road, Building F, Ste. 240 Tallahassee, FL 32303 (850) 488-7082 or (800) 955-8770 fchr.state.fl.us	Race, color, religion, sex, national origin, age, handicap, marital status, familial status, AIDS, sickle-cell trait, political opinion or affiliation, and tobacco use. FLA. STAT. ANN. §§ 110.112(4); 448.075; 760.10; 760.50(2); City of North Miami v. Kurtz, 653 So.2d 1025 (Fla. 1995). Government contractors are covered by the public employment physical handicap discrimination statute. FLA.STAT.413.08
Georgia	The state and its agencies that employ at least 15 employees. For age discrimination in employment only: public and private employers with at least one employee. For sex discrimination in wages only: public and private employers with 10 or more employees. For disability discrimination: employers in the state that employ 15 or more individuals.	For public employees: Georgia Commission on Equal Opportunity 2 Martin Luther King, Jr. Dr. Ste. 1002 - West Tower Atlanta, GA 30334 800-473-6736 www.gceo.state.ga.us.	Race, color, religion, national origin, sex, disability, and age (40-70, public employees only) GA. CODE ANN. §§ 45-19-20 et seq.); age (40-70, in addition to general prohibition of age discrimination), GA. CODE ANN. § 34-1-2); sex (for equal pay purposes only) GA. CODE ANN. § 34-5-3. There is no generally applicable fair employment practices law in Georgia.
Hawaii	All public and private employers, employment agencies, and labor organizations other than the United States.	Hawaii Civil Rights Commission 830 Punchbowl St., Rm 411 Honolulu, HI 96813 (808) 586-8636 ww.state.hi.us/hcrc	Race, sex, or pregnancy, national origin, sexual orientation, age, religion, color, ancestry, disability, marital status, politics, and arrest, court record. HAW. REV. STAT. ANN. §§ 76-1; 76-44; 378-2
Idaho	All public and private employers who hire five employees for each working day in 20 or more calendar weeks in the current or preceding year, employment agencies, labor organizations, joint labor-management committees and government contractors. Does not include household servants.	Idaho Commission on Human Rights 1109 Main St., Ste. 400 Boise, ID 83720 (208) 334-2873 or (888) 249-7025 www2.state.id.us/ihrc	Race, national origin, color, creed, sex, religion, ancestry, age (40+), and disability. IDAHO CODE§ 67-5909
Illinois	Public and private employers with at least 15 employees, employment agencies, labor organizations, and government contractors, but not elected public officials and members of their immediate personal staff and not nonprofit religious organizations. However, in cases of handicap discrimination or sexual harassment, only one or more employee is required.	Illinois Department of Human Rights 100 West Randolph St., Ste. 10-100 Chicago, IL 60601 (312) 917-6200 www.state.il.us/dhr	Race, color, religion, creed, national origin, ancestry, age, sex (including pregnancy), sexual orientation, marital status, physical or mental handicap, military status or unfavorable discharge from military status, arrest and criminal history information, off-duty use of lawful products, genetic information, and citizenship status. 775 ILL. COMP. STAT. ANN. §§ 5/1-101 et seq.; § 5/2-102; § 5/1-102 (A); § 55/5; ILL. ADMIN. CODE§ 5210.110

Jurisdiction	Covered Employers	Enforcement Agency	Categories Protected/ Relevant Statute
Indiana	Public and private employers that employ six or more persons, employment agencies, labor organizations and government contractors, but not nonprofit religious or fraternal organizations or social clubs. For purposes of age discrimination, only one or more employee is required.	Indiana Civil Rights Commission, 100 N. Senate Ave. Rm 103 Indiananapolis IN 46204 (317) 232-2600 or (800) 628-2909 www.state.in.us/icrc	Race, religion, color, sex, disability, national origin, ancestry, tobacco use, and age (40-70). IND. CODE ANN. §§ 22-9-1-1; 22-9-2-1 et seq.
Iowa	Public and private employers of employees within the state, employment agencies, labor organizations, and government contractors.	Iowa Civil Rights Commission Grimes State Office Bldg. 400 E. 14th St. Des Moines, IA 50319 (515) 281-4121 or (800) 457-4416 www.state.ia.is/government/crc	Age, race, color, creed, national origin, religion, sex, pregnancy, childbirth and related medical conditions, physical or mental disability (including HIV), and genetic testing (not for government contractors). IOWA CODE §§ 216.6; 729
Kansas	Public and private employers with at least four employees, employment agencies, labor organizations, organizations engaged in social service work, and government contractors who employ at least four employees and whose contracts cumulatively total more than $5,000 in the fiscal year, but not nonprofit fraternal or social organizations.	Kansas Human Rights Commission 900 SW Jackson, Ste. 568-S Topeka, KS 66612 (3 other area offices) (785) 296-3206 or (888) 793-6874 www.khrc.net	Race, religion, color, sex (including pregnancy), disability, national origin or ancestry, age (40-70), marital status, and HIV infection. KAN. STAT. ANN. §§ 44.1001. In addition, the law also prohibits discrimination based on an employee's, or prospective employee's, genetic screening or testing information. KAN. STAT. ANN. § 44-1009, 44-1111
Kentucky	Employers with at least eight employees within the state, employment agencies, labor organizations, joint labor-management committees, licensing agencies, and government contractors. For purposes of disability discrimination, "employer" means employing 15 or more employees and shall not include the U.S. government, Native American tribes or bona fide private membership clubs.	Kentucky Commission on Human Rights The Heyburn Bldg., Ste. 700 332 W. Broadway Louisville, KY 40202 (502) 595-4024 or (800) 292-5566 www.state.ky.us/agencies2/kchr	Age (40+), race, color, national origin, religion, sex, disability, familial status, HIV status, pregnancy, childbirth and related medical conditions, smokers/ nonsmokers, and Sabbath observance. KY. REV. STAT. §§ 207.130; 344.010; 344.040; 436.165. The Kentucky Equal Employment Opportunity Act of 1978 prohibits discrimination by government contractors (with certain exceptions) with respect to race, color, religion, sex, national origin, and age. KY. REV. STAT. § 45.570
Louisiana	Employers of 20 or more employees (in cases of pregnancy, childbirth and related medical condition discrimination, more than 25), labor organizations, joint labor-management committees, apprenticeship and training programs, and agencies of state and local governments, and government contractors.	Louisiana Commission on Human Rights P.O. Box 94094 Baton Rouge, LA 70804 (225) 342-6969 www.gov.state.la.us/HumanRights/ humanrightshome.htm	Race, color, religion, sex, disability, age (50+), sickle cell trait, pregnancy, national origin, genetic information, childbirth and related medical conditions, and smoking. LA. REV. STAT. 23:301 et seq.; 23:302 et seq.; 23:311; 23:322 et seq.;23:331 et seq.; 23:342 et seq.; 23:352 et seq.; 23:966 et seq.; 23:368 et seq.

Jurisdiction	Covered Employers	Enforcement Agency	Categories Protected/ Relevant Statute
Maine	All public and private employers and their agents, employment agencies, labor organizations, and government contractors. Except for purposes of disability discrimination, does not include nonprofit religious or fraternal corporations or associations, with respect to its members of the same religion, sect, or fraternity.	Maine Human Rights Commission 51 State House Station Augusta, ME 04333 (207) 624-6050 www.state.me.us/mhrc	Race, color, religion, national origin, ancestry, physical or mental disability, age, sex (including pregnancy and related medical conditions), having made a claim under workers' compensation law, and smoking. ME. REV. STAT. ANN. §§ 4551 et seq., 4572; tit. 26, § 597. Government contractors are covered by the public employment and government contractor law, which prohibits discrimination with respect to race, color, religious creed, sex, national origin, ancestry, and physical or mental handicap. ME. REV. STAT. ANN. tit. 5, §§ 783 et seq. In addition, health care facilities are prohibited from discriminating on the basis of AIDS. ME. REV. STAT. ANN. tit. 5, §§ 1920 et seq.
Maryland	Public and private employers with at least 15 employees, employment agencies, labor organizations, joint labor- management committees and government contractors, but not bona fide private membership club that is tax-exempt.	Maryland Commission on Human Relations 6 Saint Paul St. Ste. 900, Schaefer Towers Baltimore, MD 21202 (410) 767-8600 or (800) 637-6247 (3 other area locations) www.mchr.us.state.md	Race, color, religion, sex (including pregnancy, childbirth and related medical conditions), age, national origin, marital status, sexual orientation, genetic information, disability unrelated in nature and extent so as to reasonably preclude the performance of the employment (including AIDS), because of the individual's refusal to submit to a genetic test or make available the results of a genetic test and Sabbath observance. MD. CODE art. 49B, § 15-18; MD. CODE ANN., LAB. & EMPL. § 3-219. Government contractors are covered by the government procurement statute, which prohibits discrimination based on race, color, creed, national origin, age, or sex. MD. CODE ANN., STATE FIN. & PROC. § 13-219
Massachusetts	Public and private employers with at least six employees, employment agencies, labor organizations and government contractors, but not nonprofit private social clubs, associations and fraternal organizations.	Massachusetts Commission Against Discrimination One Ashburton Pl., Rm 601 Boston, MA 02108 (617) 727-3990 Springfield Office: 436 Dwight St., Second Fl., Rm. 220 Springfield, MA 01103 (413) 739-2145 www.state.ma.us/mcad	Age (40+), race, color, religious creed, national origin, ancestry, sex (including pregnancy and maternity leave), sexual orientation (except pedophilia), genetic information, AIDS, failure to furnish information regarding mental health treatment and handicap. MASS. GEN. LAWS ch. 151B, § 4

Jurisdiction	Covered Employers	Enforcement Agency	Categories Protected/ Relevant Statute
Michigan	All public and private employers with one or more employees, employment agencies, labor organizations, training committees, and government contractors.	Michigan Department of Civil Rights Executive Office Capitol Tower Bldg., Ste. 800 Lansing, MI 48913 (517) 335-3165 Detroit Office: Service Center, Cadillac Place 3054 W. Grand Blvd., Ste. 3600 Detroit, MI 48202 (other area locations throughout state) (313) 456-3700 www.michigan.gov/mdcr	Religion, race, color, national origin, ancestry, sex, disability, age, marital status, familial status, pregnancy, childbirth, and related conditions except nontherapeutic abortions, arrest records, height, and weight. MICH. COMP. LAWS§§ 37.2201 et seq.
Minnesota	Public and private employers with one or more employees, employment agencies, labor organizations, and government contractors.	Minnesota Department of Human Rights Army Corps of Engineers Centre 190 East 5th St., Ste. 700 St. Paul, MN 55101 (651) 296-5663 or (800) 657-3704 www.humanrights.state.mn .us	Race, color, creed, religion, national origin, ancestry, sex (including pregnancy, childbirth, and related disabilities), marital status, status with regard to public assistance, membership or activity in a local commission, disability, age, and sexual orientation. MINN. STAT., ch. 363A
Mississippi	All public and private employers.	Not applicable	Mississippi does not have a comprehensive fair employment practices law, and all other prohibited forms of discrimination in employment apply solely to public employers.
Missouri	Employers with at least six employees within the state, employment agencies, labor organizations, and government contractors, but not corporations and associations owned and operated by religious or sectarian groups.	Missouri Commission on Human Rights 3315 W. Truman Blvd., Rm. 212 Jefferson City, MO 65102 (573) 751-3325 www.dolir.mo.gov/hr	Race, color, religion, national origin, sex, ancestry, age (40-70), disability, AIDS, genetic testing, and off-duty tobacco and alcohol use. RSMO ch. 213 et seq.
Montana	All public and private employers, employment agencies, and labor organizations, but not non-profit private membership clubs.	Montana Human Rights Bureau 1625 11th Ave. P.O. Box 1728 Helena, MT 59624 (406) 444-2884 or (800) 542-0807 erd.dli.state.mt.us/humanright/ hrhome.asp	Race, creed, religion, color, sex, physical or mental disability, age, national origin, marital status, and pregnancy. Montana Human Rights Act § 49-2-303(1)(a). § 49-2-310, 311
Nebraska	Private and nonprofit employers with at least 15 employees, and any party whose business is financed in whole or in part under the Nebraska Investment Finance Authority Act regardless of the number of employees, including the State of Nebraska, governmental agencies, and political subdivisions, regardless of the number of employees; employment agencies; and labor organizations, but not the United States, Native American tribes, or bona fide tax-exempt private membership clubs.	Nebraska Equal Opportunity Commission 301 Centennial Mall S., 5th Floor Lincoln, NE 68509 (401) 471-2024 or (800) 642-6112 www.neoc.ne.gov	Race, color, national origin, religion, sex (including pregnancy), disability, marital status, age (40-70), and HIV/AIDS. NEB. STAT. §§ 20-168(1), 48-1004, 648-1101 et seq.

Jurisdiction	Covered Employers	Enforcement Agency	Categories Protected/ Relevant Statute
Nevada	Employers with 15 or more employees, employment agencies, and labor organizations, but not the United States, Native American tribes, or tax-exempt private membership clubs.	Nevada Equal Rights Commission 1515 E. Tropicana, Ste. 590 Las Vegas, NV 89119 (702) 486-7161 Reno: 1325 Corporate Blvd. Reno, NV 89502 775-688-1288 www.nvdefr.org	Race, color, religion, sex, (gender and/or sexual orientation) pregnancy, age (40+), disability, and national origin. NEV. REV. STAT. §§ 613.310 et seq.
New Hampshire	Employers with six or more employees, employment agencies, and labor organizations, but not nonprofit religious organizations or nonprofit social, fraternal, or charitable clubs and associations.	New Hampshire Commission for Human Rights 2 Chenell Dr. Concord, NH 03301 (603) 271-2767 www.state.nh.us/hrc	Age, sex (including pregnancy and pregnancy-related medical conditions), race, religion, creed, color, marital status, physical or mental disability, national origin, and tobacco use. N.H. REV. STAT. §§ 275:37-a; 354:A-7
New Jersey	All public and private employers, state and municipal contractors, employment agencies, and labor organizations.	New Jersey Dept. of the Attorney General Division on Civil Rights 140 East Front St., 6th Floor P.O. Box 090 Trenton, NJ 08625 (609) 292-4605 (4 other locations) www.state.nj.us/lps/dcr	Race, creed, color, national origin, nationality, ancestry, age (18-70), sex (including pregnancy and sexual harassment), marital status, affectional or sexual orientation, domestic partnership status, atypical hereditary, cellular, or blood trait, genetic information (or refusal to submit to a genetic test or make available the results of a genetic test to an employer), liability for military service, tobacco use, and mental and physical disability (including AIDS and HIV-related illnesses). N.J. STAT. §§ 10:5-1 et seq., 34:6B-1
New Mexico	Employers with four or more employees, the state and all its political subdivisions, employment agencies, government contractors, and labor organizations.	New Mexico Human Rights Division 1596 Pacheco St. Aspen Plaza, Ste. 103 Santa Fe, NM 87502 (800) 566-9471 www.dol.state.nm.us/dol_qhrd.html	Race, color, national origin, ancestry, religion, sex, age, physical or mental handicap, serious medical condition, genetic information, HIV testing, and tobacco use. If the employer has 50 or more employees, spousal affiliation is protected. If the employer has 15 or more employees, sexual orientation or gender identity is protected. N.M. STAT. §§ 24-21-4(D), 28-1-1 et seq., 50-11-3
New York	Employers with four or more employees, licensing agencies, employment agencies, labor organizations, and government contractors.	New York State Division of Human Rights One Fordham Plaza, 4th Fl. Bronx, NY 10458 (headquarters) (718) 741-8400 www.dhr.state.ny.us	Age (18+), race, creed, color, national origin, ancestry, sex, pregnancy, disability, sexual orientation, arrest or conviction, genetic predisposition or carrier status, and marital status. N.Y. CONSOL. LAWS, ch. 18, art. 15, § 296

Jurisdiction	Covered Employers	Enforcement Agency	Categories Protected/ Relevant Statute
North Carolina	Employers with at least 15 employees, the state and its agencies, and local government entities.	North Carolina Human Relations Commission 1318 Mail Service Center Raleigh, NC 27699 (919) 733-7996 www.doa.state.nc.us/doa/ hrc/hrc.htm	Age, sex, race, color, national origin, religion, creed, disability/ handicap, sickle cell or hemoglobin C trait, genetic testing, and AIDS/HIV. N.C. GEN. STAT. §§ 95-28.1A, 130A-148, 143-422.2, 168.A-1 et seq.
North Dakota	Private employers, the state and its agencies, employment agencies, and labor organizations.	North Dakota Department of Labor Human Rights Division 600 E. Boulevard Ave., Dept. 406 Bismarck, ND 58505 (701) 328-2660 or (800) 582-8032 www.state.nd.us/labor/services/ human-rights	Race, color, religion, sex, pregnancy-related disabilities, national origin, age (40+), mental or physical disability, status with regard to marriage or public assistance, and participation in lawful activities during nonwork hours off the employer's premises. N.D. CENT. CODE§§ 14-02.4 et seq.
Ohio	The state and its agencies, employers with four or more employees, employment agencies, joint labor-management committees, labor organizations, and government contractors.	Ohio Civil Rights Commission Central Office 1111 E. Broad St., Ste. 301 Columbus, OH 43205 (614) 466- 7742 or (888) 278-7101 (Ohio has 5 other regional offices and two satellite offices) crc.ohio.gov	Race, color, religion, sex (including pregnancy and related conditions), national origin, handicap, age (40+), and ancestry. OHIO REV. CODE § 4112.01-02. There is a separate public works contractor statute that contains a nondiscrimination provision specifying that no discrimination may occur based on race, creed, sex, disability, or color. OHIO REV. CODE § 153.59
Oklahoma	Public and private employers with at least 15 employees, employment agencies, and labor organizations, but not Native American tribes or bona fide nonprofit membership clubs.	Oklahoma Human Rights Commission, Jim Thorpe Building 2101 North Lincoln Blvd, Rm 480 Oklahoma City, OK 73105 (405) 521-2360 or (888) 456-2558 www.youroklahoma.com/ohrc	Race, color, religion, sex, pregnancy, national origin, age (40+), tobacco use, genetic testing, and handicap. OKLA. STAT. §§ 25-1201 et seq., 3614.2. OKLA. ADMIN. CODE§ 335:15-9-2
Oregon	All public and private employers, employment agencies, and labor organizations.	Oregon Bureau of Labor & Industries Civil Rights Division 800 N.E. Oregon St., Ste. 1045 Portland, OR 97232 (503) 731-4075 www.oregon.gov/BOL / CRD/ index.htm/	Race, color, national origin, ancestry, sex, pregnancy, childbirth, pregnancy-related conditions, religion, age (18+), physical or mental disability (employers with 6 or more employees), genetic screening, juvenile records, personal associations and marital status. OR. REV. STAT. §§ 659A.001 et seq.
Pennsylvania	Employers with at least four employees in Pennsylvania, the Commonwealth and any political subdivisions, employment agencies, labor organizations, and government contractors. Does not include religious, fraternal, charitable or sectarian corporations or associations (unless supported by government appropriations), except with respect to claims related to race, color, age, sex, or handicap discrimination.	Pennsylvania Human Relations Commission Central Office 301 Chestnut St., Ste. 300 Harrisburg, PA 17101 (707) 787-4410 www.phrc.state.pa.us	Race, color, religious creed, ancestry, age, sex, pregnancy, national origin, familial status, non-job-related handicap or disability, use of a guide or support animal, willingness or refusal to perform or participate in abortion, and persons who hold general education development certificates rather than high school diplomas. 43 PA. STAT. §§ 951 et seq.

Hiring and Firing

Jurisdiction	Covered Employers	Enforcement Agency	Categories Protected/ Relevant Statute
Rhode Island	The state and its political sub-divisions, employers with at least four employees, employment agencies, labor organizations, licensing agencies, and government contractors.	Rhode Island Commission for Human Rights 180 Westminster St., 3rd Fl. Providence, RI 02903 (401) 222-2661 www.rchr.state.ri.us	Race, color, sex, pregnancy, ancestral origin, disability, age (40+), sexual orientation, religion, AIDS testing, genetic testing, and tobacco use outside of employment. R.I. GEN. LAWS §§ 28-5 et seq., 23-6-22 and 23-6-23, 42-87. Employers, employment agencies, and licensing agencies are prohibited from discriminating against victims of domestic violence. R.I. GEN. LAWS § 12-28-11 The public employment and government contractor law prohibits discrimination on the basis of race, color, religion, sex, pregnancy, national origin, age, or handicap by government contractors. R.I. GEN. LAWS § 28-5.1-10
South Carolina	Employers with at least 15 employees, employment agencies, and labor organizations, but not Native American tribes and bona fide private membership clubs other than labor organizations.	South Carolina Human Affairs Commission P.O. Box 4490 Columbia, SC 29240 (803) 737-7800 or (800) 521-0725 www.state.sc.us/schac	Race, religion, color, sex, age (40+), national origin, ancestry, disability, and tobacco use outside the workplace. S.C. CODE §§ 1-13-10 et seq., 41-1-85
South Dakota	Public and private employers, employment agencies, and labor organizations.	South Dakota Division of Human Rights Director: James Marsh 700 Governors Dr. Pierre, SD 57501 (605) 773-4493 www.state.sd.us/dol/boards/hr	Race, color, creed, religion, sex, disability, blindness and partial blindness, ancestry, national origin, and tobacco use outside the workplace. S.D. COD. LAWS, §§ 20-13-1 et seq., 60-4-11
Tennessee	The state and its political sub-divisions, employers with at least eight employees within the state, employment agencies, and labor organizations.	Tennessee Human Rights Commission 530 Church St., Ste. 300 Nashville, TN 37243 (615) 741-5825 or (800) 251-3589 (3 other regional offices) www.state.tn.us/humanrights	Race, creed, color, religion, sex, age (40+), and national origin. TENN. CODE §§ 4-21-401 to 4-21-404 Discrimination by all employers against people who use tobacco is prohibited. TENN. CODE § 50-1-304 Discrimination by public and private employers against the handicapped is prohibited. TENN. CODE § 8-50-103
Texas	State and local government entities, employers with at least 15 employees, employment agencies, and labor organizations.	Texas Commission on Human Rights 1117 Trinity St., Room 144T Austin, TX 78778 (512) 463-2642 or (888) 452-4778 www.twc.state.us	Race, color, disability, religion, sex (including pregnancy, childbirth, or related medical conditions), national origin, and age (40+). TEX. LABOR CODE, ch. 21

Hiring and Firing

Jurisdiction	Covered Employers	Enforcement Agency	Categories Protected/ Relevant Statute
Utah	The state and its political subdivisions, employers with at least 15 employees, employment agencies, and labor organizations, but not religious organizations, corporations, or associations.	Utah Labor Commission, Antidiscrimination & Labor Division 160 East 300 South, 3rd Fl. Salt Lake City, UT 84111 (801) 530-6801 or (800) 222-1238 laborcommission.utah. gov/Utah_ Antidiscrimination_Labor/utah_ antidiscrimination_labo.htm	Race, color, sex, pregnancy (including childbirth and pregnancy-related conditions), age (40+), religion, national origin, and disability. UTAH CODE, tit. 34A, ch. 5
Vermont	Public and private employers with one or more employees, employment agencies, and labor organizations that represent at least five employees.	Vermont Human Rights Commission 135 State St., Drawer 33 Montpelier, VT 05633 (802) 828-2480 or (800) 416-2010 www.hrc.state.vt.us	Race, color, religion, sex, sexual orientation, national origin, ancestry, place of birth, age, HIV status, and physical/ mental condition. 21 VT. STAT. ANN. tit. 21, § 495
Virginia	Public and private employers and government contractors and subcontractors with contracts of more than $10,000.	Virginia Council on Human Rights 900 E. Main St. Pocahontas Bldg., 4th Fl Richmond, VA 23219 (804) 225-2292 or (800) 633-5510 chr.vipnet.org	Race, color, religion, national origin, sex, pregnancy, childbirth or related medical conditions, age, marital status, disability (mental or physical impairments), and genetic characteristics or test results. VA. CODE, § 2.2-3900 (Human Rights Act); § 40.1-28.7:1 (genetic characteristics and test results)
Washington	Employers with at least eight (8) employees, employment agencies, and labor organizations, but not nonprofit religious or sectarian organizations.	Washington State Human Rights Commission 711 S. Capitol Way, #402 P.O. Box 42490 Olympia, WA 98504 (360) 753-6770 or (800) 233-3247 www.hum.wa.gov	Age (40+), sex, marital status, family with children status, sexual orientation, race, creed, color, national origin, the presence of any sensory, mental or physical disability, use of a trained dog guide or service animal by a disabled person, the results of a HIV or Hepatitis C test, and using sick leave to care for a child or family member. WASH. REV. CODE §§ 49.12.157, 49.44.090, 49.60.010, 49.60.030, 49.60.172, 49.60.180
West Virginia	The state and its political subdivisions, employers with at least 12 persons within the state, employment agencies, and labor organizations, but not private clubs.	West Virginia Human Rights Commission 1321 Plaza E, Rm 108A Charleston, WV 25301 (304) 558-2616 or (888) 676-5546 www.wvf.state.wv.us/wvhrc	Race, religion, color, national origin, ancestry, sex, age (40+), blindness, disability, pregnancy, and tobacco use outside the workplace. W.VA. CODE §§ 5-11-1 et seq.

Jurisdiction	Covered Employers	Enforcement Agency	Categories Protected/ Relevant Statute
Wisconsin	The state and its agencies, private employers, employment agencies, and labor organizations, but not social clubs or fraternal societies with respect to a particular job for which the club or society seeks to employ or employs a member.	Wisconsin Department of Workforce Development Equal Rights Division 201 E. Washington Ave., Rm A300 P.O. Box 8928 Madison, WI 53708 (608) 266-6860 www.dwd.stat.wi.us	Age (40+), race, creed, color, genetic testing, disability, marital status, sex (including pregnancy, childbirth, maternity leave, or related medical condition), national origin, ancestry, sexual orientation, arrest or conviction record, membership in the national guard or military service, use/nonuse of lawful products off the employers premises during nonworking hours, and lie detector testing. WIS. STAT. §§ 103.15, 111.31-111.395
Wyoming	The state and its political subdivisions, employers with two or more employees, employment agencies, and labor organizations, but not religious organizations or associations.	Wyoming Dept. of Employment Labor Standards Office 1510 E. Pershing Blvd., West Wing Cheyenne, WY 82002 (307) 777-7261 wydoe.state.wy.us	Age (40+), sex, race, creed, color, national origin, ancestry, disability, and use/ nonuse of tobacco products. WYO. STAT. §§ 27-4-302, 27-9-105

TEMPLATE OFFER LETTER

[COMPANY LETTERHEAD]

_____, 200_

[Name]

[Address]

Dear _____:

I am pleased to offer you employment with _____. This letter sets forth the terms and conditions of your employment with _____. To be certain that you understand and agree with the terms of this employment offer, please review this letter, which you will need to sign as a condition of employment. Once you have signed and dated this letter and the attached agreements where indicated, return them to _____, by no later than _____, 200_. This offer is conditioned upon your presenting evidence of your authorization to work in the United States and your identity sufficient to allow _____ to complete the Form I-9 required by law.

Position: Your position will be _____, reporting to _____.

Start Date: Your first day of employment will be _____, 200_, unless you and _____ later agree in writing to a different start date.

Base Salary: Your annual base salary will be $_____. Your base salary will be reviewed from time to time by _____ to determine whether, in _____'s judgment, your base salary should be changed.

[_Option 1: Your base salary will be paid in accordance with _____'s normal payroll procedures and will be subject to applicable withholding required by law.] [Option 2: Your base salary will be paid in two equal installments per month, less applicable withholding required by law.] [Option 3: Your base salary will be paid at the end of each two-week period, less applicable withholding required by law._]

Bonuses: You will be eligible to participate in any bonus programs _____ may decide to establish from time to time to the same extent as other employees at your level with the company, subject to the provisions of the applicable bonus program.

[OPTIONAL – Stock Options: _____ will recommend to its Board of Directors that you be granted an option to purchase [an amount of shares/ # of shares] of _____'s Common Stock. The terms and conditions of the option grant will be set out in a stock option agreement that will be executed by you and _____at the time the grant is made and will be subject to and governed by the terms of the applicable stock option plan adopted by the Board of Directors. During your employment, _____'s Board of Directors may from time to time grant _____ employees at your level additional options to purchase shares of common stock.]

Major Responsibilities: Your primary responsibilities will be those normally associated with the position of _____, including but not limited to [brief description of major duty or duties], as well as such other duties as your supervisor may from time to time assign to you. _____ requires that you perform your assigned duties to the best of your ability and faithfully observe your obligations to _____. From time to time, _____ may impose additional or more specific work rules for you.

Conflicting Activities: While employed by _____, you may not work as an employee or consultant of any other organization or engage in any other activities which conflict or interfere with your obligations to _____, without the express prior written approval of _____. It is understood that you will not be employed by any other person or organization when you commence employment with _____.

At-Will Employment: Your employment with _____ is for no specified duration and is at the will of both you and _____, which means that either you or _____ may end the employment relationship at any time for any reason, with or without notice. The at-will nature of your employment may not be altered by any policy, practice, or representation of _____, but only by a written agreement expressly modifying or waiving it, signed both by you and _____'s CEO.

Reimbursements: You will be reimbursed on a regular basis for reasonable, necessary, and properly documented business and travel expenses incurred for the purpose of conducting _____'s business, in accordance with Company policy.

Benefits: You will be eligible to participate in any employee benefit plans or programs maintained or established by _____, including but not limited to [vacation and sick leave, group health benefits, deferred compensation, life insurance, etc.] to the same extent as other employees at your level within _____, subject to the generally applicable terms and conditions of the plan or program in question and the determination of any committee administering such plan or program.

Confidential Information and Inventions: Your employment is conditioned upon your execution, return of, and adherence to the Company's standard Confidential Information, Nonsolicitation and Invention Assignment Agreement [or however the agreement is titled].

Third Party Information: You agree that you will not, during your employment with _____, improperly use or disclose any proprietary information or trade secrets of any former or concurrent employer or other person or entity and that you will not bring onto the premises of _____ any unpublished document or proprietary information belonging to any such employer, person, or entity unless consented to in writing by such employer, person, or entity.

Arbitration: You and the Company agree to submit all disputes arising out of your employment to final and binding arbitration before an arbitrator associated with the American Arbitration Association [**option:** provided that disputes relating to matters dealt with in the Confidential Information, Nonsolicitation and Invention Assignment Agreement between you and the Company will be subject to the terms of that agreement]. The arbitrator selected will have the authority to grant you or the Company or both all remedies otherwise available by law. The arbitrator will be mutually agreed to by you and the Company. In the event we cannot agree upon the arbitrator within fifteen (15) days of submission of notice of intent to arbitrate a dispute, the arbitrator will be selected from a neutral panel pursuant to the Employment Dispute Resolution Rules of the American Arbitration Association ("AAA Rules").[**Alternatively:** pursuant to the applicable rules of Judicial Arbitration and Mediation Services/Endispute ("JAMS") ("JAMS Rules").] The arbitration will be conducted in accordance with the AAA Rules [JAMS Rules], and will provide (i) for written discovery and depositions adequate to give the parties access to documents and witnesses that the arbitrator concludes are essential to the dispute and (ii) for a written decision by the arbitrator that includes the essential findings and conclusions upon which the decision is based. Except in disputes where you assert a claim under a state or federal statute prohibiting discrimination in employment or where otherwise required by law (an "*Excepted Claim*"), you and the Company will split equally the fees and administrative costs charged by the arbitrator and AAA [JAMS]. (In Excepted Claim disputes, you will be required to pay only an amount equal to the fee you would have to pay to file a complaint in state or federal court.) This mutual agreement to arbitrate disputes does not limit either your or the Company's right to seek equitable relief from a court, including but not limited to injunctive relief, pending the resolution of a dispute by arbitration..

Miscellaneous: This letter agreement is to be governed by [*State Name*] law, without respect to [*State Name*]'s choice of law provisions. This agreement is the sole and entire agreement between you and _____ with respect to the subject of your employment and supersedes all prior or contemporaneous agreements or negotiations on that subject. This agreement may not be modified except in a writing signed by the _____ of _____ and you. The unenforceability of any provision of this letter agreement will not affect the validity or enforceability of any other provision of the agreement. This letter agreement may be executed in two or more counterparts, which together will constitute the entire agreement.

Sincerely, _____
I have reviewed and understand the terms and conditions set forth in this letter and agree to them.

Dated: _____   _____
                               Name

COMPUTER, E-MAIL, AND INTERNET USE POLICY

The computer and e-mail systems and internet access to global electronic information resources on the World Wide Web are provided by [COMPANY], Inc. ("the Company") to assist employees in performing their job duties and obtaining work-related data and technology. The following guidelines have been established to help ensure responsible and productive use of the computer and e-mail systems and the internet. While computer, e-mail, and internet usage is intended for job-related activities, incidental and occasional brief personal use is permitted within reasonable limits.

I. The Use of Computers, E-Mail, and the Internet

The equipment, services, and technology that comprise our computer and e-mail systems and that provide access to the internet remain at all times the property of the Company. All data that is composed, transmitted, accessed, or received via our computer, e-mail, and internet systems is considered to be part of the official records of the Company and, as such, is subject to disclosure to the Company, law enforcement, or other third parties. Consequently, employees should always ensure that the information transmitted through and contained in the computer, e-mail, and internet systems is accurate, appropriate, ethical, and lawful. *The Company reserves the right, in its sole discretion, without notice, to access, monitor, read, or download any data composed, transmitted, accessed, or received through or stored in our computer, e-mail, or internet systems.*

Passwords are intended to prevent unauthorized access to information. Passwords do not confer any right of privacy upon any employee of the Company. Thus, even though employees may maintain passwords for accessing the computer system, employees must not expect that any information maintained on system, including e-mail and voice mail messages, are private. Employees are expected to maintain their passwords as confidential. Employees must not share passwords and must not access coworkers' systems without express authorization.

The Company purchases and licenses the use of various computer software for business purposes and does not own the copyright to this software or its related documentation. Unless authorized by the software developer, the Company does not have the right to reproduce such software for use on more than one computer. Employees may only use software on local area networks or on multiple machines according to the software license agreement. The Company prohibits the illegal duplication of software and its related documentation.

Internet and e-mail users should take the necessary anti-virus precautions before downloading or copying any file from the internet or e-mail. All downloaded files are to be checked for viruses; all compressed files are to be checked before and after decompression.

The Company strives to maintain a workplace free of harassment and discrimination, and one that is sensitive to the diversity of its employees. Therefore, the Company prohibits the use of the computer and e-mail systems and the internet in ways that are disruptive, offensive to others, or harmful to morale.

Data that is composed, transmitted, accessed, received, or displayed via the computer or e-mail systems or the internet must not contain content that could be considered discriminatory, offensive, obscene, threatening, harassing, intimidating, or disruptive to any employee or other person. Examples of unacceptable content may include, but are not limited to, sexual comments, messages, cartoons, or images; racial or ethnic slurs or comments; off-color jokes; comments or images that could reasonably offend someone on the basis of sex, gender, race, color, religion, national origin, creed, citizenship status, ancestry, age, sexual orientation, marital status, pregnancy, cancer-related medical condition, mental and physical disability (actual or perceived), veteran status, or any other characteristic protected by applicable law or local ordinance; or other content that may be construed as harassment or discrimination.

The following are examples of previously stated or additional conduct that is prohibited and can result in disciplinary action, up to and including termination of employment:

- Sending or posting discriminatory, harassing, or threatening messages or images
- Sending or posting the Company's confidential business information, proprietary information, or trade secrets, except as required to perform the Company's business

- Engaging in unauthorized transactions that may incur a cost to the company or initiate unwanted internet services and transmissions
- Sending or posting messages or material that could damage the Company's image or reputation
- Participating in the viewing or exchange of pornography or obscene materials
- Sending or posting messages that defame or slander other individuals
- Jeopardizing the security of the Company's electronic communications systems
- Sending or posting messages that disparage another organization's products or services
- Passing off personal views as representing those of the Company
- Sending anonymous e-mail messages
- Engaging in illegal activities

Employees who violate this policy will be subject to disciplinary action, up to and including termination of employment. Employees should notify their supervisor, the network administrator, human resources, the president, or a person designated in writing by the president upon learning of a violation of this policy.

II. Use of Phone and Voice Mail Systems

The telephone and voice mail systems are provided for business purposes. Personal calls should be limited in number and length. The telephone and voice mail systems remain at all times the property of the Company. The Company reserves the right, in its sole discretion, without notice, to access these systems, including employees' voice mail.

III. Use of Other Equipment and Property

All equipment, working areas including desks, and other areas including storage spaces on the Company's premises, and all materials issued to or created by employees of the Company during their employment, remain at all times the property of the Company. The Company reserves the right, in its sole discretion, without notice, to open, access, or search any of its equipment, working areas, or other areas, and to retrieve or review any of its materials.

When using the Company's property, employees are expected to exercise care, perform required maintenance, and follow all operating instructions, safety standards, and guidelines. Employees should notify their supervisor if they have any questions or if any equipment or machines appear to be damaged, defective, or in need of repair. Prompt reporting of damages, defects, and the need for repairs could prevent deterioration of equipment and possible injury.

Employees are responsible for all the Company property, including materials and written information issued to them or in their possession. All the Company property must be returned on or before an employee's last day of work.

The Company's name, letterhead, supplies, and copy services are for the Company's business and may not be used for personal needs. Use of company postage for personal correspondence is not permitted. The reputation and influence of the Company can be adversely affected by the way in which its name or letterhead are used. Company letterhead cannot be used for correspondence of a purely personal nature without prior approval of the president or any person designated in writing by the president.

IV. Employee Acknowledgment

I have read, understand, and agree to abide by these guidelines.

_____

Employee Signature   Date

HIPAA POLICY FOR EMPLOYERS HANDLING PROTECTED HEALTH INFORMATION

What Do the HIPAA Privacy Rules Mean To Me?

From the perspective of an employee who has day-to-day contact with protected health information or "PHI," there are four principal things to remember:

1. PHI should be kept confidential at all times. Treat PHI as you would your pocketbook or wallet.

2. Only certain employees of the Company are entitled to access PHI, and PHI may not be shared for any reason with unauthorized employees.

3. PHI cannot be used for "employment" decisions (hiring, firing, promotions, or fixing compensation) or for the Company's non-health plans and programs, such as its Family and Medical Leave Act ("FMLA") program or its disability plans.

4. Even if medical information about employees and their dependents is not PHI because it does not have the necessary connection with the Company's health plans, employees should still be very sensitive about its confidentiality.

Recognizing PHI

PHI is information about an individual's mental or physical health (past, present, or future) that identifies the individual (or could be used to do so) and has a connection with one of the Company's health plans. The Company's health plans are its medical, dental, vision, employee assistance, and health care flexible spending account (Medcap) plans. PHI also includes information about payment for an individual's health care and information held by a health plan as to whether an individual is enrolled in or disenrolled from the plan.

The following are examples of PHI:

- A participant in the Company's medical plan comes to you and complains that an insurer has denied a claim for reimbursement of his other expenses for a medical procedure or questions the amount paid. When you call the insurer to discuss the claim and information about the participant's procedure is discussed, PHI is involved.

- A report from the Company's health care flexible spending account plan provider that notes the Social Security numbers of participants in the plan with the amounts of the claims reimbursed to each participant during the preceding month would constitute PHI.

- A monthly large claims report from a health care provider notes that an individual from the Company location Y (which has only five employees) made a large claim in a certain amount may be PHI as the identity of the participant in question might reasonably be deduced (for example, you may know that one of the five employees has recently been on STD for a period).

Practical Tips for Safeguarding PHI in the Workplace

PHI should be kept confidential at all times. Treat PHI as you would your pocketbook or wallet. Access to areas (individual offices and workstations) where PHI is maintained should be monitored, as appropriate, for employees, business associates, and visitors. All PHI in paper form should be kept in drawers, cabinets, or offices that are locked when you leave your workstation for any reason. If you receive or transmit PHI electronically:

- Ensure that your computer screen is not visible to employees who are not authorized to access PHI or who do not need to know about the on-screen information.

- Ensure that computer monitors are not located in high-traffic areas

- Make sure that your computer is turned off when you leave your workstation. Place an automatic log-off in the system that will log your computer off after several minutes if no activity occurs.

- Use email encryption where PHI needs to be transmitted internally within the Company. Please contact the IT Help Desk for the encryption software package if not already installed at your workstation.

- Use an additional "boot-up" password. Please contact the IT Help Desk to add a boot-up password to your workstation.

- Do not use a "remember password" feature for access to your computer.

Paper or electronic records containing PHI concerning an individual should be kept in a separate PHI file for that individual. These records should not be kept in the employee's general personnel file or even in a "medical" file that contains non-PHI medical information about the employee such as disability plan determinations, sick leave doctors certificates, or FMLA request information.

All PHI should be promptly returned to the relevant health plan provider or participant or destroyed once it is no longer needed:

- All paper records containing PHI that are to be destroyed should be shredded as soon as practicable or placed in locked shredding bins until destroyed. They should not be discarded in ordinary wastebaskets.

- Electronic PHI that is no longer needed should be deleted.

Ensure that private areas and enclosed spaces are available for employee discussions about health plan issues. If you are in a cubicle and do not have a private office, ensure that a meeting room is available for discussions with employees involving PHI and close the door during discussions.

Take steps to ensure confidentiality during telephone discussions regarding PHI with individuals, relatives, and service providers. If you cannot conduct the conversation in an office with the door closed, ensure that your voice is low and that names and medical diagnoses are used as little as possible. Try not to leave voice mail messages that mention names and medical diagnoses.

Designate a fax machine for PHI transmissions and place it in a secure location. Alternatively, ensure that an authorized individual monitors the fax machine for confidential transmissions. If PHI must be faxed, verify the fax number and request immediate pick-up of the faxed information.

Protect hardware to ensure that only authorized personnel have access to the hardware and that the hard drive is cleared of all data when the hardware is discarded.

Consider steps to protect records containing PHI against threats such as fire and burglary. Install backup systems for emergencies and consider off-site storage of backup data.

Only Authorized Individuals may Access Records Containing PHI

Only certain employees of the Company are entitled to access PHI. These are:

- Designated human resources employees

- All Benefits Department employees

- The individual appointed as privacy official (the "Privacy Official") and contact person responsible for receiving complaints and providing further information under the privacy rules and their delegates, and

- Any temporary employee under the control of the Company or an Affiliate performing services for or on behalf of any of the above listed employees or classes of employees.

This list may be updated from time to time.

Because HR Generalists may be involved in employment decisions, HR Generalists are generally not entitled to access PHI. Should matters involving PHI require escalation to management, you should contact [name of designated "Privacy Official" AND contact information (telephone and email address)].

Should any unauthorized employee need or request access to PHI, please contact [name of designated "Privacy Official" AND contact information (telephone and email address)].

Can the Company use PHI for other employment purposes matters such as the administration of its other benefit programs?

The Company, as a health plan sponsor, cannot use an individual's PHI for employment related purposes such as for its other benefit plans and programs without the individual's express authorization.

Of course, health information concerning an individual created by a Company health plan (which is PHI) cannot be used in making employment decisions about the individual, such as promotion or compensation decisions.

In addition, PHI cannot be used by the Company to assess an individual's eligibility for FMLA leave, to determine whether the individual is disabled for the purposes of its disability plans, or to make an Americans With Disabilities Act ("ADA") reasonable accommodation assessment without the individual's written authorization. That means that you may not contact the Company's health plan providers to obtain information on an employee's health condition for these (non-health plan) purposes. However, it is more likely that the information that the Company receives for these non-health plan purposes comes from outside health care providers (the employees' physicians) or directly from the affected employees. The Company does not have any HIPAA privacy concerns with this information because it does not come from a Company group health plan. The outside health care provider is likely to be a covered entity under the privacy rules, and will generally require the employee to provide an authorization before it will release the information to the Company. However, once in the Company's records, the health information forms part of the Company's "employment records" and is *not* PHI.

How should medical information relating to drug testing be handled?

The HIPAA privacy rules do not affect employment-related drug tests as long as the Company does not seek to obtain this health information *from its group health plans*. The Company receives this sort of testing information from an outside vendor, which is a covered health care provider under the HIPAA privacy rules and requires an authorization from the employee before it will release the employee's drug testing information to the Company. This authorization is required from all new employees and is included in offer packages. Once the drug testing information on a new employee is released by the outside vendor to the Company, the information will form part of the Company's "employment records" for HIPAA privacy purposes and will *not* be PHI.

How should individually identifiable health information that is *not* PHI be treated?

Although individually identifiable health information may not be PHI, employers should be sensitive to its confidentiality. Many other laws, both state and federal, provide confidentiality protections. For example, medical information obtained by an employer for ADA purposes is subject to special confidentiality requirements, including the requirement that the information be kept in separate files apart from personnel records. FMLA requires that health information provided by an employee in support of a request for FMLA leave be kept confidential. Many state privacy laws protect the privacy of various categories of personal health information. You should continue to maintain the confidentially of health information that is not PHI in accordance with the Company's standard practices.

The HIPAA privacy rules add to a web of federal and state laws that require employers to keep the personal health information of their employees and their dependents confidential and to ensure that employment decisions are not based on employees' health conditions or treatment. All sorts of medical information about individuals should be kept separately from other personnel information, under lock and key, and made available to persons only on a strict need-to-know basis. Employees should continue to be very sensitive to the confidentiality of employee health information in all contexts.

Please direct any questions on the HIPAA privacy rules to [name of designated "Privacy Official" AND contact information (telephone and email address)].

AUTHORIZATION FOR RELEASE OF HEALTH INFORMATION OR RECORDS

Section A

I authorize the disclosure to and use by my employer, [COMPANY], of my personal health information as described in Section B below. I understand this authorization is voluntary and made to confirm my directions. I hereby give my permission to:

_____

[name of physician or other health care provider or name of group health plan]

to disclose my personal health information in the manner described herein.

Name: _____

Address: _____

Telephone: _____ Member Number: _____

Section B: Personal Health Information to Be Disclosed

Describe the personal health information you are authorizing to be used and/or disclosed:

_____

_____

_____

Persons/Entities Authorized to Receive and Use

Name and address or description of the persons and/or entities to whom you are authorizing the plan/provider named above to disclose or let use the personal health information described above:

_____

Name of Individual

_____

Title

Purpose of the Disclosure

The disclosure is being made for the following reason:

_____

_____

_____

Right to Revoke

I may revoke this authorization at any time by notifying [COMPANY], Inc., in writing to [name], [title], [COMPANY], [address] or fax: [fax number]. I understand that the revocation is effective only after it is received and logged by [COMPANY]. I further understand that if I revoke my authorization and when the revocation is effective, [name of doctor or other provider or name of health plan from which records are sought] will no longer disclose medical information about me for the reasons covered by the written authorization, except to the extent of information released or action taken in reliance upon the authorization prior to the revocation. If I do not revoke it, this authorization will expire on [date or event]. I understand and agree that I will refer to the Privacy Notice of [name of provider/plan] for any further exceptions to my right to revoke this authorization.

Redisclosure

I understand that after the information referenced above is disclosed, federal law might not protect it, and the recipient might redisclose it in a manner consistent with this authorization and consistent with applicable law.

Term and Condition of Employment

I understand that my initial and continued employment and position are subject to my agreement to this authorization and any additional authorization [COMPANY] requests.

Entitlement to a Copy

I understand that I am entitled to receive a copy of this authorization after I sign it and that I may see and copy the information described on this form if I ask for it.

Conditioning Benefits or Treatment

Neither the plan or provider to whom this authorization is given nor the person/organization authorized to receive my PHI may condition treatment, payment, enrollment, or eligibility for benefits on whether or not I sign this authorization.

SIGNATURE

I, _____, have had full opportunity to read and consider the contents of this authorization, and I confirm that the contents are consistent with my direction to the plan named above. I understand that, by signing this form, I am confirming my authorization that the plan named above may use and/or disclose to the persons and/or organizations named in this form the nonpublic personal health information described in this form.

Signature: _____ Date: _____

PERSONAL REPRESENTATIVES SECTION

If a personal representative on behalf of the individual signs this authorization, complete the following:

Signature of Personal Representative: _____

Personal Representative's Name: _____

Description of Representative's authority to act: _____

SAMPLE TELECOMMUTING AGREEMENT

This Telecommuting Agreement is entered into as of _____, 200__ between _____,

a _____ corporation with its principal offices located at _____ ("Company"),

and _____, a resident of _____ ("Employee").

Company and Employee agree to participate in the telecommuting program and adhere to the terms and conditions set forth in this agreement. This agreement is effective in conjunction with Employee's existing employment contract and any other agreements between the parties.

This telecommuting opportunity is an alternative approach to fulfilling Company's work requirements. It is not to be construed as an employee benefit that creates any right to telecommute on the part of Employee. The option to allow Employee to telecommute remains at the discretion of Company.

The following criteria must be satisfied in order for Employee to be eligible for participate in the telecommuting program.

1. **Eligibility.** Telecommuting is available for employees that meet the following criteria:

   a. Employees who have worked at Company for more than one year.

   b. Employees who have demonstrated an ability to work independently.

   c. Employees who do not have an employment record reflecting poor performance.

2. **Duration of Agreement.** The duration of this agreement is subject to the discretion of Company.

3. **Minimum Requirements for Home Office.** Telecommuters must have an appropriate work space available to allow for maximum productivity. This space must be separate from the living area of the home unless otherwise approved by Company. This space will constitute the "work area" and Employee must limit performance of the job duties to this location unless otherwise approved by Company.

4. **Work Hours.** Employee shall work a total of _____hours per _____. These hours are to be designated as "work hours." Employee must be able to be contacted via telephone, e-mail, pager, or fax during Company's ordinary working hours.

5. **Overtime.** Employee shall not work any hours in excess of the above agreed amount unless prior approval is obtained from Company.

6. **Record-Keeping Requirements.** Employee shall record all hours and tasks accomplished. These records and any other work related documentation are the property of Company.

7. **Business-Owned Equipment.** All office equipment, supplies, and software supplied by Company to Employee shall remain the exclusive property of Company. Employee shall be liable for any lost or damaged items, regardless of fault, that are under the care and control of Employee and exceed normal wear and tear. Equipment owned by Company shall be maintain and serviced at the expense of Company. Any communication or correspondence that takes place through the use of Company's equipment is not private and is subject to review by Company.

8. **Employee-Owned Equipment.** All office equipment, supplies, and software that are supplied by Employee shall remain the property of Employee. Company is not liable for any lost or damaged items that are in the care and control of Employee. Company is also not responsible for any wear on the equipment due to regular use.

9. **Inspection**. Company reserves the right to inspect the "work area" of Employee's home for the purpose of ascertaining that it is a safe working environment. This includes the equipment used by Employee in the work area regardless of whether Company or Employee is the owner of the equipment.

10. **Liability**. Company shall not be liable for any damages that occur to Employee's home due to participation in this telecommuting agreement or any other cause.

11. **Workers' Compensation**. Employee is still covered by workers' compensation if Employee is injured in the course of performing duties in the designated work area during work hours. Employee shall promptly report any such injuries to Employer.

12. **Reimbursement**. Company shall not be responsible for any operating costs that accrue from participation in this telecommuting agreement, unless otherwise agreed by the parties. Employee does not give up any right to reimbursement that would otherwise be warranted for any expenses incurred while conducting business for Company.

13. **Pay**. All pay, leave, and travel entitlement shall be accrued in the same manner as if Employee were not telecommuting.

14. **Leave**. Employee must request for and gain approval for any leave taken in the same manner as if Employee were not telecommuting.

15. **Security Measures**. Employee shall continue to follow Employer's safeguards to protect the records and assets of Company. All work product done at the home work area shall be treated in the same manner as work product from Company's primary location and is the property of Company. Employee shall safeguard all records, computer files, and correspondence for return to Company's primary location. Employee shall back up and save computer files regularly.

16. **Measurement of Performance**. Company shall continue it regular evaluation of Employee's performance, based on work product and record keeping.

17. **Childcare**. This telecommuting agreement does not represent an approval to eliminate Employee's normal childcare requirements during work hours. Employees with small children shall continue to make alternative childcare arrangements.

18. **Modifications; Reasonable Accommodation**. Any amendments or modifications to this agreement shall be in writing and signed and dated by Employer and Employee. An employee who requests a modification to this telecommuting agreement as a reasonable accommodation for a disability shall follow the Employer's reasonable accommodation request procedure available at ___[*fill in web address or other location where employee can obtain reasonable accommodation request procedure*].

19. **Termination of Agreement**. Employee's failure to comply with the terms and conditions of this agreement may, at Company's sole discretion, result in the termination of this telecommuting agreement by Company. If this agreement is terminated, all equipment, work product, papers, and records that are the property of Company shall be returned to Company by Employee within one week of termination.

_____

Employee Signature

_____

Date

NEW EMPLOYEE ORIENTATION TO PROTECT TRADE SECRETS

Offer Letter Guidelines

The following language may be inserted into employee-specific offer letters from your company:

This offer is being extended to you solely based on your skill, experience, education, and our view of your potential for success here. [The COMPANY] does not want, and you must never use or disclose during your employment with [The COMPANY], any confidential or proprietary information or trade secrets from any previous employer. Consequently, we instruct you to abide by any contractual or legal obligations which you have to maintain the confidentiality of information which you are obligated to protect. By accepting employment with [The COMPANY], you agree not to use or disclose proprietary information or trade secrets from any previous employer in the course of performing your duties for [The COMPANY] under any circumstances. You must not keep any items or materials related to your former employer or use such materials during your employment with [The COMPANY]. If you have any questions regarding what constitutes such information, I encourage you to contact your former employer(s).

As a condition of your employment with [The COMPANY], you must sign and abide by [The COMPANY] Proprietary Information And Inventions Agreement and [The COMPANY] New Employee Proprietary Information Guidelines. By so doing, you are representing that your performance as an employee of [The COMPANY] does not and will not breach any agreement with any prior employer. Further, by signing these agreements, you are representing that you have not and will not enter into any agreement in conflict with your employment with [The COMPANY].

New Employee Proprietary Information Guidelines

As a new employee of [The COMPANY] it is important that you read and follow these guidelines. [The COMPANY] respects the right of every company to protect its confidential and proprietary information. No company employee should have, use, or disclose at [The COMPANY], any confidential or proprietary information of any other company. Similarly, no company employee should have, use, or disclose any confidential or trade secret information of [The COMPANY], except as necessary to perform his or her duties as a company employee.

Understand the Company's Intellectual Property Agreement

All Company employees must sign [The COMPANY]'s Intellectual Property Agreement. This Agreement prohibits you from improperly using or disclosing any confidential information or trade secrets of any former employer. It is critical that you understand your obligations to [The COMPANY] under this Agreement. If you have any questions about it, contact a member of the human resources department immediately.

Return All Property Belonging to Your Former Employer

DO return any property of your former employer **immediately**. This includes all business, marketing, sales, technical, financial, and other company documents, any keys, badges, equipment (including laptop computer, computer disks, hardware, modems, cell phones, pagers, etc.), or other tangible property, and any calendars, notebooks, Rolodexes™ in paper or electronic form, Daytimers,™ and other business papers concerning your former employer's business.

DO NOT bring any property or papers of your former employer onto the company's premises, and DO NOT use any such material for **any** purpose while working for [The COMPANY].

Protect Proprietary Information of Your Former Employer and the Company

DO NOT use **any** confidential or proprietary information of any former employer in performing your job duties for the Company, and DO NOT disclose such information to any company employee.

DO NOT access your former employer's e-mail, voice mail, or other computer systems for any purpose (either directly or by forwarding it to some other e-mail or voice mail address), **unless** your former employer has authorized it **in writing**.

DO NOT disclose the company's confidential and proprietary information to anyone outside of the company, unless you are expressly authorized to do so.

DO NOT use any of the company's confidential or proprietary information except for the company's benefit, and only as necessary to do your job as a [The COMPANY] employee.

Soliciting Employees of Your Former Employer

Some companies include provisions in their proprietary information agreements prohibiting employees who leave the company from soliciting its employees to work elsewhere for a period of time after termination of employment. Comply with any reasonable agreement you signed prohibiting you from soliciting employees of your former employer. If you have questions about your former employer's nonsolicitation clause, please contact a member of the human resources department.

If you are subject to a reasonable nonsolicitation clause, follow these guidelines:

Do not initiate discussions with employees of your former employer about the possibility of working for [The COMPANY]. However, you can inform them that you are now working at [The COMPANY].

If your friends or acquaintances at your former employer contact you about possible employment at [The COMPANY], tell them that you can **not** talk with them about joining [The COMPANY]. Refer them to [The COMPANY] human resources department. Do not participate in interviews or recruiting functions (e.g., dinners or lunches) with employees of your former employer.

When In Doubt, Ask

If you have any questions about [The COMPANY]'s proprietary information guidelines, or if you become aware of possible violations of these guidelines, contact a member of [The COMPANY]'s human resources department or legal department immediately.

Acknowledgment

I have read the above New Employee Guidelines; I understand them; and I will abide by them at all times while employed at [The COMPANY].

Date: _____   _____

                                                      Signature

                                                 _____

                                                 Name of Employee (typed or printed)

SCREENING FOR RESTRICTIVE COVENANTS

Interview Questions

This form is designed to help employers discover whether a prospective employee has proprietary information, or nonsolicitation and noncompetition obligations to current or past employers.

Have you signed any type of agreement with a current or prior employer which could prevent or interfere with your working for [The COMPANY]?　❑ Yes　❑ No

For example, do you have a:

* A fixed-term employment agreement?　❑ Yes　❑ No

* A noncompete agreement?　❑ Yes　❑ No

* A stock option agreement with forfeiture provisions?　❑ Yes　❑ No

Do any of your former co-workers (at any employer) now work for [The COMPANY]?　❑ Yes　❑ No

If so, have you talked to any of them about working at [The COMPANY]?　❑ Yes　❑ No

Have you discussed possible employment at [The COMPANY] with any current employees of your current employer?　❑ Yes　❑ No

Have you signed any type of nonsolicitation agreement that could prevent you from soliciting your current or any prior employer's employees, suppliers, independent contractors or customers?　❑ Yes　❑ No

Have you removed or not returned any property of any kind belonging to your current or most recent employer?　❑ Yes　❑ No

For example, do you have any:

* Business documents (e.g., PowerPoint presentations, marketing plans, product descriptions, manufacturing and product plans, business strategies, customer lists and information, sales information, financial information, or forecasts, personnel information, or correspondence)?　❑ Yes　❑ No

* Software, source code, technical specifications, hardware designs and prototypes, or any other technical documents?　❑ Yes　❑ No

* Keys, badges, credit cards, or equipment (e.g., a laptop, computer disks, hardware, modem, cell phone, or pager)?　❑ Yes　❑ No

* Have you made or forwarded copies of any of your voice mail or e-mail messages received at your former employer?　❑ Yes　❑ No

Any job offer from [The COMPANY] would be conditioned upon your not having, using, or disclosing at [The COMPANY] any confidential or trade secret information of your former employers.

If the prospective employee answered "yes" to any of the above questions, please ask them to explain, and note the explanations below:

_____

_____

_____

CONFIDENTIAL INFORMATION, NONSOLICITATION, AND INVENTION ASSIGNMENT AGREEMENT

THIS CONFIDENTIAL INFORMATION, NONSOLICITATION, AND INVENTION ASSIGNMENT AGREEMENT (*"Agreement"*) is made and entered into as of the date set forth below (*"Effective Date"*) by and between _____, and _____ corporation, and the undersigned individual (*"Employee"*), on the other. Unless the context otherwise requires, the term "Company" shall also include all subsidiary, parent, or related corporations of Company.

Agreement

Employee acknowledges that Employee's employment by Company, creates a relationship of confidence and trust between Employee and Company with respect to all Confidential Information (as defined below) of Company.

In consideration and as a condition of Employee's employment by Company, the compensation paid therefore and the benefits received therefore, the sufficiency of which is hereby acknowledged, it is hereby agreed as follows:

Confidential Information

Confidentiality. Except as herein provided, Employee agrees that during and after termination of his or her employment with Company, he or she (i) shall keep Confidential Information (as defined below) confidential and shall not directly or indirectly, use, divulge, publish, or otherwise disclose or allow to be disclosed any aspect of Confidential Information without Company's prior written consent; (ii) shall refrain from any action or conduct which might reasonably or foreseeably be expected to compromise the confidentiality or proprietary nature of the Confidential Information; and (iii) shall follow recommendations made by the Board of Directors, officers, or supervisors of Company from time to time regarding Confidential Information. *"Confidential Information"* includes but is not limited to inventions (as defined in section 2(b)), trade secrets, confidential information, knowledge or data of Company, or any of its clients, customers, consultants, shareholders, licensees, licensors, vendors, or affiliates, that Employee may produce, obtain, or otherwise acquire or have access to during the course of his or her employment by Company (whether before or after the date of this Agreement), including but not limited to: business plans, records, and affairs; customer files and lists; special customer matters; sales practices; methods and techniques; merchandising concepts, strategies and plans; sources of supply and vendors; special business relationships with vendors, agents, and brokers; promotional materials and information; financial matters; mergers; acquisitions; equipment, technologies, and processes; selective personnel matters; inventions; developments; product specifications; procedures; pricing information; intellectual property; know-how; technical data; software programs; algorithms; operations and production costs; processes; designs; formulas; ideas; plans; devices; materials; and other similar matters which are confidential. All Confidential Information and all tangible materials containing Confidential Information are and shall remain the sole property of Company.

Limitation. Employee shall have no obligation under this Agreement to maintain in confidence any information that (i) is in the public domain at the time of disclosure, (ii) though originally Confidential Information, subsequently enters the public domain other than by breach of Employee's obligations hereunder or by breach of another person's or entity's confidentiality obligations, or (iii) is shown by documentary evidence to have been known by Employee prior to disclosure to Employee by Company.

Former Employer Information. Employee agrees that he or she has not and will not, during the term of his or her employment, (i) improperly use or disclose any proprietary information or trade secrets of any former employer or other person or entity with which Employee has an agreement or duty to keep in confidence information acquired by Employee, if any, or (ii) bring onto the premises of Company any document or confidential or proprietary information belonging to such employer, person or entity unless consented to in writing by such employer, person or entity. Employee will indemnify Company and hold it harmless from and against all claims, liabilities, damages, and expenses, including reasonable attorneys' fees and costs of suit, arising out of or in connection with any violation of the foregoing.

Third Party Information. Employee recognizes that Company may have received, and in the future may receive, from third parties their confidential or proprietary information subject to a duty on Company's part to maintain the confidentiality of such information and to use it only for certain limited purposes. Employee agrees that Employee owes Company and such third parties, during Employee's employment by Company and thereafter, a duty to hold all such confidential or proprietary information in the strictest confidence and not to disclose it to any person or firm and to use it in a manner consistent with, and for the limited purposes permitted by, Company's agreement with such third party.

Conflicting Activities. While employed by Company, Employee will not work as an employee or consultant of any other organization or engage in any other activities which conflict with the obligations to Company, without the express prior written approval of Company.

Inventions

Inventions Retained and Licensed. Employee has attached hereto, as *Exhibit A*, a list describing all inventions, ideas, improvements, designs, and discoveries, whether or not patentable and whether or not reduced to practice, original works of authorship and trade secrets made or conceived by or belonging to Employee (whether made solely by Employee or jointly with others) that (i) were developed by Employee prior to Employee's employment by Company (collectively, *"Prior Inventions"*), (ii) relate to Company's actual or proposed business, products, or research and development, and (iii) are not assigned to Company hereunder; or, if no such list is attached, Employee represents that there are no such Prior Inventions. Except to the extent set forth on *Exhibit A*, Employee hereby acknowledges that, if in the course of his or her service for Company, Employee incorporates into a Company product, process or machine a Prior Invention owned by Employee or in which he or she has an interest, Company is hereby granted and shall have a nonexclusive, royalty-free, irrevocable, perpetual, worldwide right and license to make, have made, modify, use, sell, sublicense, and otherwise distribute such Prior Invention as part of or in connection with such product, process, or machine.

Assignment of Inventions. Except as provided in Section 2(e) hereof, Employee hereby assigns and transfers to Company his or her entire right, title, and interest in and to all inventions, ideas, improvements, designs, and discoveries (the *"Inventions"*), whether or not patentable and whether or not reduced to practice, made, or conceived by Employee, whether solely by Employee or jointly with others, during the period of his or her employment with Company that (i) relate in any manner to the actual or demonstrably anticipated business, work, or research and development of Company, its affiliates, or subsidiaries, (ii) are developed in whole or in part on Company's time or using Company's equipment, supplies, facilities or Confidential Information, or (iii) result from or are suggested by any task assigned to Employee or any work performed by Employee for or on behalf of Company, its affiliates, or subsidiaries, or by the scope of Employee's duties and responsibilities with Company, its affiliates, or subsidiaries. In the event that Employee believes that he or she is entitled to ownership, either in whole or in part, of an Invention pursuant to Section 2(c) hereof, he or she shall notify Company of such in writing. Except in such cases as the CEO of Company confirms in writing that Employee is entitled to ownership, Employee agrees that all Inventions are the sole property of Company; provided, however, that this Agreement does not require assignment of an Invention that qualifies fully for protection under [check applicable state law]. Employee further acknowledges that all original works of authorship that are made by Employee, solely or jointly with others, within the scope of and during the period of Employee's employment by Company and that are protectible by copyright are "works made for hire," as defined in the U.S. Copyright Act.

Disclosure of Inventions. Employee agrees that in connection with any Invention: (i) Employee shall promptly disclose such Invention in writing to his or her immediate supervisor at Company (which shall be received in confidence by Company), with a copy to the Chief Executive Officer of Company, regardless of whether Employee believes the Invention is protected by [check applicable state law], in order to permit Company to claim rights to which it may be entitled under this Agreement; and (ii) Employee shall, at Company's request, promptly execute a written assignment of title to Company for any Invention required to be assigned by Section 2(b) (an *"Assignable Invention"*), and Employee will preserve any such Assignable Invention as Confidential Information of Company.

Patent and Copyright Registrations. Employee agrees to assist Company, or its designee, at Company's expense, in every proper way to secure Company's rights in the Assignable Inventions and any copyrights, patents, mask work rights, or other intellectual property rights relating thereto in any and all countries, including the disclosure to Company of all pertinent information and data with respect thereto, the execution of all applications, specifications, oaths, assignments, and other instruments that Company shall deem necessary in order to apply for and obtain such rights and in order to assign and convey to Company, its successors, assigns, and nominees the sole and exclusive rights, title, and interest in and to such Assignable Inventions, and any copyrights, patents, or other intellectual property rights relating thereto. Employee further agrees that his or her obligation to execute or cause to be executed, when it is in his or her power to do so, any such instrument or papers shall continue after the termination of Employee's employment by Company. If Company is unable because of Employee's mental or physical incapacity or for any other reason to secure Employee's signature to apply for or to pursue any application for any U.S. or foreign patents or copyright registrations covering Assignable Inventions or original works of authorship assigned to Company as above, then Employee hereby irrevocably designates and appoints Company and its duly authorized officers and agents as Employee's agent and attorney-in-fact, to act for and in Employee's behalf and stead to execute and file any such applications and to do all other lawfully permitted acts to further the prosecution and issuance of letters patent or copyright registrations thereon with the same legal force and effect as if executed by Employee.

Exception to Assignments. Employee understands that the provisions of this Agreement requiring assignment of Inventions to Company may not apply to any Invention that qualifies fully under the [check applicable state law]. Nevertheless, Employee shall advise Company promptly in writing of any Inventions that Employee believes meet the criteria in [check applicable state law] and are not otherwise disclosed on *Exhibit A.*

Other Obligations. Employee acknowledges that Company from time to time may have agreements with other persons or with the U.S. Government, or agencies thereof, that impose obligations or restrictions on Company regarding Inventions made during the course of work thereunder or regarding the confidential nature of such work. Employee agrees to be bound by all such obligations and restrictions and to take all action necessary to discharge the obligations of Company thereunder.

Return of Confidential Material

In the event of Employee's termination of employment with Company for any reason whatsoever, Employee agrees promptly to surrender and deliver to Company all records, materials, equipment, drawings, documents, and data of any nature pertaining to any Confidential Information or to his or her employment, and Employee will not retain or take with him or her any tangible materials or electronically stored data, containing or pertaining to any Confidential Information that Employee may produce, acquire, or obtain access to during the course of his or her employment.

Notification of New Employer

If employee leaves Company's employ, Employee hereby consents to Company notifying Employee's new employer about Employee's rights and obligations under this Agreement.

Nonsolicitation

[Check applicable state law.] Employee agrees that during the period of his or her service to Company and for _____ (_) years after the date of termination of his or her employment with Company, he or she will not, directly or indirectly, (i) induce, solicit, recruit, or encourage any employee of Company to leave the employ of Company, or (ii) solicit the business of any client or customer of Company (other than on behalf of Company).

Non-Hiring

[Check applicable state law.] Employee agrees that during the period of his or her service to Company and for one (1) year after the date of termination of his or her employment with Company, he or she will not employ, directly or indirectly, any employee of Company who was employed during Employee's employment with Company (other than on behalf of Company).

Representations

Employee agrees to execute any proper oath or verify any proper document required to carry out or evidence compliance with the terms of this Agreement. Employee represents that his or her performance of all the terms of this Agreement, and as an employee of Company, will not breach any agreement to keep in confidence proprietary information acquired by Employee in confidence or in trust prior to Employee's retention by Company. Employee has not entered into, and Employee agrees that he or she will not enter into, any oral or written agreement in conflict herewith.

Arbitration and Equitable Relief

Arbitration

Except as provided in Section (d), below, if there is a dispute between Employee and Company arising out of or relating to this Agreement, including but not limited to an alleged violation, breach or termination of this Agreement, the parties shall resolve the dispute by final and binding arbitration before a neutral arbitrator in accordance with the [applicable rules for such arbitration]. The arbitration shall occur in [city/town, state].

Selection of Arbitrator

There shall be a single arbitrator mutually agreed upon in writing by the parties. If the parties cannot agree upon the selection of an arbitrator within 30 days after the demand for arbitration given by one party to the other, the selection of the arbitrator shall be made by obtaining a list of seven arbitrators from the [location_____] office of the [Arbitration Provider]. After obtaining this list, the parties shall alternately strike names from the list, with Employee to be the party striking first. After each party has stricken three names from the list, the remaining name shall be the single arbitrator for this proceeding.

Arbitrator's Decision

The arbitrator may grant injunctions or other relief in such dispute or controversy. The decision of the arbitrator shall be final, conclusive, and binding on the parties to the arbitration. The arbitrator's award shall be in writing and shall be accompanied by a written opinion including the essential findings and conclusions upon which the decision is based. The arbitration will be conducted in accordance with the [Arbitration Provider] Rules. [In some states, including California] Notwithstanding anything to the contrary in the [Arbitration Provider] Rules, however, in disputes where Employee asserts a claim otherwise assertable under a state or federal statute prohibiting employment discrimination (*"a Statutory Claim"*), the arbitrator shall provide for written discovery and depositions adequate to give the parties access to documents and witnesses that are essential to the dispute. Judgment may be entered on the arbitrator's decision in any court having jurisdiction. The prevailing party, as determined by the arbitrator, in such arbitration shall be awarded its reasonable attorneys' fees and costs, in addition to any other remedy provided by the arbitrator. The parties shall split equally the fees and administrative costs charged by the arbitrator and [Arbitration Provider], except in disputes where Employee asserts a Statutory Claim against Company. In disputes in which disputes the asserts a Statutory Claim, Employee shall be required to pay only the [Arbitration Provider] filing fee to the extent such filing fee does not exceed the fee to file a complaint in state or federal court. Company shall pay the balance of the arbitrator's fees and administrative costs.

Equitable Remedies

Employee agrees that it would be impossible or inadequate to measure and calculate Company's damages from any breach of the covenants set forth in this Agreement. Accordingly, Employee agrees that if Employee breaches this Agreement, including without limitation the provisions of Paragraph 5, hereunder, Company will have available, in addition to any other right or remedy available, the right to obtain an injunction from a court of competent jurisdiction restraining such breach or threatened breach and to specific performance of any such provision of this Agreement. Employee further agrees that no bond or other security shall be required in obtaining such equitable relief and Employee hereby consents to such injunction's issuance and to the ordering of specific performance. In any legal proceeding commenced under this Paragraph 7(d), the losing party shall pay the prevailing party's actual attorneys' fees and expenses incurred in the preparation for, conduct of, or appeal or enforcement of judgment from the proceeding. The phrase "prevailing party" shall mean the party who is determined in the proceeding to have prevailed or who prevails by dismissal, default, or otherwise.

Governing Law; Consent to Personal Jurisdiction

This Agreement will be governed by the laws of the State of _____, without regard to the choice of law provisions thereof. Employee hereby expressly consents to the personal jurisdiction of the state and federal courts located in _____ for any lawsuit arising from or relating to this Agreement.

Entire Agreement

This Agreement sets forth the entire agreement and understanding between Company and Employee relating to the subject matter herein and merges all prior discussions and agreements between the parties with respect that subject matter. No modification of or amendment to this Agreement, nor any waiver of any rights under this Agreement, will be effective unless in writing signed by the party to be charged. Any subsequent change or changes in Employee's duties, salary or compensation will not affect the validity or scope of this Agreement.

Severability

If one or more of the provisions in this Agreement are deemed void by law, then the remaining provisions will continue in full force and effect.

Successors and Assigns

This Agreement will be binding upon Employee's heirs, executors, administrators, and other legal representatives and will be for the benefit of Company, its successors, and its assigns.

Counterparts

This Agreement may be signed in two counterparts, each of which shall be deemed an original and both of which shall together constitute one and the same instrument.

No Employment Contract

Nothing in this Agreement shall be construed to create a contract of employment, either express or implied-in-fact, for any fixed term or requiring cause for termination.

IN WITNESS WHEREOF, the parties hereto have executed this Agreement as of the Effective Date.

EFFECTIVE DATE: _____

[EMPLOYEE]   [COMPANY]

By:_____   By:_____

Name:_____   Name:_____

                                                  Title:_____

EXHIBIT A: List of Prior Inventions

	Title	Date Developed	Description
1.			
2.			
3.			
4.			
5.			
6.			
7.			
8.			
9.			

❏　　Additional sheets attached.

❏　　No prior inventions, improvements or works of authorship to disclose.

_____

Signature of Employee

_____

Print Name

Date: _____

NONDISCLOSURE, NONSOLICITATION, AND NONCOMPETITION AGREEMENT

[Check state law.]

In consideration for my employment by [Name of Employer] or one or more of its subsidiaries or affiliates (referred to collectively as the "Company"), I, _____, agree to the following:

Please Print Name

Proprietary Information

I recognize that my relationship with the Company is one of high trust and confidence by reason of my access to and contact with the Company's trade secrets and confidential and proprietary information. I will not at any time, either during my employment with the Company or thereafter, disclose to others, or use for my own benefit or the benefit of others, any confidential, proprietary, or secret information owned, possessed, or used by the Company (collectively, "Proprietary Information"). Proprietary information is all business information that: 1) is not generally known to, and cannot be readily ascertained by others, 2) has actual or potential economic value to the Company, and 3) is treated as confidential by the Company including information regarding the Company's: (i) actual or antici-pated products, software, research, inventions, processes, techniques, designs, or other technical data; (ii) administrative, financial or marketing activities; (iii) clients, customers, investors, subscribers, employees, contractors, and/or other third parties who have deal-ings with the Company. [Optional but preferred: Specific examples include but are not limited to: (*describe the specific things at your company that are regarded **and treated** as confidential or proprietary. True Trade secrets generally will have limited distribution, limited access, should be marked "confidential" or "trade secret" and maintained in a secure location or password protected. Some examples are strategic plans, financial data, page rates and employee personnel information such as salary and benefits.*)]

My undertaking and obligations under this Section 1 will not apply, however, to any Proprietary Information which: (i) is or becomes generally known to the public through no action on my part, (ii) is generally disclosed to third parties by the Company without restric-tion, or (iii) is approved for release by written authorization of an executive officer of the Company.

Upon termination of my employment with the Company or at any other time upon request, I will promptly deliver to the Company all notes, memoranda, notebooks, drawings, records, reports, files, diskettes, any other documents and any other storage media (and all copies or reproductions of such materials) in my possession or under my control, whether prepared by me or others, which contain Proprietary Information. I acknowledge that this material is the sole property of the Company.

Absence of Restrictions Upon Disclosure & Competition

Except as I have disclosed in writing to the Company, I am not bound by the terms of any written agreement with any previous employer or other party to refrain from using or disclosing any trade secret or confidential or proprietary information during my employment with the Company or to refrain from competing, directly or indirectly, with the business of such previous employer or any other party. Whether or not I am bound by the terms of any such written agreement, I agree that while employed by the Company I will not disclose to or induce the Company to use any confidential information or material belonging to any previous employer or others.

Ownership of Works

While I am employed by the Company, the Company shall own all rights, including all trade secrets and copyrights, in and to the fol-lowing works created by me, including program codes and documentation, whether created on Company premises or at some other location, within or outside normal working hours, regardless of whether I used my own equipment or the Company's: (i) works relating to the Company's actual or anticipated business of which I had knowledge and (ii) works which result from or are derived from any task assigned to me or work performed by me for the Company (collectively the "Works"). I will assist the Company in obtaining and enforcing copyright and other forms of legal protection for all such written material in any country, including without limitation by signing all copyright applications, assignments, and other documents that I am requested to sign. To the extent that any such Works do not qualify as works made for hire under U.S. copyright law, this Agreement will constitute an irrevocable assignment by me to the Company of the ownership of, and all rights of copyright in, such Works. I agree to give the Company or its designees all assistance reasonably required to perfect such rights. [This paragraph is optional but should be used if employee will be creating material subject to copyright.]

Inventions

If I individually or jointly make or conceive of any invention, technique, process, or other know-how, whether patentable or not, in the course of performing services for the Company, which relates in any manner to the actual or anticipated business of the Company of which I had knowledge or results from any task assigned to me or work performed by me for the Company (collectively, "Inventions"), I will and hereby do assign to the Company my entire right, title, and interest in such Inventions. I will disclose any such Inventions to an officer of the Company and will, upon request, promptly sign a specific assignment of title to the Company, and do anything else reasonably necessary to enable the Company to secure patent, trade secret, or any other proprietary rights in the United States or foreign countries. Any Inventions I have made or conceived before my employment with the Company are listed and described below. These items are excluded from this Agreement. [This paragraph is optional but should be used if employee will be creating any invention or process.]

Other Individual Projects

I may continue to work on, and retain rights to, projects of my own interest outside of the Company which do not compete or conflict with the Company's current or planned business if: (i) they do not fall under the paragraphs titled "Ownership of Works" or "Inventions" above; and (ii) they do not interfere in any way with my time at work or duties for the Company. I understand that I am not permitted to engage in any outside business activities while employed by the Company which compete or conflict with the current or planned business of the Company.

Non-Competition

a) **Non-Competition During Employment.** While employed by the Company, I agree not to engage in any employment, consulting, or business activity, other than for the Company, which would conflict with my obligations to the Company.

b) **Non-Competition After Employment. [Check state law.]** If employed in a state which permits it, I agree that for a period of one year after the termination of my employment, I will not directly or indirectly own, manage, operate, control, finance, or otherwise be interested or participate in the ownership, management, operation, or control of, or be employed by, consult, or be a joint venturer with, render services to or be otherwise connected in any manner with any business or activity which is competitive with the actual or planned business of the Company of which I had knowledge, in any part of the U.S. in which such business of the Company is then being conducted or planned; provided, however, that nothing herein contained shall be deemed to prohibit my ownership of not more than 1% of the publicly traded securities of any such entity.

c) **No Services for Direct Competitor. [Check state law.]** For a period of one year after termination of my employment, I will not directly or individually own, manage, operate, consult with, advise, work for, or render services to i) [name specific competitor company(ies) or publication that is in direct competition with your Company.] or ii) any other company engaged in [describe your Company's business focus in specific terms.]

d) **Non-Competition by Use of Trade Secrets or Proprietary Information.** I agree that I will not use any "Proprietary Information" by the Company to divert or attempt to divert from the Company any business or customers of the Company or to engage in any business activity that is or may be competitive with the Company.

e) It is further agreed that the Non-Competition Period described in Sections b and c above will be extended by the amount of time of any violation of these Sections.

No Solicitation

a) **No Solicitation During Employment.** I agree that while employed by the Company, I will not, directly or indirectly, either for myself or any other person or entity, induce, influence, or solicit any person who is engaged as an employee, agent, independent contractor, or otherwise by the Company to terminate his or her employment or engagement with the Company. I further agree that while employed with the Company I will not approach or solicit in any manner, either for myself or any other person or entity, any customer of the Company to cease doing business with the Company or to do business with me or with any other person or entity.

b) **No Solicitation After Employment. [Check state law.]** I agree that for a period of one year following the termination of my employment from the Company, I will not, directly or indirectly:

   i)   either for myself or any other person or entity, induce, influence, or solicit any person who is engaged as an employee, agent, independent contractor, or otherwise by the Company to terminate his or her employment or engagement with the Company.

   ii) solicit any customer, client, investor, subscriber, contractor or other third-party vendor or supplier of the Company to the extent the identity of said individual or entity constitutes a trade secret or is proprietary or confidential information as defined in Section 1 above.

   iii) use any trade secret, proprietary, or confidential information of the Company as defined in Section 1 above to solicit any customer, client, investor, subscriber, contractor, or other third-party vendor or supplier.

Remedies

As any material breach of this Agreement will cause irreparable harm to the Company, I agree that, in addition to any other rights and remedies existing in the Company's favor, the Company may apply to any court having jurisdiction to enforce the specific performance of the provisions, and shall be entitled to injunctive relief against any act which would violate those provisions. In any equity proceeding relating to the enforcement of this Agreement, I will not raise the defense that the Company has an adequate remedy at law. In the event of a breach of this Agreement by me or anyone acting on my behalf or at my direction, the Company shall be entitled to any damages arising from this breach, including, but not limited to, lost profits, and that the Company shall also be entitled to recover all of its costs and expenses (including attorney's fees) incurred to enforce its rights.

Miscellaneous

If any provision of this Agreement is found to be invalid or unenforceable, it will not affect the validity or enforceability of any other provision of this Agreement.

This Agreement supersedes all prior agreements, written or oral, between me and the Company in relation to the subject matter of this Agreement. This Agreement may not be modified, changed, or discharged in whole or in part, except by an agreement in writing signed by me and the Company. This Agreement does not constitute an employment agreement, and no changes in my compensation, title, or duties or any other terms or conditions of my employment, including without limitation, the termination of my employment, shall affect the provisions of this Agreement except as stated herein.

I acknowledge that my employment with the Company is at will, and that either the Company or I am free to end the relationship at any time, for any reason.

This agreement will be binding upon my heirs, executor, and administrators and will inure to the benefit of the Company and its successors and assigns.

No delay or omission by the Company in exercising its rights under this Agreement shall constitute a waiver of that or any other right. A waiver or consent given by the Company on any one occasion is effective only in that instance and is not a bar to or waiver of any right on any other occasion.

I agree to be bound by the provisions of this Agreement for the benefit of the Company or any subsidiary, parent, or affiliate by which I am originally employed, or become employed without needing to execute a new Agreement at the time of such change in employment.

This Agreement shall be deemed to be a sealed instrument and shall be governed by and construed in accordance with the laws of the state in which I am employed.

I have had an opportunity to thoroughly review this Agreement and to consult with independent counsel concerning the meaning and impact of this Agreement.

If any one or more of the provisions of this Agreement shall for any reason be held to be excessively broad as to time, duration, geographical scope, activity, or subject, it shall be construed, by limiting and reducing it, so as to be enforceable to the extent compatible with the applicable law as it shall then appear.

I HAVE CAREFULLY READ ALL OF THE PROVISIONS OF THIS AGREEMENT, I HAVE HAD AN OPPORTUNITY TO CONSULT WITH LEGAL COUNSEL FOR THE PURPOSES OF REVIEWING THE AGREEMENT, AND I UNDERSTAND AND VOLUNTARILY AGREE TO EACH OF SUCH PROVISIONS.

Agreed to and accepted:

_____   _____
Witness   Signature of Employee

_____   _____
Date   Print Name

[NAME OF EMPLOYER]

_____
Officer

_____
Date

Prior inventions to be excluded from this Agreement are listed and briefly described below: [Include only if using paragraph "Inventions."]

_____

_____

_____

_____

_____

_____

EXIT INTERVIEW FORM

[COMPANY] Exit Interview

We would like to have your comments regarding your employment with our company. The exit interview is entirely voluntary. If you choose to participate, please complete this form and return it to us to go over with you in the exit interview. Alternatively, a company representative will complete it based on your comments during the exit interview.

_____   _____

Name of Departing Employee   Date

_____   _____   _____

Forwarding Address City   State   Zip

1. Why are you leaving the company? _____

   _____

2. What did you enjoy most about working here? _____

   What did you enjoy least about working here? _____

4. What could the company have done or provided to help you become even more productive or to improve your work environment?

   _____

   _____

5. How was your relationship with your supervisor(s)? _____

   _____

6. Do you think the compensation you received is competitive with what others doing the same or similar jobs for other companies receive? _____

7. If you are leaving the company for another job, we would appreciate the following information:

   New company: _____ New job title and duties: _____

   Is the new job a step up for you in terms of compensation and/or status? ❑ Yes   ❑ No

8. Do you have any other comments? _____

9. Was this form completed by the departing employee or by the company representative conducting the exit interview?

   ❑ Departing employee   ❑ Company representative

_____   _____

Signature of departing employee   Company representative conducting the exit interview

Thank you for your assistance. Good luck to you in the future.

EMPLOYEE HANDBOOK

[COMPANY] Employee Handbook

Effective Date: _____, 200___

Contents

Introduction

Welcome

On behalf of your colleagues, I welcome you to [COMPANY], Inc. and wish you every success here.

We believe that each employee contributes directly to the Company's growth and success, and we hope you will take pride in being a member of our team.

This Employee Handbook was developed to describe some of the expectations of our employees and to outline the policies, programs, and benefits available to eligible employees. Employees should familiarize themselves with the contents of the Employee Handbook as soon as possible, for it will answer many questions about employment with the Company.

We hope that your experience here will be challenging, enjoyable, and rewarding. Again, welcome!

Sincerely,

_____

Introductory Statement

One of our objectives at the Company is to provide a work environment that is conducive to both personal and professional growth. This Employee Handbook is designed to acquaint you with the Company, provide you with information about working conditions, employee benefits, and some of the policies affecting your employment, and prevent and clarify any misunderstanding of the policies and procedures implemented by the Company. You should read, understand, and comply with all provisions of the Employee Handbook. It describes many of your responsibilities as an employee and outlines the programs developed by the Company to benefit employees. This Employee Handbook is not a contract of employment, either express or implied, nor is it intended to create any legally enforceable obligations on the part of the Company.

No Employee Handbook can anticipate every circumstance or question about policy. As the Company continues to grow, the need may arise, and the Company reserves the right, to revise, supplement, or rescind any policies or portion of the Employee Handbook from time to time as the Company deems appropriate, in its sole and absolute discretion and without advance notice. Employees will, of course, be notified of such changes to the Employee Handbook as they occur. The only exception is that the Company's employment at-will policy permitting you or the Company to end our relationship with or without good cause, at any time, with or without advance notice, is not subject to change.

No one other than the president of the Company may enter into any employment or other agreement that modifies the policies stated in this Employee Handbook or the nature of the employment at-will relationship between you and the Company. Any agreement modifying the employment at-will relationship between you and the Company must be in writing and must be signed by the president of the Company and you.

Policy Changes

Policies set forth in this Employee Handbook are not intended to create a contract, nor are they to be construed to constitute contractual obligations of any kind or a contract of employment between the Company and any of its employees. The provisions of the Employee Handbook have been developed at the discretion of management and, except for its policy of employment at-will, may be amended or canceled at any time, at the Company's sole discretion. These provisions supersede all existing policies and practices and may not be amended or added to without the express written approval of the president of the Company.

Nature of Employment

At-Will Status

The best employment relationship is one that is mutually satisfying for both parties, the employee and the Company. To protect both parties' rights, employment with the Company is voluntarily entered into, and the employee is free to resign at-will, for any reason, at any time, with or without advance notice. Similarly, the Company may terminate the employment relationship at-will, for any reason, at any time, with or without advance notice, so long as there is no violation of applicable federal or state law.

No one other than the president of the company may enter into any employment or other agreement, including any oral, express, or implied agreement, that modifies the nature of the employment at-will relationship between you and [The COMPANY]. Any agreement modifying the employment at-will relationship between you and [The COMPANY] must be in writing and must be signed by the president of [The COMPANY] and you.

All employees are required to sign an Employee Acknowledgment of Employee Handbook and At-Will Status, in which they expressly acknowledge and agree to the at-will relationship, and a Confidential Information, Invention Assignment, and Nonsolicitation Agreement.

Equal Employment Opportunity

[COMPANY] is committed to a policy of equal employment opportunity for all applicants and employees. In order to provide equal employment and advancement opportunities to all individuals, employment decisions at [The COMPANY] are based on merit, qualifications, and abilities. [COMPANY] does not discriminate in employment opportunities or practices on the basis of sex, gender, race, color, religion, national origin, creed, citizenship status, ancestry, age, sexual orientation, marital status, pregnancy, cancer-related medical condition, mental and physical disability (actual or perceived), veteran status, or any other characteristic protected by applicable law or local ordinance. This policy governs all aspects of employment, including recruitment, recruitment advertising, promotion, job assignment, training, transfer, compensation, discipline, demotion, reduction in force, termination, and employee participation in company-sponsored benefits and social/recreational activities. Refer to the **Policy Prohibiting Discrimination and Harassment** for further information.

[COMPANY] is committed to complying fully with the federal Americans with Disabilities Act and the ensuring equal opportunity in employment for qualified persons with disabilities. All employment practices and activities are conducted on a nondiscriminatory basis. [COMPANY] will make reasonable accommodations for qualified persons with known disabilities, where it would not result in an undue hardship to do so and is consistent with its legal obligations. An employee who would like to request reasonable accommodation of a disability should make an appointment with human resources to discuss the subject. [COMPANY] encourages employees to discuss any need for reasonable accommodation as early as possible and to offer suggestions of possible reasonable accommodations. This will help the employee and the Company to work together to arrive at an appropriate accommodation.

Immigration Law Compliance

[COMPANY] is committed to complying with federal immigration law, which requires it to employ only United States citizens and aliens who are authorized to work in the United States. [COMPANY] does not unlawfully discriminate on the basis of national origin, ancestry, or citizenship.

In compliance with the Immigration Reform and Control Act of 1986, each new employee, as a condition of employment, must complete the Employment Eligibility Verification Form I-9 and present documentation establishing identity and employment eligibility. Should the original employment eligibility documentation expire, employees are responsible for providing updated documentation establishing employment eligibility. Former employees who are rehired must also complete a Form I-9 if they have not completed an I-9 with the Company within the past three years, or if their previous I-9 is no longer retained or valid.

Employees with questions or seeking more information on immigration law issues are encouraged to contact human resources. Employees may raise questions or good faith complaints about immigration law compliance without fear of reprisal.

Employment Status and Records

Benefits Waiting Period

All new and rehired employees are subject to a benefits waiting period of three months. During this period, employees will be eligible only for limited benefits, in accordance with the terms of the Company's benefits plans. Employees will not earn vacation or sick leave during the benefits waiting period.

Employment Categories

It is the intent of the Company to clarify the definitions of employment classifications so that employees understand their employment status and benefit eligibility. These classifications do not guarantee employment for any specified period of time. Accordingly, the right to terminate the employment relationship at-will, with or without good cause, at any time, with or without advance notice, is retained by both the employee and the Company.

Each employee is designated as either **nonexempt** or **exempt** from federal and state wage and hour laws. Nonexempt employees are entitled to overtime pay under the specific provisions of federal and state laws. Exempt employees are excluded from specific provisions of federal and state wage and hour laws. Employees will be informed of their exempt or nonexempt status by human resources.

In addition to the above categories, each employee will belong to one other employment category:

Regular Full-Time employees are those who are not in a temporary status, have completed the benefits waiting period, and are regularly scheduled to work the Company's full-time schedule. Generally, they are eligible for the Company's full benefit package, subject to the terms, conditions, and limitations of each benefit program.

Regular Part-Time employees are those who are not in a temporary status and who are regularly scheduled to work less than 40 hours per week. Regular part-time employees receive all legally mandated benefits (such as Social Security and workers' compensation insurance), but are not eligible for all of the Company's other benefits programs.

Temporary employees are those who are hired as interim replacements, to temporarily supplement the work force, or to assist in the completion of a specific project. Employment assignments in this category are of a limited duration and usually do not exceed one year. Employment beyond any initially stated period does not in any way imply a change in employment status. Temporary employees retain that status unless and until they are given written notification of a change of status by human resources. While temporary employees receive all legally mandated benefits (such as workers' compensation insurance and Social Security), they are ineligible for all of the Company's other benefit programs. (Agency temporary employees assigned to the Company are not Company "Temporary" employees.)

Personnel Records

[COMPANY] keeps a personnel file on each employee. Employees who wish to review their own file should contact human resources. With reasonable advance notice, employees may review the contents of their own personnel files, except for letters of reference and other limited kinds of information, in the Company's offices and in the presence of an individual appointed by the Company to maintain the files. Employees may not remove anything from their personnel files, but may receive copies of documents in their file which they have signed or had the opportunity to sign.

[COMPANY] endeavors to keep employees' personnel records confidential, except where disclosure is authorized by law and necessary for business purposes or administration of benefits.

It is the responsibility of each employee to promptly notify the Company of any changes in personnel data. Personal mailing addresses, telephone numbers, number and names of dependents, individuals to be contacted in the event of an emergency, educational accomplishments, and other such status reports should be accurate and current at all times. If any personnel data has changed, notify human resources so that our records and your benefits are kept up-to-date.

Medical Records

Medical information about individual employees is treated confidentially. [The COMPANY] will take reasonable precautions to protect such information from inappropriate disclosure. Human resources, management staff, and other employees have a responsibility to respect and maintain the confidentiality of employee medical information. Anyone inappropriately disclosing such information is subject to disciplinary action, up to and including termination of employment.

Performance Evaluations

[COMPANY] strongly encourages you and your manager to discuss job performance and goals on an informal, day-to-day basis. A formal performance evaluation normally will be conducted after your first 90 days of employment or transfer or promotion into a new position. Additional formal and informal performance reviews are conducted to provide both you and your manager the opportunity to discuss job tasks, encourage and recognize strengths, identify areas of improvement, and discuss positive and specific approaches to meet performance goals. Formal performance evaluations normally are scheduled every 12 months.

Employment Termination

Since employment with the Company is based on mutual consent, both the employee and the Company have the right to terminate employment at-will, with or without good cause, at any time, with or without advance notice.

Upon termination, employees will receive their final pay in accordance with applicable law. Employee benefits will be affected by employment termination in the following manner. All accrued, vested benefits that are due and payable at termination will be paid. Some benefits may be continued at the employee's expense if the employee so chooses. The employee will be notified in writing of the benefits that may be continued and of the terms, conditions, and limitations of such continuance.

At the time of termination, employees must return all company-furnished property, including equipment, badges, keys, and all electronics and communications devices.

Exit Interviews

Exit interviews may be conducted upon termination of employment. An employee or his or her manager may arrange an appointment with human resources for an exit interview. The exit interview allows the employee to communicate views on the employment, job requirements, operations, training needs, or any other information the employee feels is relevant. It also provides the employee with an opportunity to discuss issues concerning benefits and insurance.

Employee References

[COMPANY] limits its response to inquiries about former employees to confirming the former employee's employment, dates of employment, and job titles held. Salary information will be provided only if the former employee first consents in writing. [COMPANY] will also provide further information if it is legally required to do so.

Only the president, human resources, and persons designated in writing by the president may provide information regarding former employees to any outside person or entity. Other employees may not do so. An employee who receives a request for information about a former employee must refer the person making the request to human resources. Any violation of this policy may result in disciplinary action, up to and including termination.

Employee Benefits

Group Insurance Plans

You may be eligible for Company-sponsored benefits. [Briefly set out benefits information.] Terms of the Company's benefits programs are set out in the Summary Plan Description (SPD). Please contact human resources to obtain a copy of the SPD.

Benefits Continuation (COBRA)

The federal Consolidated Omnibus Budget Reconciliation Act (COBRA) gives employees and their qualified beneficiaries the opportunity to continue health insurance coverage under the Company's health insurance plans when a "qualifying event" would normally result in the loss of eligibility. Some common qualifying events are resignation, termination of employment, or death of an employee; a reduction in an employee's hours or a leave of absence; an employee's divorce or legal separation; and a dependent child no longer meeting eligibility requirements.

Under COBRA, the employee or beneficiary pays the full cost of coverage at the Company's group rates plus an administration fee. [COMPANY] provides each eligible employee with a written notice describing rights granted under COBRA when the employee becomes eligible for coverage under the Company's health insurance plan. The notice contains important information about the employee's rights and obligations.

State Disability Insurance

If an employee is disabled from working, the employee may qualify for state disability insurance benefits. State disability benefits are calculated as a percentage of pay, up to a maximum specified by law, for a duration of 52 weeks. The cost of this insurance is fully paid for by the employee through payroll deductions.

Employees who are absent due to illness or injury, or who are on a disability leave of absence other than a work-related disability leave of absence, for eight or more calendar days and who are not eligible for the company's disability insurance are responsible for applying for state disability benefits. Each employee is responsible for filing his or her own claim and other forms promptly and accurately with the State [agency]. Upon request, the Company will provide an employee with a claim form for his or her use, or an employee may obtain one at the [state agency] offices. [COMPANY] will integrate the employee's vacation or sick leave, where applicable, with state disability payments.

Worker's Compensation Insurance

[COMPANY] provides a comprehensive workers' compensation insurance program at no cost to employees. This program covers any injury or illness sustained in the course of employment that requires medical, surgical, or hospital treatment. Subject to applicable legal requirements, workers' compensation insurance provides benefits after a short waiting period or, if the employee is hospitalized, immediately.

Employees who are involved in a work-related accident or who sustain a work-related injury or illness must inform their supervisor immediately. No matter how minor an on-the-job accident, injury, or illness may appear, it is important that it be reported immediately. This will enable an eligible employee to qualify for coverage as quickly as possible. Refer to the Work-Related Disability Leave policy for further information.

Neither the Company nor its workers' compensation insurance carrier shall be liable for the payment of workers' compensation benefits for injuries that occur during an employee's voluntary participation in off-duty recreational, social or athletic activity sponsored by the Company.

Payroll and Timekeeping

Paydays

All employees are paid [indicate paydays, no less than twice per month.] Each paycheck will include earnings for all work performed through the end of the previous payroll period. If the regularly scheduled payday falls on a holiday or a Saturday, the paycheck will be given on the day before. If the payday falls on a Sunday, the paycheck will be given on Monday. [COMPANY] will not provide employees pay advances or extensions of credits on unearned or unpaid wages.

Administrative Pay Corrections

[COMPANY] takes all reasonable steps to ensure that employees receive the correct amount of pay in each paycheck and that employees are paid promptly on the scheduled payday. In the unlikely event that there is an error in the amount of pay, the employee should promptly bring the discrepancy to the attention of human resources so that corrections can be made as quickly as possible.

Pay Deductions

The law requires that the Company make certain deductions from every employee's compensation. Among these are applicable federal and state income taxes, social security, and state disability insurance. [COMPANY] also must withhold any court-ordered wage garnishment or family support from wages, where applicable. [COMPANY] may from time to time offer programs or benefits for which eligible employees may voluntarily authorize deductions from their paychecks to participate in those programs or receive those benefits.

Timekeeping for Nonexempt Employees

Employees have the responsibility to accurately record time worked. Federal and state laws require the Company to keep an accurate record of time worked in order to calculate employee pay and benefits. Time worked is all the time actually spent on the job performing assigned duties.

Non-exempt employees should accurately record the time they begin and end their work, as well as the beginning and ending time of each meal period. They should also record the beginning and ending time of any split shift or departure from work for personal reasons.

Altering, falsifying, tampering with time records, or recording time on another employee's time record may result in disciplinary action, up to and including termination of employment.

Working Hours, Breaks, and Meals

[Check state law.] [COMPANY]'s normal office hours are from [__am] to [__pm], Monday through Friday. Non-exempt employees must take an unpaid [___hour/minute – must be at least 30 minutes] lunch break, which may be taken between [__am] and [__pm], depending on the needs of the work being done and with the approval of the employee's manager. Non-exempt employees must also take two paid rest breaks, one in the mid-morning and one in the mid-afternoon, of no more than [must be at least 10] minutes each. The weekly and daily work schedules of part-time employees will depend on the nature of their job assignments. Exempt employees' duties may regularly include evening and weekend work depending upon the needs of the work they are performing. All employees are expected to devote their full attention to their work duties during working hours.

Overtime Pay

[Check state law.] Employees may be asked to work beyond their normally scheduled hours. Although an attempt will be made to give an employee advance notice of the need to work overtime where it is feasible to do so and to accommodate special circumstances, this is not always possible.

Nonexempt employees who work more than **[check state law]** 8 hours in a day or 40 hours in a work week will receive overtime pay computed as follows:

- Overtime at the rate of 1 [____] times the employee's regular rate of pay will be paid for all hours worked in excess of **[check state law]** 8 hours in 1 day or 40 hours in 1 work week;

- Overtime at 2 times the employee's regular rate of pay will be paid for time worked in excess of 12 hours in 1 day;

- Overtime at 1 [____] times the employee's regular rate of pay will be paid for the first 8 hours worked on the seventh consecutive day of work in a workweek; and

- Overtime at 2 times the employee's regular rate of pay will be paid for hours worked in excess of 8 hours on the seventh consecutive day of work in a workweek.

Only those hours that are actually worked are added together to determine an employee's overtime pay. For example, paid vacations, holidays, sick leave, and disability pay are not hours worked (even if compensated) and, therefore, are not counted for overtime calculations.

[COMPANY] does not permit employees to take compensatory time off.

Non-exempt employees may not work overtime without the express prior approval of their manager. This includes all work, whether performed inside or outside the office. If you work overtime without this authorization, you may be subject to disciplinary action, up to and including termination.

Exempt employees are not eligible for overtime pay.

Make-Up Time [Check state law]

[COMPANY] may allow nonexempt employees to make up work time that is or would be lost as a result of personal obligations. The decision to permit make-up time will be at the discretion of the employee's supervisor. The employee must provide his or her supervisor with a signed written request for each occasion of make-up work. Supervisors may not encourage or solicit an employee to make such a request.

The make-up work time must be performed in the same workweek in which the personal time off was taken, and will not be paid as overtime, except for hours worked in excess of 11 hours in one work day or 40 hours in one workweek. Make-up time may not exceed 3 hours in one work day.

Work Conditions

Safety

To assist in providing a safe and healthful work environment for employees, customers, and visitors, the Company has established a workplace safety program. This program is a top priority for the Company. The office manager has responsibility for implementing, administering, monitoring, and evaluating the safety program. Its success depends on the alertness and personal commitment of all employees.

[COMPANY] provides information to employees about workplace safety and health issues through regular internal communication channels such as supervisor-employee meetings, bulletin board postings, memos, or other written communications. Employees and supervisors receive periodic workplace safety training. The training covers potential safety and health hazards and safe work practices and procedures to eliminate or minimize hazards.

Some of the best safety improvement ideas come from employees. Those with ideas, concerns, or suggestions for improved safety in the workplace are encouraged to raise them with their supervisor, or with another supervisor or manager, or bring them to the attention of the office manager. Reports and concerns about workplace safety issues may be made anonymously if the employee wishes. All reports can be made in good faith without fear of reprisal.

Each employee is expected to obey safety rules and to exercise caution in all work activities. Employees must immediately report any unsafe condition to the appropriate supervisor. Employees who violate safety standards, who cause hazardous or dangerous situations, or who fail to report or, where appropriate, remedy such situations, may be subject to disciplinary action, up to and including termination of employment.

In the case of accidents that result in injury, regardless of how insignificant the injury may appear, employees should immediately notify human resources or the appropriate supervisor. Such reports are necessary to comply with laws and initiate insurance and workers' compensation benefits procedures.

Workplace Violence Prevention

[COMPANY] is committed to preventing workplace violence and to maintaining a safe work environment. [COMPANY] has adopted the following guidelines to deal with intimidation, harassment, or other threats of or actual violence that may occur during business hours or on its premises.

All employees, including supervisors and temporary employees, should be treated with courtesy and respect at all times. Employees are expected to refrain from fighting, "horseplay," or other conduct that may be dangerous to others. Firearms, weapons, and other dangerous or hazardous devices or substances are prohibited from the premises of the Company without proper authorization.

Conduct that threatens, intimidates, or coerces another employee, a customer, or a member of the public at any time, including off-duty periods, will not be tolerated. This prohibition includes all acts of harassment, including sexual harassment and harassment that is based on an individual's sex, gender, race, color, religion, national origin, creed, citizenship status, ancestry, age, sexual orientation, marital status, pregnancy, cancer-related medical condition, mental and physical disability (actual or perceived), veteran status, or any other characteristic protected by applicable law or local ordinance.

Employees should report all threats of or actual violence, both direct and indirect, as soon as possible to their supervisor, human resources, the president, or any person designated in writing by the president. This includes threats by employees, as well as threats by customers, vendors, solicitors, or other members of the public. When reporting a threat of violence, employees should be as specific and detailed as possible.

Employees also should report all suspicious individuals or activities as soon as possible to their supervisor, human resources, the president, or any person designated in writing by the president. Employees should not place themselves in peril. If employees see or hear a commotion or disturbance near their work station, they should not try to intercede or see what is happening.

[COMPANY] will promptly and thoroughly investigate all reports of threats of or actual violence and of suspicious individuals or activities. The identity of the individual making a report will be protected as much as is practical. In order to maintain workplace safety and the integrity of its investigation, the Company may suspend employees, either with or without pay, pending investigation.

Anyone determined to be responsible for threats of or actual violence or other conduct that is in violation of these guidelines will be subject to prompt disciplinary action up to and including termination of employment.

[COMPANY] encourages employees to bring their disputes or differences with other employees to the attention of their supervisor, human resources, the president, or any person designated in writing by the president before the situation escalates into potential violence. [COMPANY] is eager to assist in the resolution of employee disputes, and will not discipline employees for raising such concerns in good faith.

Smoking

In keeping with the Company's intent to provide a safe and healthful work environment and in compliance with state law, smoking is prohibited anywhere inside the facilities. Employees are requested to ask business and personal visitors to comply with this policy as well.

Company Property

Confidential Business Information, Proprietary Information, and Trade Secrets

The protection of confidential business information, proprietary information, and trade secrets is vital to the interests and the success of the Company. This information is and at all times remains the company's property. Such confidential business information, proprietary information, and trade secrets include, but are not limited to, the following: [THIS LIST SHOULD BE CONSISTENT WITH ANY SUCH LISTS IN EMPLOYEE CONFIDENTIAL INFORMATION AGREEMENTS] inventions, mask works, ideas, processes, formulas, source and object codes, data, programs, other works of authorship, know-how, improvements, discoveries, developments, designs, techniques, information regarding plans for research, development, new products, marketing and selling, business plans, budgets and unpublished financial statements, licenses, prices and costs, suppliers and customers, and information regarding the skills and compensation of employees or other independent contractors of the Company.

All employees will be required to sign a Confidential Information, Invention Assignment, and Nonsolicitation Agreement as a condition of employment. Employees who improperly use or disclose confidential business information, proprietary information, or trade secrets will be subject to disciplinary action, up to and including termination of employment, even if they do not actually benefit from the disclosed information. Employees may not use the Company's confidential business information, proprietary information, or trade secrets for any purpose other than as required to perform their jobs with the Company, and may not use it after leaving employment with the Company. Employees must return all originals and copies of the Company's confidential business information, proprietary information, and trade secrets upon leaving employment with the Company. Refer to the Confidential Information, Invention Assignment, and Nonsolicitation Agreement for further information.

Use of Computers, E-Mail, and the Internet

The computer and e-mail systems and internet access to global electronic information resources on the World Wide Web are provided by the Company to assist employees in performing their job duties and obtaining work-related data and technology. The following guidelines have been established to help ensure responsible and productive use of the computer and e-mail systems and the internet. While computer, e-mail, and internet usage is intended for job-related activities, incidental and occasional brief personal use is permitted within reasonable limits.

The equipment, services, and technology that comprise our computer and e-mail systems and that provide access to the internet remain at all times the property of the Company. All data that is composed, transmitted, accessed, or received via our computer, e-mail, and internet systems is considered to be part of the official records of the Company and, as such, is subject to disclosure to the Company, law enforcement, or other third parties. Consequently, employees should always ensure that the information transmitted through and contained in the computer, e-mail, and internet systems is accurate, appropriate, ethical, and lawful. [COMPANY] reserves the right, in its sole discretion, without notice, to access, monitor, read, or download any data composed, transmitted, accessed, or received through or stored in our computer, e-mail, or internet systems.

Passwords are intended to prevent unauthorized access to information. Passwords do not confer any right of privacy upon any employee of the Company. Thus, even though employees may maintain passwords for accessing the computer system, employees must not expect that any information maintained on system, including e-mail and voice mail messages, are private. Employees are expected to maintain their passwords as confidential. Employees must not share passwords and must not access coworkers' systems without express authorization.

[COMPANY] purchases and licenses the use of various computer software for business purposes and does not own the copyright to this software or its related documentation. Unless authorized by the software developer, the Company does not have the right to reproduce such software for use on more than one computer. Employees may only use software on local area networks or on multiple machines according to the software license agreement. [COMPANY] prohibits the illegal duplication of software and its related documentation.

Internet and e-mail users should take the necessary anti-virus precautions before downloading or copying any file from the internet or e-mail. All downloaded files are to be checked for viruses; all compressed files are to be checked before and after decompression. [COMPANY] strives to maintain a workplace free of harassment and discrimination, and one that is sensitive to the diversity of its employees. Therefore, the Company prohibits the use of the computer and e-mail systems and the internet in ways that are disruptive, offensive to others, or harmful to morale.

Data that is composed, transmitted, accessed, received, or displayed via the computer or e-mail systems or the internet must not contain content that could be considered discriminatory, offensive, obscene, threatening, harassing, intimidating, or disruptive to any employee or other person. Examples of unacceptable content may include, but are not limited to, sexual comments, messages, cartoons, or images; racial or ethnic slurs or comments; off-color jokes; comments or images that could reasonably offend someone on the basis of sex, gender, race, color, religion, national origin, creed, citizenship status, ancestry, age, sexual orientation, marital status, pregnancy, cancer-related medical condition, mental and physical disability (actual or perceived), veteran status, or any other characteristic protected by applicable law or local ordinance; or other content that may be construed as harassment or discrimination. The following are examples of previously stated or additional conduct that is prohibited and can result in disciplinary action, up to and including termination of employment:

- Sending or posting discriminatory, harassing, or threatening messages or images
- Sending or posting the company's confidential business information, proprietary information, or trade secrets, except as required to perform the company's business
- Engaging in unauthorized transactions that may incur a cost to the company or initiate unwanted internet services and transmissions
- Sending or posting messages or material that could damage the company's image or reputation
- Participating in the viewing or exchange of pornography or obscene materials
- Sending or posting messages that defame or slander other individuals
- Jeopardizing the security of the company's electronic communications systems
- Sending or posting messages that disparage another organization's products or services
- Passing off personal views as representing those of the company
- Sending anonymous e-mail messages
- Engaging in illegal activities

Employees who violate this policy will be subject to disciplinary action, up to and including termination of employment. Employees should notify their supervisor, the network administrator, human resources, the president, or a person designated in writing by the president upon learning of a violation of this policy.

Use of Phone and Voice Mail Systems
The telephone and voice mail systems are provided for business purposes. Personal calls should be limited in number and length. The telephone and voice mail systems remain at all times the property of the Company. [COMPANY] reserves the right, in its sole discretion, without notice, to access these systems, including employees' voice mail.

Use of Other Equipment and Property
All equipment, working areas including desks, and other areas including storage spaces on the Company's premises, and all materials issued to or created by employees of the Company during their employment, remain at all times the property of the Company. [COMPANY] reserves the right, in its sole discretion, without notice, to open, access, or search any of its equipment, working areas, or other areas, and to retrieve or review any of its materials.

When using the Company's property, employees are expected to exercise care, perform required maintenance, and follow all operating instructions, safety standards, and guidelines. Employees should notify their supervisor if they have any questions or if any equipment or machines appear to be damaged, defective, or in need of repair. Prompt reporting of damages, defects, and the need for repairs could prevent deterioration of equipment and possible injury.

Employees are responsible for all the Company property, including materials and written information issued to them or in their possession. All the Company property must be returned on or before an employee's last day of work.

[COMPANY]'s name, letterhead, supplies, and copy services are for the Company's business and may not be used for personal needs. Use of company postage for personal correspondence is not permitted. The reputation and influence of the Company can be adversely affected by the way in which its name or letterhead are used. Company letterhead cannot be used for correspondence of a purely personal nature without prior approval of the president or any person designated in writing by the president.

Employee Conduct and Disciplinary Action

Employee Conduct and Work Rules

To ensure orderly operations and provide the best possible work environment, the Company expects employees to follow rules of conduct that will protect the interests and safety of all employees and the organization.

It is not possible to list all the forms of behavior that are considered unacceptable in the workplace. The following are examples of infractions of rules of conduct that may result in disciplinary action, up to and including termination of employment:

- Sexual harassment or other inappropriate behavior or harassment

- Discriminatory conduct

- Retaliation

- Theft or inappropriate removal or possession of property

- Working under the influence of alcohol or illegal drugs

- Possession, distribution, sale, transfer, or use of alcohol or illegal drugs in the workplace, while on duty, or while operating employer-owned vehicles or equipment

- Conviction for the sale or use of illegal drugs on or off company premises

- Fighting, or threatening or engaging in violence in the workplace

- Bringing dangerous materials or weapons onto Company property

- Boisterous or disruptive activity in the workplace

- Negligence or improper conduct leading to damage of employer-owned or customer-owned property

- Unsatisfactory performance or conduct

- Falsification of time records or reports

- Insubordination or other disrespectful conduct

- Violation of safety or health rules

- Smoking in prohibited areas

- Engaging in a conflict of interest or unethical conduct

- Unauthorized use or disclosure of confidential business information, proprietary information, or trade secrets

- Excessive absenteeism or tardiness or any absence without notice

- Violation of personnel policies

Notwithstanding these examples of unacceptable conduct, employment with the Company is nevertheless at the mutual consent of the Company and the employee, and is held at-will. Therefore, either the Company or the employee may terminate the relationship with or without good cause, at any time, with or without advance notice.

Policy Prohibiting Discrimination and Harassment

We are committed to providing a work environment that is free of discrimination. In keeping with this policy, the Company strictly prohibits illegal or inappropriate discrimination or harassment of any kind, including discrimination or harassment on the basis of sex, gender, race, color, religion, national origin, creed, citizenship status, ancestry, age, sexual orientation, marital status, pregnancy, medical condition, mental and physical disability (actual or perceived), veteran status, or any other characteristic protected by applicable law or local ordinance. It is the responsibility of each employee, whether or not employed in a supervisory or managerial capacity, to conscientiously follow this policy in all of his or her daily work activities.

Unlawful Harassment

Unlawful harassment may take many forms but most commonly includes the following:

- Verbal harassment such as jokes, epithets, slurs, and unwelcome remarks about an individual's body, dress, clothing, color, physical appearance or talents, derogatory comments, questions about a person's sexual practices, and/or patronizing terms or remarks;

- Physical harassment such as physical interference with normal work, impeding or blocking movement, assault, unwelcome physical contact or touching, staring at a person's body, and threatening, intimidating, or hostile acts that relate to a protected characteristic; and

- Visual harassment such as offensive or obscene photographs, calendars, posters, cards, cartoons, drawings, and gestures; displays with sexually suggestive or lewd objects; and unwelcome letters, notes, or any other graphic material that denigrates or shows hostility or aversion toward an individual because of the individual's protected characteristic.

Sexual Harassment

Sexual harassment occurs when submission to or rejection of unwelcome sexual conduct by an individual is used as a basis for employment decisions affecting that individual. Sexual harassment also occurs when unwelcome sexual conduct unreasonably interferes with an individual's job performance or creates an intimidating, hostile, or offensive working environment, even if it does not lead to tangible or economic job consequences. Sexual harassment includes verbal harassment, physical harassment, visual harassment, and unwanted sexual advances. It also includes retaliation for having reported acts of harassment. Sexual harassment includes harassment of women by men, men by women, and gender-based harassment of individuals of the same sex as the harasser.

Responsibility of Employees and Complaint Procedure

It is the responsibility of each employee to ensure that discrimination or harassment on any of these bases does not occur within the workplace. If you believe that any kind of illegal or inappropriate discrimination or harassment is occurring by an employee, vendor, client, or visitor, you are requested to immediately bring your concerns to the attention of your supervisor, the office manager, or any officer of the Company. **You are not required to report the incident to your supervisor first.** Do not allow an inappropriate situation to continue by not reporting it, regardless of who creates the situation. No employee is exempt from this policy. We encourage the prompt reporting of complaints so that we may respond rapidly and take appropriate remedial action, if necessary.

Any supervisor or manager who becomes aware of any unlawful harassment or discrimination must immediately contact the president.

Reported incidents of harassment or discrimination will promptly be investigated and investigations will be conducted in a discreet manner. Information obtained from the investigation will be disclosed only on a need-to-know basis. Every investigation requires a determination based on all the facts in the matter. At the conclusion of the investigation, the Company will determine whether harassment or discrimination in violation of this policy has occurred. However, a finding that an employee has violated the Company's policy against discrimination and harassment does not necessarily mean that the employee has violated any law prohibiting harassment or discrimination. [COMPANY] will communicate its findings to the accused, the complainant, and, when appropriate, other persons who are directly concerned.

The reporting employee and all employees participating in any investigation have the assurance of the Company that no reprisals will be taken as the result of the complaint, unless the complaint was filed in bad faith or for an improper purpose.

Any employee of the Company who is determined to have violated the Company's policy will be subject to appropriate disciplinary action, up to and including immediate termination. Steps will be taken as necessary to prevent any further discrimination or harassment.

Discrimination, harassment, including sexual harassment, retaliation for opposing such discrimination and harassment, and retaliation for participating in investigations of discrimination and harassment are illegal. We encourage all employees to use the Company's procedures for resolving complaints of harassment and retaliation. Employees should also be aware that the [State EEO enforcement agency, if any] and the federal Equal Employment Opportunity Commission (EEOC) investigate and prosecute complaints of unlawful harassment in employment. If an employee or applicant thinks he or she has been harassed, he or she may file a complaint with the appropriate agency. The nearest office is listed in the phone book. The [State EEO enforcement agency, if any] agency will conduct an investigation and attempt to resolve the dispute. If [the agency] finds evidence of harassment, the matter may go to a public hearing before the [State EEO enforcement agency, if any] or the EEOC. Possible remedies include reinstatement, backpay, promotion, changes in company policies and procedures, emotional distress damages, and fines. [COMPANY] will not tolerate, nor does the law allow, retaliation against an employee for filing a complaint with, or otherwise participating in an investigation, proceeding, or hearing conducted by any government agency or commission.

Drug- and Alcohol-Free Workplace

It is the Company's desire to provide a drug- and alcohol-free, healthful, and safe workplace. To promote this goal, employees are required to report to work in appropriate mental and physical condition to perform their jobs in a satisfactory manner.

While on the Company's premises and while conducting business-related activities off the Company's premises, no employee may use, possess, manufacture, distribute, sell, or be under the influence of alcohol or illegal drugs. No employee's work or fellow employees' work may be impacted or influenced by an employee's use, possession, manufacture, distribution, sale, or being under the influence of alcohol or illegal drugs. Violations of this policy may lead to disciplinary action, up to and including termination of employment or required participation in a substance abuse rehabilitation program.

In accordance with law, we will make reasonable efforts to accommodate anyone who voluntarily enters an alcohol or drug abuse rehabilitation program. We reserve the right to discharge an employee for any legal reason.

Business Ethics and Conflicts of Interest

The successful business operation and reputation of the Company is built upon the principles of fair dealing and ethical conduct of our employees. Our reputation for integrity and excellence requires strict observance of the spirit and letter of all applicable laws and regulations, as well as a scrupulous regard for the highest standards of conduct and personal integrity. The purpose of these guidelines is to provide general direction so that employees can seek further clarification on issues related to the subject of acceptable standards of operation.

The continued success of the Company is dependent upon our customers' trust and we are dedicated to preserving that trust. Employees owe a duty to the Company and its customers to act in a way that will merit the continued trust and confidence of the public. [COMPANY] will comply with all applicable laws and regulations and expects its directors, officers, and employees to conduct business in accordance with the letter, spirit, and intent of all relevant laws and to refrain from any illegal, dishonest, or unethical conduct.

In general, the use of good judgment, based on high ethical principles, will guide employees with respect to lines of acceptable conduct. If a situation arises where it is difficult to determine the proper course of action, employees should discuss the matter openly with their supervisors and, if necessary, with the management staff for advice and consultation.

Employees are required to conduct business within guidelines that prohibit actual or potential conflicts of interest. In general, an actual or potential conflict of interest occurs when an employee is in a position to influence a decision that may result in a personal gain for that employee or for a relative as a result of the Company's business dealings. For the purposes of this policy, a relative is any person who is related by blood or marriage, or whose relationship with the employee is similar to that of persons who are related by blood or marriage, such as a domestic partner. **Employees must disclose to a member of the Company's management staff as soon as possible the existence of any actual or potential conflict of interest so that safeguards can be established to protect all parties.** Engaging in or failing to disclose potential or actual conflicts of interest could lead to disciplinary action, up to and including termination of employment.

During their employment with the Company, employees may not engage in outside employment for a competitor of the Company. You must disclose outside employment to management so that we can determine if a conflict of interest exists. If we find that there is a conflict, we may ask that you terminate your outside employment if you wish to remain employed by the Company. Failure to disclose outside employment may lead to disciplinary action, up to and including termination.

Attendance and Punctuality

To maintain a safe and productive work environment, the Company expects employees to be reliable and to be punctual in reporting for scheduled work. Absenteeism and tardiness place a burden on other employees and on the Company. In the rare instances when employees cannot avoid being late to work or are unable to work as scheduled, they should notify their supervisor as soon as possible in advance of the anticipated tardiness or absence.

Poor attendance and excessive tardiness are disruptive. Either may lead to disciplinary action, up to and including termination of employment.

Solicitation and Postings

In an effort to ensure a productive and harmonious work environment, persons not employed by the Company may not solicit or distribute literature in the workplace at any time for any purpose.

[COMPANY] recognizes that employees may have interests in events and organizations outside the workplace. However, employees may not solicit or distribute literature concerning these activities during working time, and may not solicit or distribute literature at any time in work areas. Working time does not include lunch periods, work breaks, or any other periods in which employees are not on duty.

In addition, the posting of written solicitations on company bulletin boards is restricted. These bulletin boards display important information, and employees should consult them frequently for:

- Discrimination and sexual harassment notice
- Payday notice
- State disability insurance/unemployment insurance information
- Workers' compensation insurance information

If employees have a message of interest to the workplace they would like considered for posting, they must submit it to human resources for approval before posting.

Time Off Work

Vacation

[COMPANY] offers vacation benefits to regular full-time employees. Regular full-time employees receive two weeks paid vacation per year. Vacation is earned monthly at a rate of [_____] working days per month. Part time and temporary employees are not eligible for vacation time. Employees will not earn vacation during the benefits waiting period or while on a leave of absence. Vacation pay consists of the employee's regular wages, excluding overtime and other special forms of compensation.

Vacation time off is intended for rest, recreation, extra time with your family, or other personal pursuits. It is our opinion that an annual break away from the daily routine will renew your energy and enthusiasm upon returning to work. Employees may not accrue more than 3 weeks of vacation. If an employee's accrued but unused vacation reaches that maximum amount, the employee will cease earning and accruing vacation. If the employee later uses vacation and his or her accrued vacation balance falls below the maximum, he or she will resume accruing vacation time up to that maximum. Employees may not receive pay in lieu of taking vacation, except upon termination of employment.

An employee who resigns or is terminated with accrued but unused vacation time will be paid for that time. In the event a terminating employee has taken advance vacation time not yet earned, such time will be deducted from the employee's final paycheck. Before an employee will be allowed to take vacation time not accrued, he or she must sign an acknowledgment authorizing the Company to deduct the advance vacation pay from the employee's final paycheck.

Holidays

[COMPANY] observes the holidays listed below:

New Year's Day (January 1)

Memorial Day (last Monday in May)

Independence Day (July 4)

Labor Day (first Monday in September)

Thanksgiving (fourth Thursday in November)

Friday after Thanksgiving

Christmas (December 25)

[COMPANY] will grant paid holiday pay to all regular full-time employees who have completed the benefits waiting period. Holiday pay will be calculated based on the employee's straight-time pay rate (as of the date of the holiday) times the number of hours the employee would otherwise have worked on that day. The standard number of hours is based on an eight-hour workday.

To be eligible for paid holiday time off, the holiday must fall or be observed on a day that the employee would normally be scheduled to work and the employee must work either on the last scheduled day before the holiday or the first scheduled day after the holiday, unless excused in advance by the Company. If a recognized holiday falls during an eligible employee's paid absence (such as a vacation), holiday pay will be provided instead of the paid time off that would otherwise have applied.

Sick Leave [Check state and local law]

In order to help prevent loss of earnings caused by accident or illness, the Company has established paid sick and emergency leave.

All regular full-time employees are eligible for [__] days' sick leave per calendar year. Employees do not accrue sick leave during the benefits waiting period. Temporary employees are ineligible to earn or receive sick-leave benefits.

- Sick leave may be taken for personal illness or injury. Employees may use up to half of their sick leave each year for the illness or injury of the employee's child, parent, spouse, or domestic partner.

- Hours absent for medical and dental appointments will be treated as sick leave.

- Non-exempt employees who are absent due to illness or disability during their benefits waiting period will not be compensated.

- Unused sick days do not carry over from one calendar year to the next.

- [COMPANY] retains the right to request verification from a licensed health-care provider for all absences due to illness or disability. Sick pay may be withheld if a satisfactory verification is not received.

- Sick leave will not accrue during any leave of absence.

No employee will receive pay in lieu of sick leave under any circumstances, and employees will not receive pay for unused sick leave on termination of employment.

Leave of Absence for Disability for Pregnancy, Childbirth, or Related Medical Conditions [Check state law]

Terms of the Leave

You are considered to be "actually disabled" when you cannot work at all or are unable to perform any one or more of the essential functions of your job or to perform them without undue risk to yourself, the successful completion of your pregnancy, or to other persons. This term also applies to severe morning sickness or if you need to take time off for prenatal care.

[COMPANY] will transfer you (if you are affected by pregnancy) to a less strenuous or hazardous position if:

- You request a transfer

- Your request is based upon the certification of your health care provider as medically advisable

- The transfer can be reasonably accommodated

You are "affected by pregnancy" if you are pregnant or have a related medical condition. No additional position will be created and the Company will not discharge another employee, transfer another employee with more seniority or promote any employee who is not qualified to perform the new job.

Notification Requirements

To request a leave of absence, you are required to submit to your manager a completed request for time off. You must give at least 30 days' advance notice before your leave or transfer is to begin if the need for the leave or transfer is foreseeable. When 30 days' notice is not possible, notice must be given as soon as possible.

As a condition of your disability leave or transfer, you must provide a written certification signed by your health care provider, in the form provided by human resources.

If you continue to be disabled at the expiration of the time period your health care provider originally estimated you needed, you must obtain recertification to continue your leave.

Reinstatement

If you and the Company have agreed upon a definite date of return, you will be reinstated on that date if you notify the Company that you can return on or before that date. If the length of your leave has not been established, or if it differs from the original agreement, you will be returned to work within two business days, where feasible, after you notify us of your readiness to return.

When you are ready to work after a leave or transfer, you must obtain a written release from your health care provider certifying that you are able to perform all of the essential duties of your original job, with or without reasonable accommodation.

[COMPANY] will reinstate you on the job you held before your leave or transfer began, unless one of the following conditions exists:

- You would not otherwise have been employed in your same job at the time reinstatement is requested

- Your job could not be kept open or filled by a temporary employee without substantially undermining the ability of the Company operate safely and efficiently

- You have directly or indirectly indicated your intention not to return to your job

- You can no longer safely perform the essential functions of your job with or without reasonable accommodation

- You are no longer qualified for the job

If we cannot reinstate you to your job, we will offer you a comparable position provided that a comparable position exists and is available. A position is "available" if there is a position open on your scheduled date of return or within 10 working days thereafter, for which you are qualified. A "comparable position" is virtually identical to your original position in terms of pay, benefits, promotional opportunities, and working conditions, and involves the same or substantially similar duties and responsibilities. We can deny you a comparable position if one is available but filling it with you would substantially undermine our ability to operate efficiently and safely.

If you were laid off during your leave and no comparable position is available, the employment relationship will be terminated.

Integration with Other Benefits:
Your leave will be unpaid. You may substitute your accrued vacation and sick leave for unpaid leave.

When you become disabled, you should apply for [State Disability Insurance, if any] benefits. SDI forms are available from your health care provider. Any state disability benefits for which you are eligible will be integrated with your accrued vacation and sick leave so that you do not receive over 100% of your regular pay.

You will not accrue vacation or sick leave during any unpaid portion of your leave, and you will not be eligible to receive Holiday pay.

During your leave, you may be eligible to elect to continue your insurance coverage under COBRA.

Leave of Absence for Work-Related Disability
You may take an unpaid leave of absence when you are disabled because of an occupational illness or injury. When you are on leave, you must be examined by a doctor and certified to be disabled from returning to work.

Your leave of absence will end at the conclusion of the leave, or when a doctor certifies that you can safely perform the essential functions of your job, with or without reasonable accommodation. If we receive medical evidence that you will be permanently unable to perform all of the essential functions of your job, with or without reasonable accommodation, and if reassignment to a vacant position is not possible, your employment will be terminated. You may then be eligible for vocational rehabilitation benefits.

You will be reinstated when a doctor certifies that you can safely perform all of the essential functions of your job, with or without reasonable accommodation. We will not reinstate you when one of the following circumstances exists:

- When you directly or indirectly indicate to us that you do not intend to return to our employ

- When your former position no longer exists

- When you had to be replaced as a business necessity

- When you are no longer qualified for your former job

- When you cannot return to your former job without posing a direct threat to your health or safety or to the health and safety of another employee

During your leave, you may receive workers' compensation benefits in accordance with state law. Your group health plan coverage for you and your dependents will be maintained at the level and under the conditions coverage would have been provided if you had remained continuously employed.

You will not accrue vacation or sick leave during your leave or be entitled to holiday pay, but you will be credited with service for the period of the disability.

Military Leave

[COMPANY] grants unpaid military leaves of absence for active duty or training. In order to be eligible for a military leave of absence, employees must submit written verification from the appropriate military authority. Vacation time, sick leave, and holiday time do not accrue during any period of a military leave in excess of 30 calendar days. An employee's health and life insurance will be continued during a military leave under the terms explained in those policies.

Members of the National Guard or military reserves are entitled to a leave of absence not to exceed, except in the event of an emergency or extenuating circumstances, 17 calendar days per year for required training or similar duty, plus reasonable travel time.

To be eligible for reinstatement after other military leaves, an employee must: (1) have a certificate of satisfactory completion of service; (2) apply within 90 days after release from service or training, or within 90 days after release from hospitalization that continued following discharge, or within such extended period, if any, as the employee's rights are protected by law; and (3) be qualified to perform the essential functions of his or her former position. The company will reinstate eligible employees returning from military leave to their same position or to one of comparable seniority, status, and pay, unless a change in the Company's circumstances makes it impossible or unreasonable to do so. Exceptions to this policy will occur wherever necessary to comply with applicable laws.

Time Off to Vote [Check state law]

[COMPANY] encourages employees to fulfill their civic responsibilities by participating in elections. Generally, employees are able to find time to vote either before or after their regular work schedule, because election polls now open early in the morning and remain open until late in the evening. If employees are registered voters and are unable to vote in an election during their non-working hours, the Company will grant up to two hours of paid time off to vote.

An employee should request time off to vote from the office manager at least two working days prior to the election day. Advance notice is required so that the necessary time off can be scheduled at the beginning or end of the work shift, whichever provides the least disruption to the normal work schedule. Employees must submit a voter's receipt on the first working day following the election to qualify for paid leave.

Jury Duty and Witness Duty [Check state law]

[COMPANY] encourages employees to fulfill their civic responsibilities by serving jury duty when required. Employees may take an unpaid leave of absence while serving on a jury. So that the Company may make arrangements to accommodate the employee's absence during jury duty, an employee must show the jury duty summons to the office manager as soon as possible after it is received. The employee is expected to report for work whenever the court schedule permits.

An employee who is required by law to appear in court as a witness may take unpaid time off for this purpose, provided that the employee provides the Company with reasonable advance notice. The employee must show the subpoena to the office manager as soon as possible after it is received so that operating requirements can be adjusted, where necessary, to accommodate the employee's absence. The employee is expected to report for work whenever the court schedule permits.

Leave for Children's School Activities [Check state law]

School Participation Leave

An employee who is the parent, guardian, or grandparent with custody of a child or children enrolled in kindergarten or grades 1 through 12 or attending a licensed child care facility may take time off work, up to 40 hours per school year, not to exceed 8 hours per calendar month, to participate in the activities of the school or licensed child care facility. You must provide reasonable advance notice of your planned absence to your manager, and you must use any accrued vacation time for the absence. If requested, you must provide documentation from the school verifying the date and time of your visit(s).

School Conferences Involving Suspension

If you are the parent or guardian of a child who has been suspended from school and you receive a notice from the child's school requesting that you attend a portion of a school day in the child's classroom, you may take unpaid time to appear at the child's school. You must, prior to your planned absence, give reasonable notice to your manager that you have been requested to appear in your child's school.

Leave for Victims of Domestic Violence [Check state law]

[COMPANY] understands that an employee who is the victim of domestic violence may need to take time off from work to obtain relief from such violence. An employee who is the victim of domestic violence may take time off to seek medical attention, obtain services from a domestic violence program, obtain psychological counseling, or participate in safety planning. In addition, an employee may take time off to appear in court in an effort to obtain relief from domestic violence. An employee must give the Company reasonable notice that he or she will need time off to obtain relief from domestic violence. If the need for leave is unscheduled or an emergency, advance notice is not required, but the employee may be required to provide certification establishing the need for the leave.

Bereavement Leave

An employee who suffers the death of an immediate family member (father/mother, daughter/son, spouse or domestic partner, grandparent, sibling), may take up to three days of paid bereavement leave. Bereavement pay is calculated based on the base pay rate at the time of absence and will not include any special forms of compensation, such as incentives, commissions, bonuses, or shift differentials. Employees may, with the office manager's approval, use any available paid leave for additional time off as necessary.

ACKNOWLEDGMENT OF RECEIPT OF EMPLOYEE HANDBOOK

Employee's Name _____
(Type or print)

This is to acknowledge that I have received my copy of the Company Employee Handbook which outlines the policies and practices of Company, Inc. (the Company), referred to herein as the "Company." I will promptly read and familiarize myself with the information contained in this Handbook. I understand I must comply with its contents.

I understand that the policies and procedures in this handbook are not intended to be contractual commitments or to create a contract of employment, but are merely descriptions of recommended procedures to be followed and policies necessary for the safe and efficient operation of the business. I further understand that with the exception of its policy of at-will employment and those policies compelled by law, the Company reserves the sole right to revoke, change, or supplement its policies and guidelines at any time without notice. No policy is intended as a guarantee that benefits or rights will continue.

I understand and agree that my employment is at will, which means that either I or the Company may end the relationship at any time, for any legal reason, with or without cause, with or without notice. No one except the president of the Company can enter into an agreement for employment for a specified period of time, or make any agreement contrary to this policy of at-will employment. Any such agreement must be in writing, and must be signed by both the president and by me.

My signature below further signifies that I have carefully read this acknowledgement of receipt. I agree to observe the policies set forth in the handbook.

_____
Employee's Printed Name

_____
Employee's Signature

_____
Date

Note to the employee: The original of this form will go into your personnel file and you will receive a copy.

SAMPLE EMPLOYEE COUNSELING/DISCIPLINE FORM

[COMPANY] Employee Counseling/Discipline Form

❑ Record of Verbal Counseling and/or Reprimand (#_____)

❑ Written Counseling and/or Reprimand (#_____)

❑ Suspension ❑ Termination

Name of Employee: _____

Work Location _____ Date _____

Explanation of counseling and/or discipline

_____

_____

Reason for counseling and/or discipline

_____

_____

To avoid further counseling and/or discipline, employee must:

_____

_____

Employee response

_____

_____

Further unacceptable conduct may lead to further counseling and/or discipline, up to and including termination. Nevertheless, because employment is at will, employer reserves the right to terminate the employment relationship with or without good cause, at any time, with or without advance notice.

Counseling and/or Discipline Given By

_____   _____

Signature   Date

Suspension Period (if applicable): Effective Dates: _____ to _____ ❑ paid ❑ unpaid

For all actions except verbal counseling and/or reprimand:

By signing this document, I am acknowledging that I have been counseled and/or disciplined as stated above.

_____   _____

Employee Signature   Date

PERFORMANCE EVALUATION FORM

[COMPANY] Performance Evaluation Form

_____   _____
Employee   Date of Evaluation

_____   _____
Title   Date of Hire

_____
Work Location

_____
Evaluator

As you complete this performance evaluation, use the following scale as a guideline for rating each category:

5 = Outstanding. Performance well beyond expectations; positive attitude reflecting a keen interest in excellence and exceeding company goals.

4 = Above expectations. Performance above average; attitude constantly reflects interest in improving and attaining higher level of achievement for self and company.

3 = Meets expectations. Performance at average level; some interest in improving and positive attitude about the job and the company.

2 = Below expectations. Performance is below average; attitude reflects little concern for improving.

1 = Unsatisfactory. Performance is unacceptable; negative attitude about the job and the company.

CRITERIA	5	4	3	2	1
Performance					
Completes tasks on time	❑	❑	❑	❑	❑
Work quality	❑	❑	❑	❑	❑
Productivity	❑	❑	❑	❑	❑
Works independently	❑	❑	❑	❑	❑
Communication					
Reports to proper supervisor(s)	❑	❑	❑	❑	❑
Understands instructions easily	❑	❑	❑	❑	❑
Communication skills	❑	❑	❑	❑	❑
Interpersonal Skills					
Working relationship with others	❑	❑	❑	❑	❑
Relationship with customers/clients	❑	❑	❑	❑	❑
Relationship with supervisor	❑	❑	❑	❑	❑
Attendance					
Punctuality	❑	❑	❑	❑	❑
Absenteeism	❑	❑	❑	❑	❑
Overall attendance record	❑	❑	❑	❑	❑
Safety Compliance					
Attends safety meetings	❑	❑	❑	❑	❑
Keeps workplace in safe condition	❑	❑	❑	❑	❑
Puts safety over production	❑	❑	❑	❑	❑
Knowledge/Skills					
Meets job requirements	❑	❑	❑	❑	❑
Applies knowledge/skills to job	❑	❑	❑	❑	❑
Adds to knowledge and skills	❑	❑	❑	❑	❑
Other					
_____	❑	❑	❑	❑	❑
_____	❑	❑	❑	❑	❑
_____	❑	❑	❑	❑	❑
_____	❑	❑	❑	❑	❑
_____	❑	❑	❑	❑	❑

Evaluator's Comments:

1. Has employee met goals set during last evaluation? (If applicable)

_____

_____

_____

_____

_____

2. In what specific areas, if any, has the employee excelled since last evaluation?

_____

_____

_____

_____

_____

3. In what specific areas does the employee need improvement?

_____

_____

_____

_____

_____

4. What goals should the employee plan to meet before the next scheduled evaluation?

_____

_____

_____

_____

_____

5. Other comments?

_____

_____

_____

_____

_____

Employee's Comments:

1. What could the company do to better use your skills and strengths?

_____
_____
_____
_____
_____

2. What areas do you need improvement in, and what steps will you take to improve?

_____
_____
_____
_____
_____

3. Other comments

_____
_____
_____
_____
_____

Signatures:

_____
Evaluator

_____
Employee

Copy to: ❑ Employee

Signed Original to: ❑ Personnel File

MUTUAL AGREEMENT TO ARBITRATE CLAIMS [CHECK STATE LAW]

I recognize that differences may arise between [COMPANY], Inc. ("the Company") and me during or following my employment with the Company, and that those differences may or may not be related to my employment. I understand and agree that by entering into this Mutual Agreement to Arbitrate Claims ("Agreement"), I anticipate gaining the benefits of a speedy, impartial, final, and binding dispute-resolution procedure.

Except as provided in this Agreement, the Federal Arbitration Act shall govern the interpretation, enforcement, and all proceedings pursuant to this Agreement. To the extent that the Federal Arbitration Act is inapplicable, or held not to require arbitration of a particular claim or claims, state law pertaining to agreements to arbitrate shall apply.

Claims Covered by the Agreement

The Company and I mutually consent to the resolution by arbitration of all claims or controversies ("claims"), past, present, or future, whether or not arising out of my employment (or its termination), that the Company may have against me or that I may have against any of the following: 1) the Company, 2) its officers, directors, employees, or agents in their capacity as such or otherwise, 3) the Company's parent, subsidiary, and affiliated entities, 4) the Company's benefit plans or the plans' sponsors, fiduciaries, administrators, affiliates, and agents, and/or 5) all successors and assigns of any of them.

The only claims that are arbitrable are those that, in the absence of this Agreement, would have been justiciable under applicable state or federal law. The claims covered by this Agreement include, but are not limited to: claims for wages or other compensation due; claims for breach of any contract or covenant (express or implied); tort claims; claims for discrimination (including, but not limited to, race, sex, sexual orientation, religion, national origin, age, marital status, physical or mental disability or handicap, or medical condition); claims for benefits (except claims under an employee benefit or pension plan that either 1) specifies that its claims procedure shall culminate in an arbitration procedure different from this one, or 2) is underwritten by a commercial insurer which decides claims); and claims for violation of any federal, state, or other governmental law, statute, regulation, or ordinance, except claims excluded in the section of this Agreement entitled "Claims Not Covered By The Agreement."

Except as otherwise provided in this Agreement, both the Company and I agree that neither of us shall initiate or prosecute any lawsuit or administrative action (other than an administrative charge of discrimination to the Equal Employment Opportunity Commission, California Department of Fair Employment and Housing or similar fair employment practices agency, or an administrative charge within the jurisdiction of the National Labor Relations Board), in any way related to any claim covered by this Agreement.

Claims Not Covered by the Agreement

Claims for workers' compensation or unemployment compensation benefits are not covered by this Agreement.

Also not covered are claims by the Company or by me for temporary restraining orders or preliminary injunctions ("temporary equitable relief") in cases in which such temporary equitable relief would be otherwise authorized by law. Such resort to temporary equitable relief shall be pending and in aid of arbitration only, and in such cases the trial on the merits of the action will occur in front of, and will be decided by, the Arbitrator, who will have the same ability to order legal or equitable remedies as could a court of general jurisdiction.

Time Limits for Commencing Arbitration and Required Notice of All Claims

The Company and I agree that the aggrieved party must give written notice of any claim to the other party no later than the expiration of the statute of limitations (deadline for filing) that the law prescribes for the claim. Otherwise, the claim shall be void and deemed waived. I understand that the aggrieved party is encouraged to give written notice of any claim as soon as possible after the event or events in dispute so that arbitration of any differences may take place promptly.

Written notice to the Company, or its officers, directors, employees, or agents, shall be sent to _____ at the Company's then-current address. I will be given written notice at the last address recorded in my personnel file.

The written notice shall identify and describe the nature of all claims asserted, the facts upon which such claims are based and the relief or remedy sought. The notice shall be sent to the other party by certified or registered mail, return receipt requested.

Representation

Any party may be represented by an attorney or other representative selected by the party.

Discovery

Each party shall have the right to take the deposition of two individuals and any expert witness designated by another party. Each party also shall have the right to make requests for production of documents to any party and to subpoena documents from third parties. Requests for additional discovery may be made to the Arbitrator selected pursuant to this Agreement. The Arbitrator may grant an order for such requested additional discovery if the Arbitrator finds that the party requires it to adequately arbitrate a claim, taking into account the parties' mutual desire to have a fast, cost-effective dispute resolution mechanism.

Designation of Witnesses

At least 30 days before the arbitration, the parties must exchange lists of witnesses, including any experts, and copies of all exhibits intended to be used at the arbitration.

Subpoenas

Each party shall have the right to subpoena witnesses and documents for the arbitration as well as documents relevant to the case from third parties.

Arbitration Procedures

The arbitration will be held under the auspices of a sponsoring organization, either the American Arbitration Association ("AAA") or Judicial Arbitration & Mediation Services ("J·A·M·S"), with the designation of the sponsoring organization to be made by the party who did not initiate the claim.

The Company and I agree that, except as provided in this Agreement, the arbitration shall be in accordance with the sponsoring organization's then-current employment arbitration rules/procedures. The Arbitrator shall be either a retired judge, or an attorney who is experienced in employment law and licensed to practice law in the state in which the arbitration is convened (the "Arbitrator"). The arbitration shall take place in or near the city in which I am or was last employed by the Company.

The Arbitrator shall be selected as follows: The sponsoring organization shall give each party a list of eleven (11) arbitrators drawn from its panel of employment dispute arbitrators. Each party shall have ten (10) calendar days from the postmark date on the list to strike all names on the list it deems unacceptable. If only one common name remains on the lists of all parties, that individual shall be designated as the Arbitrator. If more than one common name remains on the lists of all parties, the parties shall strike names alternately from the list of common names until only one remains. The party who did not initiate the claim shall strike first. If no common name exists on the lists of all parties, the sponsoring organization shall furnish an additional list of eleven (11) arbitrators from which the parties shall strike alternately, with the party initiating the claim striking first, until only one name remains. That person shall be designated as the Arbitrator.

The Arbitrator shall apply the substantive law (and the law of remedies, if applicable) of the state in which the claim arose, or federal law, or both, as applicable to the claim(s) asserted. The Arbitrator is without jurisdiction to apply any different substantive law or law of remedies. The Federal Rules of Evidence shall apply. The Arbitrator shall have exclusive authority to resolve any dispute relating to the interpretation, applicability, enforceability or formation of this Agreement, including but not limited to any claim that all or any part of this Agreement is void or voidable. The arbitration shall be final and binding upon the parties, except as provided in this Agreement.

The Arbitrator shall have jurisdiction to hear and rule on pre-hearing disputes and is authorized to hold pre-hearing conferences by telephone or in person, as the Arbitrator deems advisable. The Arbitrator shall have the authority to entertain a motion to dismiss and/or a motion for summary judgment by any party and shall apply the standards governing such motions under the Federal Rules of Civil Procedure.

Either party, at its expense, may arrange for and pay the cost of a court reporter to provide a stenographic record of proceedings.

Should any party refuse or neglect to appear for, or participate in, the arbitration hearing, the Arbitrator shall have the authority to decide the dispute based upon whatever evidence is presented.

Either party, upon request at the close of hearing, shall be given leave to file a post-hearing brief. The time for filing such a brief shall be set by the Arbitrator.

The Arbitrator shall render an award and written opinion in the form typically rendered in labor arbitrations no later than thirty (30) days from the date the arbitration hearing concludes or the post-hearing briefs (if requested) are received, whichever is later. The opinion shall include the factual and legal basis for the award.

Either party shall have the right, within twenty (20) days of issuance of the Arbitrator's opinion, to file with the Arbitrator a motion to reconsider (accompanied by a supporting brief), and the other party shall have twenty (20) days from the date of the motion to respond. The Arbitrator thereupon shall reconsider the issues raised by the motion and, promptly, either confirm or change the decision, which (except as provided by law) shall then be final and conclusive upon the parties.

Arbitration Fees and Costs

The Company will be responsible for paying any filing fee and the fees and costs of the Arbitrator; provided, however, that if I am the party initiating the claim, I will contribute an amount equal to the filing fee to initiate a claim in the court of general jurisdiction in the state in which I am (or was last) employed by the Company. Each party shall pay for its own costs and attorneys' fees, if any. However, if any party prevails on a statutory claim which affords the prevailing party attorneys' fees and costs, or if there is a written agreement providing for attorneys' fees and/or costs, the Arbitrator may award reasonable attorneys' fees and/or costs to the prevailing party, applying the same standards a court would apply under the law applicable to the claim(s).

Judicial Review

Either party may bring an action in any court of competent jurisdiction to compel arbitration under this Agreement and to enforce an arbitration award.

Interstate Commerce

I understand and agree that the Company is engaged in transactions involving interstate commerce.

Requirements for Modification or Revocation

This Agreement to arbitrate shall survive the termination of my employment and the expiration of any benefit plan. It can only be revoked or modified by a writing signed by both the Company's Chief Executive Officer and me which specifically states an intent to revoke or modify this Agreement.

Sole and Entire Agreement

This is the complete agreement of the parties on the subject of arbitration of disputes (except for any arbitration agreement in connection with any pension or benefit plan). This Agreement supersedes any prior or contemporaneous oral or written understandings on the subject. No party is relying on any representations, oral or written, on the subject of the effect, enforceability, or meaning of this Agreement, except as specifically set forth in this Agreement.

Construction

If any provision of this Agreement is adjudged to be void or otherwise unenforceable, in whole or in part, such adjudication shall not affect the validity of the remainder of the Agreement. All other provisions shall remain in full force and effect.

Consideration

The promises by the Company and by me to arbitrate differences, rather than litigate them before courts or other bodies, provide consideration for each other.

Not an Employment Agreement

This Agreement is not, and shall not be construed to create, any contract of employment, express or implied. Nor does this Agreement in any way alter the "at-will" status of my employment.

Voluntary Agreement

I ACKNOWLEDGE THAT I HAVE CAREFULLY READ THIS AGREEMENT, THAT I UNDERSTAND ITS TERMS, THAT ALL UNDERSTAND-INGS AND AGREEMENTS BETWEEN THE COMPANY AND ME RELATING TO THE SUBJECTS COVERED IN THE AGREEMENT ARE CONTAINED IN IT, AND THAT I HAVE ENTERED INTO THE AGREEMENT VOLUNTARILY AND NOT IN RELIANCE ON ANY PROMISES OR REPRESENTATIONS BY THE COMPANY OTHER THAN THOSE CONTAINED IN THIS AGREEMENT ITSELF. I UNDERSTAND THAT BY SIGNING THIS AGREEMENT I AM GIVING UP MY RIGHT TO A JURY TRIAL.

Employee initials: _____

I FURTHER ACKNOWLEDGE THAT I HAVE BEEN GIVEN THE OPPORTUNITY TO DISCUSS THIS AGREEMENT WITH MY PRIVATE LEGAL COUNSEL AND HAVE AVAILED MYSELF OF THAT OPPORTUNITY TO THE EXTENT I WISH TO DO SO.

Employee: [COMPANY], Inc.

_____   _____
Signature of Employee   Signature of Authorized Company Representative

_____   _____
Print Name of Employee   Title of Representative

_____   _____
Date   Date

SAMPLE POLICY FOR INTERNAL COMPLAINTS PROCEDURE

This is a draft of a policy that a company may implement in order to establish procedures for the receipt, retention, and treatment of complaints regarding accounting, internal accounting controls, or auditing matters and employees' confidential, anonymous submission of concerns regarding accounting or auditing matters. It is important for each company to tailor this draft policy to meet its specific circumstances. This policy must be discussed and approved by the audit committee of a company's board of directors.

[COMPANY]'s Policy on Complaints of Accounting, Internal Accounting Controls, and Auditing Matters ("Whistleblower" Policy)

Section 1: Purpose

It is the policy of [COMPANY] (the "Company") to comply with all applicable legal and regulatory requirements relating to accounting, internal accounting controls and auditing matters, and to require its employees to do likewise. Every employee of Company has the responsibility to assist the Company in meeting these legal and regulatory requirements.

The Company's internal controls and operating procedures are intended to prevent, deter, and remedy any violation of the applicable laws and regulations that relate to accounting, internal accounting controls, and auditing matters. Even the best systems of control, however, cannot provide absolute safeguards against such violations. The Company has a responsibility to investigate and report to appropriate governmental authorities, as required, any violations of applicable legal and regulatory requirements relating to accounting, internal accounting controls and auditing matters, and the actions taken by the Company to remedy such violations.

This policy governs the process through which employees and others, acting on behalf of the Company, either directly or anonymously can notify the Audit Committee of the Company's Board of Directors of alleged accounting and auditing violations or concerns. In addition, this policy establishes a mechanism for responding to, and keeping records of, any complaints from employees and others regarding accounting and auditing violations or concerns. The Securities and Exchange Commission (the "SEC") must adopt rules relating to policies such as this no later than April 26, 2003. Therefore, this policy may be revised following the adoption of the SEC's rules.

Section 2: Reporting Alleged Accounting, Internal Accounting Controls, and Auditing Violations or Concerns

If an employee believes that the Company or any its employees or others, acting on behalf of the Company, have violated any accounting rules, internal accounting controls procedures or auditing rules, the employee must immediately report any such violation to either the Company's general counsel, [Name of GC] or the Company's [Controller], [Name of Controller or CFO]. If the statement is written and sent to either person via the mail, the employee should mark the envelope as "confidential and private." [COMPANY may want to consider whether these recipients should have newly established P.O. Boxes or private email addresses for the receipt of these statements.]

The statement must be in writing and sufficiently detailed and inclusive to ensure a clear understanding by the recipients of the issues raised. A report may be submitted anonymously. Otherwise, the employee must either sign and date, or send an email of, the statement of the alleged violation or concern.

The written statement submitted by an employee describing an alleged violation or concern must be candid and set forth all of the information that the employee knows regarding the allegation or concern. In addition, all reports must contain sufficient corroborating information to support the commencement of an investigation. The Company may not commence an investigation if the statement contains only unspecified wrongdoing or broad allegations without appropriate informational support.

Section 3: Investigation of Alleged Accounting, Internal Accounting Controls, and Auditing Violations or Concerns

Upon receipt of the statement by either the General Counsel or the [Controller], such recipient shall make a determination, in his reasonable judgment, whether such statement is material to the accounting, auditing and internal controls of the Company. If the statement is material, the General Counsel or the [Controller], as the case may be, will immediately notify the Audit Committee or its member designee. The Internal Audit Department of the Company shall have the responsibility for investigating all statements submitted regarding accounting and auditing alleged violations or concerns. In the event, the statement is related to an alleged violation or concern relating to the internal accounting controls of the Company, the General Counsel shall have the responsibility for investigating all statements submitted regarding alleged violations of, or concerns relating to, the internal accounting controls. In addition, other parties may become involved in investigations based on their oversight responsibility or expertise.

If the General Counsel or the [Controller] determines that the statement, in his reasonable judgment, is not material, the General Counsel or the [Controller] will oversee the investigation of such statement. At each meeting of the Audit Committee, the General Counsel and the [Controller] shall prepare a report to the Audit Committee stating the nature of each statement submitted during the quarter immediately preceding the meeting of the Audit Committee, whether or not the statement was determined to be material, and the status of each investigation.

The Audit Committee shall ensure coordination of each investigation and shall have overall responsibility for implementation of this policy. The Audit Committee shall have the authority to retain outside legal or accounting expertise in any investigation as it deems necessary to conduct the investigation in accordance with its charter.

Section 4: No Retaliation for Submitting Statements of Alleged Violations or Concerns

There will be no retaliation by the Company or any of its employees against any employee who makes a statement pursuant to this policy even if after investigation the Company determines that there has not been a violation.

Section 5: Corrective Action

It is the responsibility of the Company and each of its employees to prevent or correct noncompliance of the legal and regulatory requirements relating to accounting, internal accounting controls and auditing matters, with the oversight of the Audit Committee. This is the Company's legal obligation. A violation can cause the Company and its employees to be subjected to legal liability, regulatory investigation and adverse publicity, which can damage the Company's reputation and business.

Section 6: Retention of Statements by Employees

All statements submitted by an employee regarding an alleged violation or concern regarding accounting, internal accounting controls, or auditing matters will remain confidential to the extent practicable. In addition, all written statements, along with the results of any investigations relating thereto, shall be retained by the Company for a minimum of [six] years. [The Company may want to align the retention procedures under this policy with its more general document retention policy.]

Section 7: Violation of this Policy

All employees must follow the procedures outlined herein before any employee reports alleged violations or concerns to any news medium, government agency, or similar body. Employee complaints that do not follow this procedure will constitute a policy violation. Adhering to this policy is a condition of employment. The Company must have the opportunity to investigate and remedy any alleged violations or employee concerns, and each employee must ensure that the Company has an opportunity to undertake such an investigation.

SAMPLE SAFETY, HEALTH, AND SUBSTANCE ABUSE POLICIES

[Sample 1] Safety

Every employee is responsible for safety. To achieve our goal of providing a completely safe work place, everyone must be safety conscious. Please report any unsafe or hazardous condition directly to your supervisor immediately. Every effort will be made to remedy problems as quickly as possible.

In case of an accident involving a personal injury, regardless of how serious, please notify your supervisor or the human resources Department immediately. Failure to report accidents can result in a violation of legal requirements, and can lead to difficulties in processing insurance and benefit claims.

If an employee is injured on the job, he or she will be entitled to benefits under the state worker's compensation law in most cases. The employer carries workers' compensation insurance and will assist employees to obtain all benefits to which they are legally entitled.

[Sample 2] Safety First

The company asks you to cooperate in helping to promote safety and to prevent accidents to yourself, as well as to other employees, customers, and visitors, by observing the following common-sense rules.

1. Learn the company's posted fire rules, the location of fire alarm boxes, and your own duties in case of fire.

2. Promptly report all unsafe or potentially hazardous conditions, such as the following, to your supervisor:

   a. Wet or slippery floors

   b. Equipment left in halls or in walkways

   c. Exposed wiring

   d. Careless handling of equipment

   e. Defective equipment

3. Help to avoid all accidents by eliminating fire hazards wherever you find them.

4. Immediately report all accidents to your supervisor.

5. Always be on the alert for safety hazards.

6. Do not operate electrical equipment with went hands.

[Sample 3] Safety Policy

Every employee should understand the importance of safety in the work place. By remaining safety conscious, employees can protect their own interests as well as those of their co-workers. Accordingly, the company emphasizes safety first and expects all employees to take steps to promote safety in the work place.

In keeping with this commitment, the company has established an Injury and Illness Prevention Program as part of its safety program. The [safety manager] has been delegated responsibility for administering and implementing our Injury and Illness Prevention Program.

Compliance Is Essential

Employees must understand that compliance with safety requirements is a condition of employment and will be evaluated, together with other aspects of an employee's performance, as part of the performance appraisal process. Employees who are particularly effective in following safe and healthful work practices may receive recognition for their effectiveness. Due to the importance of safety considerations to the company, employees who violate safety standards, who cause hazardous or dangerous situations, or who allow such conditions to remain when they could be effectively remedied, may be subject to disciplinary action, up to and possibly including termination.

It is therefore essential that all employees comply fully with the standards and practices of the company that are designed to promote a safe and healthful working environment. As part of our policy, the company has established programs to train and retrain employees as appropriate to assist them to avoid dangerous or unhealthful conditions and to remedy problems or hazards before they cause accidents or injuries.

Reporting Unsafe Conditions and Risks

Whenever an employee identifies an unsafe condition or an occupational safety and health risk, the employee should report the matter immediately to his supervisor if he or she is unable to remedy the situation himself. If the supervisor is not readily available, the employee should immediately inform the [director of human resources or the safety manager] so that any dangerous condition can be corrected. Employees are strongly encouraged to report any situations of this nature and need not fear any form of reprisal as the result of their compliance with this policy. Employees who identify any hazards in the work place can also choose to report the situation anonymously to the [director of human resources or the safety manager] if they prefer not to identify themselves.

The Injury and Illness Prevention Program

Part of the company's Injury and Illness Prevention Program will include safety meetings, training programs, posting safety notices and safety tips, and providing periodic written communications to employees regarding safety matters. Representatives of the company may also conduct periodic inspections to identify unsafe conditions and work practices and will also investigate occupational injuries and illnesses. When appropriate, the company may utilize the services of outside representatives to conduct investigations where it believes that it will be helpful in our attempts to promote the interests of safety to the work place. Every effort will be made to correct unsafe or unhealthy conditions, work practices, or procedures in timely manner. It is therefore essential that all employees cooperate in achieving these objectives and assist the company to provide a safe work place for everyone.

Cooperation and Questions

Employees may occasionally be asked to assist or participate in inspections, the correction of unsafe or unhealthful conditions, or training programs and activities. Full cooperation by all employees is necessary to the accomplishment of our goals. Employees should direct any questions they have regarding their obligations under the Injury and Illness Prevention Program or the company's safety policies to the [director of human resources or the safety manager].

[Sample 4] Injury and Illness Prevention Program

Employee safety is of paramount importance to the company. In keeping with its commitment to safety in the work place, the company has established this Injury and Illness Prevention Program (the "IIPP") to explain its safety policies and procedures. Some of the key features of the program are summarized below:

Responsibility for Administration

The individual with principal authority and responsibility for implementing and administering the company's IIPP is _____, the Safety Director. This person is referred to as the "IIPP Administrator" in this IIPP statement.

Need for Compliance

All employees are required to comply with the company's safety and health policies and practices. This includes employees at every level and in all positions within the company. Performance evaluations take into consideration all aspects of an employee's perform-ance, including the employee's compliance with the company's safety standards. Consequently, strict adherence to the company's safety standards and legal obligations concerning safety will be viewed positively in an evaluation. In the same manner, employees who fail to promote the interests of safety and health in the work place may be viewed negatively in an evaluation. In addition, viola-tions of safety standards or conduct that shows either a disregard for safety concerns or negligent or reckless conduct may result in disciplinary action. In this regard, it should be remembered that the employment relationship is at the mutual consent of the employee and the company and can be terminated at will, at any time, either by the employee or by the company.

Communications

Employees will be informed of matters relating to occupational safety and health from time to time. Communications of this nature may be contained in posted notices, memos, personnel policy statements, employee newsletters, or safety guidelines. Important safety issues may also be raised at employee meetings and training programs.

Employees are, in turn, encouraged to direct any questions they have regarding safety issues or the IIPP to the IIPP Administrator. It is also the responsibility of each employee to inform his or her supervisor or the IIPP Administrator **immediately** of any hazard or unsafe condition in the work site. This can occur without fear of reprisal in any form. Employees can also notify the IIPP Administrator of any such hazards anonymously if they prefer to do so. This can be done either by calling the IIPP Administrator at [phone number] and indi-cating that the employee does not wish to identify himself or herself or by writing to the IIPP Administrator at [_____ , Safety Director, COMPANY, ADDRESS].

Inspections

The company has adopted procedures that are designed to assist it to identify and evaluate work place hazards, including unsafe con-ditions and work practices. These procedures include periodic inspections. Inspections may be scheduled at various times. In addition to the inspections that were conducted when our IIPP was first established in 1991, inspections may occur (a) when new substances, processes, procedures, or equipment that represent a new occupational safety and health hazard are introduced to the work place, and (b) when the company becomes aware of a new or previously unrecognized hazard.

Investigation of Injuries and Illnesses

The company will investigate occupational injuries and illnesses when and in the manner that it determines appropriate. This may involve a physical inspection of the location where an injury occurred, the circumstances that led to the injury or illness, and whether specific procedures, practices, or preventive measures could have helped to reduce or eliminate the danger or prevent the injury or ill-ness. Such investigations may be conducted by the IIPP Administrator or a person designated by the Administrator for that purpose.

Correction of Unsafe Conditions

Where it is determined that an unsafe or unhealthy condition, work practice, or work procedure exists, the company will take steps that it determines are appropriate under the circumstances to correct the condition, practice, or procedure in a timely manner. The severity of a hazard will be considered along with other relevant factors when evaluating the most appropriate method of correcting any hazardous situation and the time frame within which the correction will be made. If an imminent hazard exists that cannot be abated immediately without endangering one or more employees or property, the company may find it appropriate to remove all exposed personnel from the area in which the hazard exists, unless they are necessary to correct the existing condition. Where employees are found necessary to correct the hazardous condition, they will be provided necessary safeguards.

Training and Instruction

The company will also provide training and instruction to employees under the IIPP from time to time. Such training and instruction will be provided (a) when the program is first established, (b) as part of the orientation provided to new employees, (c) to employees provided new job assignments for which training has not previously been received, (d) when new substances, processes, procedures, or equipment are introduced to the work place and represent a new hazard, (e) when the company becomes aware of a new hazard or one that was previously unrecognized, and (f) to supervisors who must be familiar with the safety and health hazards to which employees under their immediate direction and control may be exposed

Records

The company will retain records of inspections and training conducted under the IIPP for the period required by law.

The objectives of the IIPP can only be fully accomplished with the cooperation of all employees. We again wish to stress the importance of safety to the company and all of its employees and urge every employee to cooperate in our goal of achieving "safety first." If you have any questions regarding the IIPP or your responsibilities with respect to work place safety, please direct them to the IIPP Administrator.

CONFIDENTIAL SEVERANCE AND GENERAL RELEASE OF ALL CLAIMS AGREEMENT

This Confidential Severance and General Release of All Claims Agreement (*"Agreement"*) is made by and between Employee, an individual (hereafter *"Employee"*), and _____, Inc. (*"Employer"*), effective on the date set forth below. Employee and Employer are sometimes referred to collectively as "*the Parties*" in this Agreement.

1. Termination of Employment

Employee resigned his employment with Employer effective _____, __, 200_. [The Parties agree that Employer will not oppose Employee's application for Unemployment Insurance benefits.]

2. General Release of Any and All Claims

Employee's employment with Employer, and any fiduciary or other positions held by Employee with Employer, are terminated effective _____, 200_. In partial exchange for the payments and promises between Employee and Employer, and for other good and sufficient consideration, the receipt of which is acknowledged by Employee, Employee hereby releases, acquits, and forever discharges Employer and each of its past, present, and future affiliates, related entities, board members, directors, managers, officers, employees, agents, insurers, attorneys, predecessors, successors, heirs, assigns, and transferees (herein individually and collectively referred to as *"Released Persons"*), from and against any and all claims, rights, demands, actions, obligations, liability, and causes of action, whether asserted or whatsoever, known or unknown, which s/he has or has had against Employer and/or Released Persons from the beginning of time until the date of execution of this Agreement (collectively referred to as *"Claims"*). Without limiting the generality of the foregoing, Employee hereby releases, acquits, and forever discharges Employer against any Claims arising from or in any way connected with or relating to: (i) Employee's employment or other relationship with Employer or the ending of such employment or other relationship; (ii) any Claims for compensation in any form, including without limitation stock, stock rights, or stock options, wages, or benefits; (iii) any and all Claims of employment discrimination of any sort arising under any local, state, or federal law; (iv) any and all Claims under any local ordinance or state or federal law or regulation of any kind or nature whatsoever; (v) any and all Claims of violation of any public policy, violation of statute, sounding in tort (either intentional or negligent), or breach of contract or covenant, whether express or implied; and (vi) any allegations for costs, fees, or other expenses, including attorneys' fees, incurred in these matters, *provided that* nothing in this Agreement will affect or limit: (i) rights created by this Agreement, (ii) any vested right that Employee may have in any 401(k) savings plan or deferred compensation plan as of the time of the termination of his employment with Employer, (iii) any right Employee may have to continue group health care coverage under COBRA, or (iv) any right Employee may have to receive unemployment or workers' compensation benefits.

If this provision at anytime is found invalid or unenforceable, this provision shall be considered divisible and shall be amended to such an extent as shall be determined by the body having jurisdiction over the matter.

3. Reinstatement or Reemployment

Employee understands and acknowledges that his employment with Employer is terminated effective _____, 200_, and Employee waives and relinquishes any and all rights, expectations, and/or Claims regarding reinstatement, recall, or reemployment of any sort to any position with Employer. Employee expressly agrees and promises not to apply for, nor otherwise affirmatively seek, nor under any circumstances accept, any employment appointment, title, or position, whether as an employee, independent contractor, or otherwise, with Employer, or with any sister, parent or subsidiary corporation of Employer. Employee agrees that Employer is not obligated to review any application submitted or offered by Employee. By waiving and relinquishing any and all rights, expectations, and/or Claims regarding reinstatement, recall, or reemployment of any sort, and by expressly agreeing not to apply for, nor otherwise affirmatively to seek, nor to accept, any employment appointment, position, or title of any sort with Employer or with any sister, parent or subsidiary corporation of Employer, Employee does completely waive and relinquish and generally release any and all rights to pursue any Claims in any forum or tribunal where such Claims assert, in whole or in part, any allegation that Employer or any sister, parent, or subsidiary of Employer failed or refused to reemploy, recall, reinstate, employ, appoint, hire, and/or otherwise retain him/her.

If this provision at anytime is found invalid or unenforceable, this provision shall be considered divisible and shall be amended to such an extent as shall be determined by the body having jurisdiction over the matter.

4. Waiver of ADEA and OWBPA

Employee specifically acknowledges that this Agreement includes a complete release and discharge of Employer from any and all claims, damages of any kind, and claims for attorneys' fees and costs, under the Age Discrimination in Employment Act of 1967 ("ADEA") as amended by the Older Worker Benefit Protection Act ("OWBPA"). Employee agrees that part of the consideration payable to him/her under this Agreement is consideration that s/he would not otherwise be entitled to and is in consideration for his /her release of claims under the ADEA as amended by the OWBPA.

Employee acknowledges that s/he understands the protections provided by the OWBPA and that the provisions of the OWBPA have been met by the terms of this Agreement. Employee states that s/he knowingly and voluntarily enters into this Agreement. Employee acknowledges that this Agreement is written in a manner calculated to be understood by him/her. Employee acknowledges that s/he has been represented by Attorney _____ in the negotiation and signing of this Agreement. Employee further acknowledges that this Agreement refers without limitation to rights under the Age Discrimination in Employment Act ("ADEA"), including without limitation claims of age discrimination in employment decisions. Employee understands that by this Agreement, s/he does not waive rights or claims that may arise after the date the Agreement is executed. Employee acknowledges that s/he is entering this Agreement in exchange for consideration in addition to anything of value to which s/he already is entitled due to his/her employment with Employer. Further, Employee acknowledges that this release of claims under the OWBPA is not requested in connection with an exit incentive program or other employment termination program offered to a group or class of employees within the meaning of OWBPA. Employee acknowledges that s/he has been allowed up to twenty-one (21) days from the date that s/he received this Agreement to review this Agreement and to accept its terms. Employee agrees that if s/he signs this Agreement before expiration of the twenty-one (21) day review period, s/he voluntarily waives his right to use the full twenty-one day period to review this Agreement. Employee acknowledges s/he has been advised in writing to consult with an attorney about the Agreement. Employee acknowledges that after s/he signs the Agreement, s/he will then be given seven (7) days following the date on which s/he signs the Agreement to revoke it and that this Agreement will only become effective at 12:01 a.m. on the eighth day after Employee signs this Agreement. Any such revocation must be in writing, signed by Employee and immediately delivered in person to _____ at Employer:

[Address at Employer]

5. Immediate Return of Personal and Company Property

Employee will return to Employer, no later than at the time s/he signs this Agreement, any documents (including electronic documents, disks, and files) that s/he accumulated, received and/or created as part of his employment with Employer and that remain in his possession, custody or control, and s/he further agrees that s/he will not, to the best of his knowledge and belief, have retained (by him/herself or through any agent) any copies thereof. Employee further agrees that s/he will return to Employer, no later than the time he signs this Agreement, all tangible property that remains in his/her possession, custody or control, including but not limited to Employer-sponsored credit cards and/or calling cards, keys, badges, computer equipment, software, lap top computers, printers, fax machines, call reports, customer lists, and all information about Employer's existing and potential customers and business plans (for example, and for illustration only, _____), and any other property owned by Employer. Employee agrees to return any unused airline tickets sponsored by Employer, and provide Employer with any information necessary for it to obtain a refund by the airlines for any unused airline tickets. **Employee also hereby certifies that sh/e: 1) has destroyed any and all remaining Employer electronic or hard copy data that he retained on his hard drive, home computer, personal laptop** computer, any other computer, Personal Device Assistant, mobile telephone, portable or other electronic device, external hard drive, or elsewhere; 2) has made no copies of any Employer electronic or hard copy data; 3) has not used any Employer electronic or hard copy data; and 4) has not disclosed to any unauthorized third party any Employer electronic or hard copy data. Employee agrees and understands that his material compliance with the requirements of this Paragraph is an express condition to his entitlement to the Consideration set forth below.

6. Assumption of Risk

Employee acknowledges that there is a risk that after signing this Agreement that s/he may discover losses or claims that s/he believes were in some way caused by or arose out of his employment or other relationship with Employer or that are otherwise released under this Agreement, but that are presently unknown to him/her. Employee assumes this risk and understands that this release shall apply to any such losses and claims.

Therefore, Employee expressly waives the provision of California Civil Code section 1542, which states:

> A general release does not extend to claims which the creditor does not know or suspect to exist in his favor at the time of executing the release, which if known by him/her must have materially affected his settlement with the debtor.

Employee understands that this Agreement includes a full and final release covering all known and unknown, suspected, or unsuspected injuries, debts, claims or damages which have arisen or may have arisen from any matters, acts, omissions, or dealings released in Paragraphs 1, 2 and 3, above. Employee acknowledges that by accepting the payment referred to in this Agreement, s/he voluntarily assumes and waives the risk that the facts and the law may be other than as s/he believes.

7. No Admission of Liability or Wrongdoing

The purpose of this Agreement is to assist Employee in connection with the termination of his employment with Employer, and Employee's transition to other opportunities for him/her, and not to resolve any claim Employee may assert against the Employer Releasees, or as any admission of liability or wrongdoing by Employer or any of its officers, directors, employees, or agents. Therefore, neither the fact that Employer entered into this Agreement nor this Agreement itself means, and cannot be interpreted or construed to mean, that Employer acted wrongfully towards Employee or anyone else or that Employer breached any duty towards Employee or anyone else. Employer expressly denies any alleged wrongdoing or liability.

8. Consideration

In consideration for the promises and releases provided in this Agreement, Employer will provide Employee a one-time severance payment in the sum of _____ Dollars and _____ Cents ($_____); payment will be made 3 days after the completion of the 7-day revocation period in Paragraph 3 by overnight delivery. This severance payment will be made by way of one payroll check, made payable to Employee from Employer , subject to all lawful payroll deductions or authorized by Employee. Employee will receive a Form W-2 in the amount of the payment to him/her of $_____.

9. Indemnification

Employee understands and acknowledges that it shall be his sole responsibility to pay any and all federal, state, or other taxes that may be required by law to be paid with respect to the payment being made under this Agreement, and s/he agrees to indemnify and hold Employer harmless from any claims, demands, deficiencies, levies, assessments, executions, judgments, or recoveries by any government entity for any amounts claimed to be due on account of this Agreement. Employee shall file all tax reporting documents regarding the payments made under this Agreement as may be required by law.

10. Trade Secret and Confidentiality Obligations

Employee acknowledges and agrees to continue to be bound and abide by his/her obligations under the "Proprietary Information and Prior Inventions Agreement" with Employer, which s/he signed on _____, _____. Employee agrees not to use or disclose, either directly or indirectly, any Confidential Information that s/he acquired or received during his employment or other relationship with Employer. For purposes of this Agreement, Confidential Information includes but is not limited to inventions, ideas, improvements, designs and discoveries, trade secrets, information regarding confidential knowledge or data of Employer, or any of its clients, customers, officers, directors, agents, employees, consultants, shareholders, licensees, licensors, vendors or affiliates, that Employee acquired or had access to during the course of his employment or other relationship with Employer. In this connection, Employee acknowledges and agrees to continue to abide by Employer's "Confidential Information" policies referenced in the Employer Employee Manual, at pages _____.

11. Confidentiality and Non-Disclosure

Employee expressly agrees that each and every term and provision of this Agreement will be maintained in a private and extremely confidential manner. Employee expressly agrees not to publicize, discuss, or disclose the facts leading to this Agreement, or any negotiations regarding this Agreement or this Agreement itself to anyone (including, but not limited to, any past, present, or prospective employees or applicants for employment with Employer), except in any proceedings conducted by the EEOC or any other governmental agency, or as required by a court of competent jurisdiction, or in testimony pursuant to a subpoena in pending litigation, or as otherwise authorized in this Agreement. Employee expressly agrees that any verbal or non-verbal communication regarding any Claims released in this Agreement will be limited to a statement that "the matter was resolved," and Employee expressly agrees that s/he shall not make any further statement or respond in any other way to any further inquiry. Employee expressly agrees not to disclose to anyone, by means of any verbal or non-verbal communication, any estimate or approximation or representation of any kind as to the consideration included this Agreement. Employee is authorized to make necessary disclosures to any governmental taxing authority. Employee also is authorized to make necessary disclosures to tax preparers, retained attorneys, and retained accountants, but only if in advance of any such disclosure, Employee makes it clear to any such person that strict confidentiality provisions exist, and obtain such person's express agreement to treat the information confidentially. If any breach of this Paragraph occurs, Employer shall have the right to seek damages for any such breach as set forth in Paragraph 11 of this Agreement. Employee further agrees that access to any and all copies of this Agreement (including any and all draft copies and photocopies of it) shall be carefully limited and restricted to Employee himself or his legal representative, with no access of any kind permitted to anyone else unless required by law.

12. Breach and Liquidated Damages

In the event of an alleged breach of Paragraph 10 of this Agreement, Employer may initiate arbitration proceedings through the American Arbitration Association, whose rules shall apply, except as follows: no party to such arbitration shall have the right to conduct any formal discovery, but the name and telephone number of all witnesses to be called by a party must be disclosed to the other party to the arbitration at least twenty-one (21) days in advance of the arbitration hearing. No undisclosed witness shall be permitted to testify at the arbitration hearing, unless the arbitrator, for good cause shown, decides to permit it. Also, a copy of any and all documentary evidence that a Party intends to introduce at the arbitration hearing, other than for impeachment or rebuttal, shall be provided to the other Party at least fourteen (14) days in advance of the arbitration hearing. No undisclosed documentary evidence shall be admitted at the arbitration hearing unless the arbitrator permits it, for good cause shown. Due to the difficulty of ascertaining the actual damages caused by each material breach of Paragraph 10 of this Agreement, the Parties agree that in lieu of proof of actual damages resulting from a breach of Paragraph 10 of this Agreement, Employer shall be awarded liquidated damages in the amount of Five Thousand Dollars and No Cents ($5,000.00) for each material breach by Employee if Employer carries its burden of proving material breach by Employee. The Parties agree that the liquidated damages are a reasonable estimate of the Employer's damages in the event of a material breach of Paragraph 10 of this Agreement and not a penalty.

13. Awareness of Claims

Employee represents and warrants that s/he is unaware of any Claims that s/he may have against Employer, and/or any of the other Released Persons, that have not been released in this Agreement.

14. Non-Disparagement

Employee will not make any comment or take any action that disparages, defames, or places in a negative light Employer or Employer's past and present officers, directors, division heads, employees, and independent contractors. If asked about facts concerning this Agreement or the ending of Employee's employment with Employer, Employee will respond by stating only that "the matter was resolved," and refuse to discuss further the ending of Employee's employment with Employer. Neither party will make disparaging comments about the other party. Employee may refer prospective employers to _____ or his/her successor in Human Resources who will only respond as follows, "Employee was an employee in good standing as the _____ from _____ through his resignation date of _____, ___. 200_." Employee's salary will be released to a prospective employer upon receipt of a written request by Employee.

15. Cooperation in Legal Matters

Employee agrees to cooperate with Employer in any legal matters brought by or against it before any court, arbitrator, mediator, or government agency. By agreeing to cooperate with Employer in any legal matters, Employee agrees, among other things, to make him/herself generally available on a date and time and at a place mutually agreeable, provide any documents within his possession, custody or control, and provide truthful information.

16. No Alleged Ambiguity in Agreement Construed Against Employer

Any alleged ambiguity in this Agreement shall not be construed against Employer because Employer or its legal counsel drafted part or all of it.

17. No Assignment

Employee represents and warrants that there has been no assignment or other transfer of any claims s/he has or may have as against Employer.

18. Entire Agreement

This Agreement contains all of the terms and understanding between the Parties to this Agreement with regard to the subject matter herein, is a fully integrated and complete agreement, and supersedes any other prior oral or written agreement or understanding between the parties to this Agreement regarding the subject matter herein.

19. Severable Provisions

If any provision of this Agreement is found invalid or unenforceable, that provision shall be considered severable and the remaining provisions shall be in effect.

20. Arbitration

Notwithstanding the provisions in Paragraph 11 of this Agreement, the Parties agree that any dispute regarding the terms, provisions or enforceability of this Agreement shall be submitted to final and binding arbitration through the American Arbitration Association. The Parties agree that such arbitration shall be conducted in full compliance with applicable statutory and decisional law. The Parties further agree that the prevailing party in such final and binding arbitration shall be entitled to recover his or its reasonable attorneys' fees. The Parties further agree that any arbitration under this Agreement will take place within 35 miles of _____, _____.

21. Voluntary Release and Authority

Employee agrees that s/he has executed this Agreement voluntarily, with full knowledge of its import and significance; that this Agreement is fair and reasonable and is not the result of any duress, overreaching, coercion, pressure or undue influence exercised by Employer upon him/her; and that Employee has been awarded the opportunity to obtain independent legal advice from counsel of his/her own selection with respect to this Agreement and his rights and obligations under this Agreement; and s/he has full personal and/or corporate power and authority to execute and deliver this Agreement.

22. Consultation with Legal Counsel

Employee agrees that s/he is not relying upon Employer or its legal counsel for any representations, or legal or tax advice. Employee agrees that Employer has afforded him/her a reasonable opportunity to consult with legal counsel before signing this Agreement.

23. Governing Law

This Agreement is to be governed by and construed in accordance with the laws of the State of _____, without regard to the choice of law provisions thereof.

24. Binding Against the Parties

This Agreement shall be binding upon and inure the benefit of the parties hereto and their respective successors and assigns.

IN WITNESS THEREOF, Employee and Employer have executed this Confidential Severance and General Release of All Claims Agreement on _____, 20____.

_____
Employee

_____
Employer

By: _____
Its

APPROVED AS TO FORM AND CONTENT:

_____
[Name of Employee's Attorney, if known] Attorney for Employee

About
the Author

Tyler M. Paetkau is an experienced labor and employment law attorney. He counsels large and small employers on a daily basis on the multitude of evolving labor and employment law obligations and compliance issues. He represents employers in litigation matters in state and federal courts and before administrative agencies, defending individual employee and collective or class claims of discrimination, sexual harassment, retaliation, and whistleblowing; breach of contract and wrongful termination; wage and hour violations, benefits; trade secret misappropriation (theft) and violations of non-competes; and privacy violations. Mr. Paetkau has significant jury trial experience, but a large part of his practice consists of counseling employers to help them avoid employment litigation and claims.

Mr. Paetkau is past chair and current advisor to the Executive Committee of the State Bar of California Labor and Employment Law Section, and is an editor for numerous labor and employment law publications, including *Bender's California Employment Law Bulletin*, the *State Bar of California Labor and Employment Law Review*, and the American Bar Association International Labor Law Committee's e-newsletter.

Mr. Paetkau earned his A.B., with high honors and high distinction, from the University of Michigan in Ann Arbor, Michigan, and his J.D., *cum laude*, from the University of Michigan Law School in 1989, where he was Articles Editor for the *Journal of Law Reform*. He is a shareholder of Littler Mendelson (www.littler.com, 415-677-3102), the largest law firm in the United States devoted exclusively to representing management in employment, employee benefits, and labor law matters.

Index